ETHNIC GROUPS IN COMPARATIVE
PERSPECTIVE • General Editor
PETER I. ROSE *Smith College*

Random House New York

Japanese Americans

Oppression and Success

William Petersen

Robert Lazarus Professor of
Social Demography
The Ohio State University

ISBN: 0-394-31220-1

Library of Congress Catalog Card Number: 71-153113

Manufactured in the United States of America
Composed by The Book Press, Inc., Brattleboro, Vt.
Printed and bound by Halliday Lithograph, Inc.
West Hanover, Mass.

Designed by Karin Batten

First Edition

9 8 7 6 5 4 3 2 1

◉ Foreword

"Nation of nations" or "Herrenvolk democracy"? Melting pot or seething caldron? How does one describe the ethnic character of the United States?

The conventional wisdom, reflected in traditional texts on American history and society, tells of the odyssey of one group of newcomers after another who came to these shores: some of their own free will and others in the chains of bondage; some to escape religious persecution, others fleeing from political oppression, and many seeking their fortunes. "Rich and poor," goes the story, "mighty and meek, white and black, Jew and Gentile, Protestant and Catholic, Irishman and Italian and Pole . . . a motley array who, together, make up the Great American Nation."

Although many a school child can recite the litany, even he knows that it has a rather hollow ring. For most people there are at least three kinds of Americans: whatever one happens to be, the members of the dominant group (viewed differently depending where one stands in the status hierarchy), and everybody else. And, if one happens to see himself as a member of the dominant group, the number of alternatives may be reduced to two: they and we.

For a variety of reasons writers of textbooks and teachers of American history have tended to overlook or underplay this essential fact of American life. While acknowledging the pluralistic character of the social structure and celebrating the extent to which "our differences make us strong," they rarely convey the true meaning of membership in an ethnic group. And none know this better than those whose life experiences belie the notion of tolerance for all. Recently, a common plea has arisen from various quarters: "Give us equal time."

In response to such demands there have been attempts to

alter the rather lop-sided image of American history and of the American people. Historians and social scientists have begun to respond to the call for a more accurate and meaningful view of race and ethnicity in America. Many have sought to "redress the balance," as they say, by upgrading the status of one group or another and rewriting their history to parallel that of the dominant group. One finds new volumes that appear to make the same strategic errors as those they wish to complement, i.e., placing emphasis on great events and prominent figures while avoiding in-depth descriptions of patterns of social organization, cultural traditions, and everyday activities.

Fortunately, there have been some other approaches tried recently, most notably studies seeking to reassess the entire ethnic experience not by playing the mirroring game (we have a hero, you have a hero; we have a holiday, you have a holiday; everybody has . . .) but by getting to the core of the social and economic and political realities of existence for the various peoples who came (or were brought) and stayed. The work of the latter scholars is far more important and, by its very nature, far more difficult. It involves new ways of looking, new perspectives. It encourages the examination of history and biography, of episode and event as before. But it also requires careful study of culture and community and character, the examination of everyday life.

Those who have and use such an imagination (C. Wright Mills called it "the sociological imagination") must possess a willingness to challenge the old homilies, to get away from stereotypes and deal with real people, and to relate that which is revealed with both detachment and compassion.

This volume is one of an original series written to provide student-readers with the sort of background material and sociological evaluation just mentioned. Like the others in this series, Ethnic Groups in Comparative Perspective, it offers information about the origins and experiences, the cultural patterns and social relationships of various groups of Americans. Taken together, the volumes in the series should provide a new and different look at the ethnic experience in the United States.

In planning the series it was decided that all books should follow a relatively common format which would include chapters on social history, descriptions of social organization of the various communities and their differing cultural characteristics, relations with others and with the wider society, and a conclusion to tie the early chapters together.

The very best qualified historians and social scientists would be invited to join in the venture, those not only informed but committed to the approach sketched earlier. Each author would be given the freedom to work within the framework in his own way and in his own literary style so that each volume would be a unique contribution to the overall project—and each could stand alone.

This volume is no exception. It is at once a comprehensive history and a sociological analysis of Japanese Americans, one of the least known—or, better stated, least understood—of the many ethnic groups in the United States. Who they are, why they came, how they fared, what they suffered, and how they eventually succeeded in becoming one of the most mobile of all minorities, are all subjects discussed by Professor William Petersen, a distinguished demographer and author of, among other works, *Planned Migration* (1955), *The Politics of Population* (1964), and *Population* (1969).

Petersen's book is unique in many ways. Most striking, I suppose, because the author—unlike those who wrote most of the other volumes in the series, including *Italian Americans, Jewish Americans, White Southerners, The Black American, The Puerto Ricans*—is not a member of the subject of his concern. In fact, by his own admission, he knew almost nothing about Japanese Americans prior to 1965. In the past five years he has devoted a substantial amount of time to exploring the trials and tribulations of Japanese Americans, both through interviewing people in many parts of the American mainland and in Hawaii and through intensive examination of the numerous studies and reports on Japanese history and settlement and on the camps in which more than 110,000 Japanese Americans were interned during World War II. And he has applied his special talents to the task of sifting through mountains of figures to present, simply and accurately, the demographic record.

In many ways, Petersen's book belies the claim that one cannot understand without belonging. He proves the importance of compassionate detachment through his handling of the very difficult material, and offers a balanced presentation.

Petersen's volume should assist American students and teachers in their quest for knowledge about Americans of Japanese ancestry and, as I discovered through discussions with Japanese students of American culture, it will prove a useful addition to American Studies in Japan. For sociological colleagues here and abroad, Petersen's description and discussion of the "deviant case" of the Japanese Americans offers serious challenge to many traditional assumptions about racial and ethnic relations.

PETER I. ROSE
General Editor

Kyoto, Japan
July 1970

◉ Preface

When the editor of *The New York Times Magazine* proposed that I write an article on Japanese Americans, I supposed that he must have asked other more likely candidates and that they had refused. For at that time, in 1965, I knew less about that subnation than the average long-time resident of the West Coast. Until 1953, when I accepted a position at the Berkeley campus of the University of California, I had never been west of Chicago; and my acquaintances in and around New York included precisely two Nisei. In retrospect, I believe this psychological distance from Japanese Americans—in great contrast to the Jews who write about Jews and the blacks who write about Negroes—was not altogether a disadvantage. I started not with a feeling of identification or even particularly of empathy, but with an interesting analytical problem: why in the case of *this* colored minority past oppression had led to phenomenal economic and social success, contradicting the generalizations derived from the experience of Negroes, American Indians, Mexican Americans, and others.

The article, entitled "Success Story: Japanese American Style," was published in the January 9, 1966, issue. Within the limits of a short piece addressed to a general audience, it made the essential point of this book. It was well received both by knowledgeable readers of *The New York Times*, who sent more letters of commendation than I had ever received concerning a work of mine, and by professional colleagues, who several times asked permission to reprint the article in anthologies on race or social problems. My own feelings were mixed, for I felt that I had raised some very important questions to which I found no satisfactory answers. Only a disappointingly small portion of the information I had collected in months of work could be fitted into the few pages of one article. It was for these reasons that I decided to develop the thesis into a book.

Further work on the subject was facilitated by grants from the National Institute of Mental Health and the American Philosophical Society. I am grateful to both these agencies for their assistance. With it I was able, among other extensions of my research, to spend a period in Hawaii and thus to lay a basis for contrasting Japanese Americans there with those on the mainland.

Since I started with no knowledge at all about the Japanese Americans, I collected obligations to a large number of persons who helped me in various ways. Some granted me interviews; some answered questions by mail; some criticized an early draft of the *Times* article; some gave me leads to new data or sources of information. They are listed (with identifications or locations that in some cases may be obsolete) in noninvidious alphabetical order; I thank them all most heartily: Mr. Yasuo Abiko, *Nichi Bei Times*, San Francisco. Miss Dorothea Andrews, Children's Bureau, Washington, D.C. Prof. Abe Arkoff, University of Hawaii. Mr. Roger N. Baldwin, American Civil Liberties Union. Prof. Edward N. Barnhart, University of California, Berkeley. Prof. Eric C. Bellquist, University of California, Berkeley. Mr. Ernest Besig, American Civil Liberties Union. Dr. Alan Blaisdell, Berkeley. Dr. Monica Boyd, Duke University. Prof. Severyn T. Bruyn, Boston College. Mr. Arthur A. Campbell, National Center for Health Statistics, Washington, D.C. Prof. C. K. Cheng, University of Hawaii. Mr. Frank F. Chuman, Los Angeles. Mrs. Martha Clifford, Punahou School, Honolulu. Mr. Wayne M. Collins, American Civil Liberties Union. Judge Gerald R. Corbett, Family Court, Honolulu. Mrs. Nansi E. Corson, Placement Center, University of California, Berkeley. Prof. George DeVos, University of California, Berkeley. Prof. Arthur A. Dole, University of Pennsylvania. Prof. Wolfram Eberhard, University of California, Berkeley. Rev. Hogen Fujimoto, Buddhist Churches of America, San Francisco. Mr. Yukio Gotanda, Hawaii Department of Social Services. Mr. Robert K. Hasegawa, Hawaii Department of Labor and Industrial Relations. Prof. Gordon K. Hirabayashi, University of Alberta. Mr. Kei Hori, San Francisco. Rev. Isao Horinouchi, Japanese Seventh-Day Adventist Church, Sacramento.

Prof. Bernhard L. Hormann, University of Hawaii. Dr. Allan Howard, Bishop Museum, Honolulu. Mr. Edward Howden, California Fair Employment Practices Division. Mrs. Edward Howden, San Francisco. Mr. M. H. Hutchins, California Bureau of Criminal Statistics. Mrs. Konmo Imamura, Honpa Hongwanji Buddhist Temple, Honolulu. Mr. Howard M. Imazeki, *Hokubei Mainichi,* San Francisco. Dr. Yukiko Kimura, University of Hawaii. Prof. Harry Kitano, University of California, Los Angeles. Mr. Michio Kunitani, Berkeley. Prof. Stanford Lyman, University of California, San Diego. Mr. Rinji Maeyama, *Hawaii Hochi,* Honolulu. Mr. Joe Grant Masaoka, Japanese American Study Project, University of California, Los Angeles. Mr. Mike M. Masaoka, Japanese American Citizens League, Washington, D.C. Dr. Mitsugu Matsuda, University of Hawaii. Mr. Masato Matsumoto, Palama School, Honolulu. Prof. Norman Meller, University of Hawaii. Mrs. Franklin Metzger, Punahou School, Honolulu. Mr. James N. Miho, Los Angeles. Mr. Donald L. Miller, U.S. Bureau of Prisons. Mr. Stanley Miyamoto, Honolulu. Dr. James K. Morishima, University of Washington. Miss Joanne Mujata, University of Hawaii. Prof. Sasumu Nakamura, University of California, Berkeley. Mr. Robert Omura, University of Hawaii. Dr. Arthur Ross, U.S. Bureau of Labor Statistics. Prof. Alvin Rudoff, San Jose State College. Leigh Sakamaki, M.D., Honolulu. Mr. Masao Satow, Japanese American Citizens League, San Francisco. Mr. Frederic F. Schneidewind, California Youth Authority. Prof. Tamotsu Shibutani, University of California, Santa Barbara. Mr. Iwao Shimizu, *Hokubei Mainichi,* San Francisco. Dr. Peter T. Suzuki, University of Maryland. Mr. Ben Taguchi, American Society of Civil Engineers, Hawaii Section. Mr. K. Tanimoto, Hawaii Employment Relations Board. Miss Karen Terao, Alameda, Calif. Mr. Norman Thomas, Post-War World Council, New York. Mr. Tom Tonemura, University of Hawaii. Mrs. Marie Viele, Hawaii Department of Health. Mr. Yori Wada, California Youth Authority. Rev. Lloyd Wake, Pine Methodist Church, San Francisco. Prof. George Won, University of Hawaii. Prof. George K. Yamamoto, University of Hawaii. Prof. Douglas Yamamura, University of Hawaii.

Various portions of an early draft of this book were read by several specialists, who were kind enough to challenge a number of dubious interpretations or plain errors. Their criticisms helped improve the manuscript, and I am happy to acknowledge my debt to them: Prof. Roger Daniels, Dept. of History, University of Wyoming. Prof. Wen L. Li, Dept. of Sociology, Ohio State University. Prof. Saad Nagi, Dept. of Sociology, Ohio State University. Prof. Peter I. Rose, Dept. of Sociology, Smith College. Prof. Henry Rosovsky, Dept. of Economics, Harvard University. Mr. Robert C. Schmitt, Hawaii State Statistician. Prof. Dorothy Swaine Thomas, Dept. of Sociology, University of Pennsylvania.

Miss Aiko Shinoda, of the East-West Center, Honolulu, translated Japanese works faithfully and intelligently. Dr. John Modell, of the Japanese American Study Project, University of California, Los Angeles, lent me a typescript of his doctoral dissertation on the history of the Los Angeles Japanese community; it lacked page numbers (as the reader will see from my references) but had an abundance of fact and stimulating exposition.

WILLIAM PETERSEN

Columbus, Ohio

◉ Contents

Japanese Americans

Chapter 1 ◉ The Anomaly of Japanese Americans

Asked which of America's ethnic minorities has been subjected to the most discrimination, the worst injustices, few persons would even think of answering, "The Japanese Americans." Yet if the question refers to those now alive, that is the correct response. Like Negroes, the Japanese[1] have been an object of color prejudice. Like Jews, they have been feared and hated as hyperefficient competitors. More than any other nationality, they have been perceived as the agents of an overseas enemy. Reactionaries, liberals, and radicals; local sheriffs, federal agencies, and the Supreme Court—all have cooperated in denying Japanese Americans their elementary rights. The notorious evacuation to internment camps during World War II was the culmination of a long and shameful record.

Generally, this kind of group experience, as we all have learned in recent years, creates what welfare workers term "problem minorities." Each of a number of interrelated factors —low income, ill health, poor education, high crime rate, unstable family pattern—reinforces all the others; together they make up the reality of slum life. And by what Gunnar Myrdal called the "principle of cumulation," this social reality both reinforces the prejudices of the majority and is reinforced by them.[2] For example, when whites defined Negroes as innately less intelligent and therefore furnished them with inferior schools, the products of those schools generally validated the original judgment. After such a cumulative degradation has continued for several generations, it is painfully difficult to reverse the trend. For when new opportunities—even equal opportunities—are opened up, many of the minority react to them with either self-defeating apathy or a hatred so all-consuming as to be self-destructive. Neither the countless more or less scholarly studies now focused on Negroes nor the routinely "experimental" programs in education, welfare, or crime prevention have informed us how really to repair the damage the slave-traders started. Moreover, since Negroes constitute the country's largest and most visible racial minority, the pessimistic conclusions derived from their history have been generalized into a theory of race relations.

The history of the United States, it is sometimes forgotten, is the history of the diverse groups that make up the country's population, and thus of their frequent discord and usual eventual cooperation. Each new nationality that arrived from Europe was typically met with such hostility as, for example, the anti-German riots in the Middle West a century ago, the American Protective Association to fight the Irish, the national-quota laws to keep out Italians, Poles, and Jews. Yet, in one generation or sometimes two, each of these minorities climbed out of the slums, took on better paying occupations, and acquired social respect and dignity. However, this is less true (or, at worst, not true) of "nonwhites." The reason usually given for the difference is that color prejudice is so great among Caucasians that anyone who carries a visible stigma has little or no possibility of rising. Manifestly, this notion has some truth, but it is altogether too simplistic. "Nonwhites" differ considerably in how successful they have been in adapting to American culture: by most indices, Indians, Mexicans, and Negroes are heavily represented at the lower end, and Chinese and Puerto Ricans are generally at a far higher level. It is obvious that the varied typical behavior patterns must reflect more than white hostility toward all colored minorities.

In particular, the Japanese case constitutes the outstanding exception to the generalization that past oppression blocks present progress. By almost any criterion of good citizenship that we choose, not only are Japanese Americans better than any other segment of American society, including native whites of native parents, but they have realized this remarkable progress by their own almost unaided effort. In the early years they got some support from Japan's consuls; but this assistance, seldom very effective in any case, became of more and more questionable value as Japanese Americans increasingly recognized that their fate, whatever it might be, was tied to that of the United States. In their new homeland, they were neither the hapless beneficiaries of social welfare nor the cause of militant placard-bearers. Out of the elements of American democracy—universal education, the free labor market, citizenship for all native-born residents, color-blind justice—to the sometimes slight degree that these were available to them, the Japanese themselves fashioned their identity as the nation's prize sub-nation.

Denied citizenship because of their race, Issei[3] became exceptionally law-abiding alien residents. Young men were typically unable to marry at the usual age because of the extreme shortage of Japanese females, but later in life they developed a family style both strong and flexible enough to help their children cross a wide cultural gap. Deprived of access to many urban jobs, both white-collar and manual, they undertook menial tasks with such perseverance that most realized a modest material success. Forbidden to own agricultural land, they acquired control of small plots through one or another subterfuge and, by hard and efficient work, helped convert the California desert into a fabulous garden. Most significantly, within a decade or two after the degrading and debilitating internment in camps, former inmates pulled themselves up above even prejudiced criticism. Every attempt to hamper the progress of Japanese Americans, in short, has resulted only in enhancing their determination to succeed. Even in a country whose patron saint is Horatio Alger's hero, there is no parallel to this success story.

This book is less a study of Japanese Americans per se than an analysis of the puzzle that they present to theorists of ethnic relations. What made them different? What gave them the strength to thrive on adversity? And, in conclusion, how must our theories of intergroup relations be amended to take account of this deviant case?

After this introductory chapter, the exposition is in three parts—respectively, on Oppression (Chapters 2–4), Success (Chapters 5–6), and Explanations (Chapters 7–10). We begin with the migrations to Hawaii and mainland United States and recount the discriminations, sometimes basic or violent and sometimes petty, to which the immigrants were subjected. Rejected by their country of permanent residence and prevented from escaping altogether from their homeland's supervision, most Issei nevertheless chose to ally themselves with America, which for their sons would be the land of promise it never was for them. How difficult this choice was no outsider can ever know, nor how empty the promise became in the spring of 1942, when the whole subnation, citizen and noncitizen alike, were evacuated under armed guard and placed in prison camps. It is the considered judgment of Edward S. Corwin, in my layman's view the country's foremost scholar of constitutional law, that the incarceration of Japanese was "the most drastic invasion of the rights of citizens of the United States by their own government that has thus far occurred in the history of our nation."[4] With this defeat, the unequal struggle between a small, isolated, guiltless minority and the vast forces of the American state seemingly came to a final end. David did not slay Goliath; right did not win out over might.

The following two chapters give evidence of various kinds demonstrating, respectively, the postwar progress of the Japanese and their low incidence of virtually every type of social pathology. Amazingly, the record is even better on the mainland than in Hawaii, where most of the Japanese were not subjected to the camp experience.

In the concluding four chapters, an effort is made to resolve the anomaly. If elements of the Japanese culture were passed on to the Nisei generation, the first task is to examine the country of emigration during the years when most of the outward movement was in progress. The principal institutions that served as means of cultural transmission, presumably, were religion and the family, but in neither case can a firm link be plausibly established. The faith of Japanese Americans, whether Buddhism or Christianity, typically constitutes a loose and vague set of sometimes self-contradictory beliefs, tolerant of great diversity. The case for the family is stronger—indeed, perhaps too strong. Of all the maxims that Nisei memorized in Japanese-language schools, none was more important than "Honor your obligations to parents and avoid bringing shame on them." But the very rigidity of the family structure, particularly when contrasted with the aspirations to individual freedom that young Nisei acquired in the American milieu, should have given rise to a rebellious second generation. Indeed, the conflict within families was often sharp, but it did not result in the general erosion of authority that sociological theories would lead us to expect.

Neither the family nor religion, nor the two in combination, can adequately explain this subnation's behavior. A third factor is that Japanese Americans constitute a self-conscious cohesive group, with which almost every member has identified virtually automatically. Of course, the coalescence is partly the consequence of outsiders' hostility, whether actual or feared, but such a negative force does not in itself create a genuine subculture. It was reinforced in this case by pride in Japan's remarkable achievements, by a determination that every overseas Japanese should also set a proud record—in short, by an identification with his race that gave every person, not only symbolically but in the material assistance due him from the group, the strength of ten. That in some respects group solidarity has been maintained (for instance, by the extremely low incidence of out-marriage) has *not* meant that assimilation in other respects was blocked. On the contrary, acculturation in public roles can be facilitated if in private roles one is supported by traditional associations. The Japanese were able to climb over the highest barriers that American society was able to fashion in part just because of their meaningful links with an alien culture. Pride in their heritage and shame for any reduction in its only partly legendary glory carried the subnation through its travail.

Such an analysis may resolve the anomaly, but it raises new questions. For according to the conventional wisdom of sociology, acculturation is a bridge. The shorter the span, the easier it will be to cross it. By this view, the minority whose subculture most closely approximates that of the general population is the most likely to adjust successfully. Eventually, moreover, as Robert Park put it in an authoritative statement of a long tradition, all groups in continuous contact will merge; to persist in identifying either oneself or others by race, nationality, religion reflects a parochial—usually a reactionary—orientation, which fortunately cannot last very long. For as "the world becomes smaller," the number of ethnic groups will decrease more and more, and the social significance of differences still remaining will decline.

Incorporating the Japanese Americans into the theory of group relations means that all these propositions, many of them axiomatic, must be amended or discarded.

Notes

[1] "Japanese American" is clumsy locution, and I considered using AJA (American of Japanese Ancestry), which is sometimes heard in Hawaii, but it is not the role of even a sympathetic outsider to instruct any people on its proper designation. On occasion, for the sake of a less cumbrous style, I have followed the analogy of other nationalities and called the group in the United States "the Japanese," but this can be done only when there is no possibility of ambiguity.

[2] Gunnar Myrdal, *An American Dilemma: The Negro Problem and Modern Democracy* (New York: Harper & Row, 1944), vol. 1, pp. 75–78.

[3] In any analysis of Japanese Americans, the relation among the three (or now four or five) generations is so important that authors typically adopt the Japanese words for them in their discussion—namely, *Issei*, the first generation of immigrants; *Nisei*, the second generation, American-born children of Issei; and *Sansei*, the third generation, children of Nisei. In more popular usage, however, "Nisei" is often a synonym for Japanese American; for instance, most of the members of the Nisei Student Clubs at the various campuses of the University of California are now, in fact, Sansei. In Hawaii, on the other hand, some of the Japanese resent the use of any of these designations for the generations.

[4] Edward S. Corwin, *Total War and the Constitution* (New York: Knopf, 1947), p. 91.

Chapter 2 ◉ The Migration

The contrast between penury at home and opportunities abroad set an economic background to emigration from Japan, but from the beginning the lives of Japanese Americans, their hopes and fears, were controlled mainly by noneconomic factors. For three and a half centuries the Japanese government had prohibited almost all contact with foreigners. Then, after the restoration of Emperor Meiji to full power in 1868, the country rushed headlong out of isolation and, in a few short decades, began to compete in economic and military power with the largest Western states. Japanese were now encouraged to emigrate and did so, in most cases, under the supervision of their government.

At the receiving end, too, politics was more important than economics. The people of California, and eventually of the United States, gradually inculcated themselves with beliefs and attitudes that prepared the way for the incarceration in concentration camps of a whole subnation, charged with no crime and guilty of none. This culmination of a decades-long degradation, which is recounted in a later chapter, can be understood only in historical perspective.

THE CHARACTERISTIC EMIGRANT

The first emigration was in the year "Meiji One," or 1868, when 148 contract laborers went to Hawaii.[1] Their experiences left an aftertaste of bitterness and distrust. Within a month of when they started work, complaints came to Hawaii's Board of Immigration both from them and from their employers, and reports of the trouble, considerably magnified, found their way back to Tokyo. An agent of the Japanese government, sent to investigate, arranged to have the most dissatisfied returned home at Hawaii's expense. The proud new regime was determined that its country should not be regarded as another China, one more storehouse of coolie labor to be maltreated by foreign overseers. For seventeen years no more contract laborers went to Hawaii; and the emigration of Japanese to any destination was placed firmly under the control of a government bureau or, later, government-sponsored emigration companies, whose ostensible purpose it was to protect even humble workers abroad from any indignities. Often this protection was at best nominal, but the supervision by agents of the Japanese government set some of the conditions of acculturation (Conroy, 1953: 15–40).

From the 1860s on, the Hawaiian economy moved continuously toward concentration on a single endeavor—sugar. Production increased from almost nothing around 1840 to more than 4 million tons at the end of the century, double that in the 1930s, and between 10 and 11 million tons in the mid-1960s. Sugar production brought an almost insatiable demand for plantation laborers, who were recruited from other islands of the Pacific, China and Japan, the West Indies, many European countries, and various parts of the United States (Conroy, 1953: 9–13). Though Walter Murray Gibson, the premier and minister of foreign affairs, was not hostile to the planters' needs, the government's main concern in his view should be to populate the islands with suitable stock—that is, persons who would work efficiently in the fields, but would also be acceptable politically and socially. But Europeans and Americans were not attracted to the poorly paid, hard work on sugar plantations; Polynesians from other Pacific islands, whom the Hawaiian rulers wanted to bring to their kingdom, were not numerous enough to satisfy the demand; and Chinese, at first praised for their obsequious diligence, were perceived—after their numbers increased somewhat—as a major economic and civic threat. A committee of the legislature recommended that "Japanese immigration under proper restrictions should be encouraged as the best partial substitute for Chinese labor in this Kingdom, bringing as it does a class who are willing to adopt Western civilization and who can be incorporated into our system without seriously disjointing it."[2]

Virtually all Japanese immigrants to Hawaii, thus, started as plantation workers. Their movement was arranged principally by Robert Walker Irwin, an American businessman living in Japan and the acting consul general for Hawaii, who in the 1880s became a special agent of Hawaii's board of immigration. As a social intimate of Japan's foreign minister, Irwin was able to organize the large migration that the sugar planters urgently demanded. His efforts were strongly reinforced by an economic crisis in Japan: a galloping inflation succeeded by a vast deflation brought widespread unemployment and social unrest, and the government was happy for the safety valve of an emigration program. The movement to Hawaii started even before the parties signed the Irwin Convention of 1886, which set the conditions of Japanese migration to that country for the next eight years and in essential terms, by its precedent, beyond that period. Under its terms, a total of 26 ships carried 28,691 Japanese to Hawaii.

The "first-year men" of 1868 had come from the area of Tokyo and Yokohama; their urban background may have been one reason they made poor plantation workers. As Irwin wrote his principals, he was seeking "agricultural laborers," and he found them in abundant numbers in southwestern Japan. The first came from the prefectures of Hiroshima and Yamaguchi. Considering it "wise and prudent to extend the privilege to other provinces also," Irwin later recruited in Kumamoto and Fukuoka as well. After the Irwin system broke down, enough overseas links existed from these prefectures to stimulate a continued movement to Hawaii and, later, to the United States (Conroy, 1953: 81–83).

In 1884, when the first call went out for contract laborers in Hawaii, 28,000 persons applied from all over Japan. Only about 600 were sent in the first shipment, and about half of these came from one small island, Oshima District in Yamaguchi Prefecture, which has been the subject of two detailed studies (Ishikawa, 1967a; Y. Doi, 1957). Since its population was too densely settled to subsist from farming and fishing alone, men traditionally took on such secondary occupations as carpentry or stone-cutting, and their wives wove cotton at home. The economic troubles were aggravated by a typhoon and a landslide. As recorded in one village, the daily meal consisted mostly of buckwheat and bean-curd refuse, flavored with aromatic leaves. The government distributed food to the worst stricken, who only thus were saved from death from starvation. Some men got jobs carrying building materials to the site of a new school under construction; at a time when the daily wages of field workers ranged from 70 to 150 *rin*, they were paid 5 *rin* for a barrel of gravel, 3 *rin* for one of earth or sand.[3] Many more applied to leave Oshima than could be accepted. Married couples were given preference; even so, most emigrants were single young men. Four out of ten returned to the village after their indenture, sufficiently well off to pay their debts, buy small plots, or build houses, thus undoubtedly stimulating others to follow their example.

Different details are given in a study of emigrants from a place on the shore of Hiroshima Bay (Ishikawa, 1967b). From this village a total of 777 went abroad over a fifteen-year period —624 to Hawaii, 151 to the United States, and small numbers to Canada, the French West Indies, Peru, and Australia. Of the 194 females, all but 10 were married. Though 58 of the migrants died overseas and almost half of the remainder had not returned by the end of the period, the village's resident population grew steadily from 2,673 in 1892 to 2,825 in 1899. This last datum, perhaps surprising at first sight, is confirmed by a study of another village, whose resident population increased from 1,967 in 1903 to 2,020 in 1916 in spite of the sizable emigration during these years (Ishikawa, 1967c). Emigration from another village started in 1887, when one man heard from a cousin of opportunities in Canada and moved to British Columbia. He prospered there and soon sent for some former neighbors to join him. Eventually not only the needy but the moderately well off were emigrating, some leaving their land to their tenants. No longer poor, the place acquired the name of "American Village." Of its 1,687 inhabitants in 1951, one-sixth had been born in Canada or the United States, and at that date 7 out of 10 families had relatives abroad, not including the 51 families that had emigrated *in toto* (Fukutake, 1962: 146–79; Population Problems Research Council, 1953).

From either the sum of such sociographs or the thinner general accounts, we know that most migrants to Hawaii were young agricultural laborers or small peasant-farmers. Four or more males left for every female. Seemingly, the most desperate left first, followed a few years later by those a bit better off. A large proportion of the emigrants to whatever destination, probably something like half the departures over the whole of the Meiji era, went abroad only to repair their fortunes and then returned home. The net movement was too small really to affect the country's population significantly, and even the villages from which the largest numbers had departed sometimes grew as a consequence of their greater prosperity. Their death rates may well have declined, their birth rates probably rose, and peasants from the surrounding area often moved in. Any improvement in the local economy was not due to a relaxation of population pressure, thus, but rather to assistance received from villagers overseas. In a single year, according to an actual count, 27,326 parcels were received from foreign countries in the various villages of Oshima District alone. The cash remittances from just Hawaii to Japan increased almost without interruption from slightly over $125,000 in 1892 to almost $3.7 million in 1907, making up a total over this period of not quite $29 million (Y. Doi, 1957). To such figures must be added the goods and cash brought back by remigrants, an amount impossible to estimate but possibly equal to the remittances.

From various types of data (for example, Taeuber, 1958: 199), it seems that Japanese who went to mainland United States came from less impoverished districts and higher social classes than migrants to Hawaii (or Latin America or the Philippines). Of the males who left one village, mostly for Hawaii, just under half reported their occupation in Japan to be in agriculture, and sizable proportions were in fishing, "seamanship," and casual labor (Ishikawa, 1967b). Of those who applied for passports to mainland United States in the years 1886–1908, in contrast, the main designations were merchants, students, and laborers (each more than 20 percent of the total), with agriculturists and fishermen together making up only 14.1 percent (Ichihashi, 1932: 66–67). One should not suppose, however, that at least by American standards Japanese immigrants

were well off. The cash that each person declared on his arrival ranged from an average of $11 in 1896 to a high of $26
in 1904; but even these tiny amounts were comparable to
those declared by Western Europeans and larger than those
brought in by Southern or Eastern Europeans (Ichihashi, 1932:
74–76).

The cultural level of Japanese migrants to the mainland was
high. Of a sample of wage earners surveyed by the Senate
Immigration Commission (1911, 23: 151–60), 97.8 percent
could read and write Japanese, and of a smaller sample of females, the percentage was 72.2. The urban residents especially
read enough news magazines and political commentaries to
suggest a lively interest in current events, even in a country
of which they could not become citizens. Partly because of their
literacy in their own language, "the Japanese have acquired the
use of the English language more quickly and more eagerly
than the Chinese, the Mexicans, and some of the European
races."

A NOTE ON STATISTICS

In the modern period, characterized by swollen populations
and efficient mass transportation, a migration must be measured in millions to be significant. And, as we know from a
hundred analyses, overpopulated Japan has been *the* country
of the world from which one might have anticipated an emigration commensurate with its growing numbers (Taeuber,
1958: chap. 3). Yet the movement from this overcrowded land
during the whole of the Meiji era totaled not many millions, but
only some hundreds of thousands. The all but universal theme
in analyses by non-Japanese, however, was "the Japanese invasion"—the actual title of an article in a reputable journal
(Chambers, 1921) and of a book introduced by Robert Park,
one of the foremost American sociologists of his day (Steiner,
1917). It was a major motif of many volumes produced by
agencies of a dozen governments. Nativist organizations clam-
ored in more frenetic tones for exclusion acts and periodically
relieved their excitation by violence against the few Japanese

they could discover. The disparity between this scholarly-offi-cial-popular fancy and statistical fact is of fundamental im-portance.

Both Japan and, at the other end, Hawaii and the United States collected statistics on the migration between the coun-tries, but all of the series are in various ways incomplete, in-accurate, and inconsistent. While it is not possible to resolve all the difficulties, neither can they be passed over, for through-out the period of immigration, one of the recurrent issues was the precise number of Japanese entering the country. It is con-venient to start with the most obvious source, the official com-pilation of U.S. immigration statistics (Table 2-1). Even the

Table 2-1. Japanese "Immigrants" to Mainland United States, 1861–1940*

PERIOD	NUMBER	PERCENT OF ALL "IMMIGRANTS"
1861–1870	218	0.01
1871–1880	149	0.02
1881–1890	2,270	0.04
1891–1900	27,982	0.77
1901–1907	108,163	1.74
1908–1914	74,478	1.11
1915–1924	85,197	2.16
1925–1940	6,156	0.03

* Not including migrants from Hawaii after its annexation.

SOURCES: Calculated from U.S. Bureau of the Census, *His-torical Statistics of the United States* (Washington, D.C.: U.S. Government Printing Office, 1960), Series C-88, C-104; Yamato Ichihashi, *Japanese Immigration: Its Status in Cali-fornia* (San Francisco: Marshall Press, 1915), p. 9.

meaning of the key term is not clear. Beginning in 1906, the United States has classified arriving aliens as either "immi-grants" (who intend to settle permanently) or "nonimmi-grants" (who do not). After the law of 1924 barred Japanese immigration, all Japanese arrivals (merchants and students in the main) were of necessity nonimmigrants. If we follow the usage of *Historical Statistics* and, as in Table 2-1, ignore this legal distinction, the conclusion is that the movement of Japanese to the United States developed slowly and never grew to be very large. The total up to 1900 was slightly over 30,000; from 1901 to the date of the Gentlemen's Agreement, almost 110,000; and from then to the beginning of World War I, almost 75,000. During the war immigration from Europe was cut off, so that the proportion of Japanese during the period up to 1924 was the highest for the whole series—2.16 percent. Thereafter, up to the year before the two countries went to war, the number of arrivals averaged 385 per year.

Even apart from the ambiguous meaning of "immigrant," no knowledgeable person would contend that the figures in Table 2–1 (the only ones that the reader of the usual book on the subject is likely to see) are more than roughly indicative. The main difficulties in interpreting such data are the following:

1. There was an indeterminate number of illegal and therefore unrecorded entries from Canada and Mexico. Japanese data suggest that both countries, and particularly the latter, were gateways to the United States: of the 12,000 Japanese passports issued for Mexico over the period 1892–1924, about three-quarters were to persons departing in 1906–1907, undoubtedly in response to the Gentlemen's Agreement then pending. But by any reasonable estimate, these surreptitious crossings over a longer period are well below the figures featured in anti-Asian propaganda.

2. Like Japanese migrants to anywhere in the world, those who remained in the United States constituted only a comparatively small percentage of the number of arrivals. The distinction between gross and net movement is fundamental, but it cannot always be made from the data that exist. From 1908 to 1924 (that is, from the Gentlemen's Agreement to the law barring Asian immigration), the 160,000 Japanese arrivals resulted in a net movement into the country of only 90,000. During these years, when the country was allegedly being flooded by "picture brides" (see pp. 43–44, 197–198), only 73,000 females arrived and almost 10,000 females departed.[4]

Japanese passport data also give only a very rough approximation of the net movement, since usually most were issued to laborers hired on short-term contracts, officials, merchants, tourists, and students, rather than emigrants in the narrow sense.[5] In Japanese, the word *dekasegi* ("going out to work") is contrasted with *teiju* ("permanent emigration and settlement abroad"), and for many years the second was almost a nul category. Virtually all who "emigrated" according to the statistics carried the dream of a triumphant return (Kihara, 1935: 559–63). Even Japanese born abroad were often sent back for a proper Buddhist education, and some of these so-called *Kibei* remained there.

3. Japanese passport compilations have another fault, for under the law a new one was required each time a person went abroad. The historian Roger Daniels interviewed Issei farmers who made as many as five round trips, and in an extreme case a merchant whose business took him back and forth across the Pacific had forty passports during his lifetime. Even so, there were fewer than 1.2 million issued to Japanese citizens over the more than half a century from 1868 to 1924, and one can agree that this datum shows that "the amount of Japanese emigration abroad has been insignificant" (Ichihashi, 1932: 8–9, 55).

4. Under American regulations, a person leaving the United States is classified as an "emigrant" if he intends to remain abroad or a "nonemigrant" if he does not. However, Japanese who had established a legal domicile in the United States did not relinquish it lightly; and in overwhelming proportion those who visited Japan classified themselves as nonemigrants until they could decide on the spot whether they wanted to stay there. In 1911–1920, according to Adams's estimate (1929), about 24,000 so designated departed permanently from mainland United States and about 17,000 from Hawaii. These remigrants thus constituted another inflation of American statistics on Japanese in the United States.

5. Confusion concerning the status of Hawaii in national statistics was a constant source of error from the time of its annexation as a territory in 1898 to its admission as a state in 1959. Parochial accounts about the islands estimated the proportions of Japanese who remained there as against those who departed "either to the mainland or back to Japan," and

works focused on the West Coast counted Japanese coming from Hawaii as new immigrants. For example, Jenks and Lauck's *Immigration Problem*, regarded for years as the most authoritative work on the subject, gave a figure for "Japanese immigration to the continent of the United States . . . excluding Alaska" that in fact included *both* the mainland and Hawaii, with the latter by far the larger part.[6]

One instance of the confusion about Hawaii is worth relating in detail. When the 1920 census reported that there were 81,338 foreign-born Japanese in the United States, many questioned the accuracy of the datum. Ten years earlier, the census count had been 67,655, and during the decade the net immigration was 67,109. Allowing for the probable excess (because of the subnation's age structure) of mortality over fertility, the 1920 figure therefore represented an underenumeration of some 45,000, or about 55 percent. The racist press made much of the supposed error, and two professors who authored responsible works on Japanese Americans (McKenzie, 1928; Mears, 1928) cited the data without comment. The discrepancy, however, was only in how two federal agencies defined "the United States." By the usage of the Bureau of the Census, it excluded Hawaii, but the Commissioner General of Immigration included territories—in both cases usually with no special warning to those using the tables. In order to correct the supposed error, one would have to estimate the natural increase of Japanese in Hawaii and on the mainland and their net movement between the two places; but this can be done only very roughly. When the figures were assigned to the proper populations and these estimates made, the counts in 1920 proved to be not significantly lower than the extrapolations from 1910, but slightly higher (Adams, 1929).

6. A final source of information, the data that both countries maintain of resident Japanese, is also inaccurate. In principle, each ethnic Japanese living abroad used to be obliged to register with a Japanese consulate, giving the place of his continuing legal residence (or *honseki*) in Japan. However, isolated groups and young children were sometimes omitted; the names of deceased persons remained on the lists for years; and in countries where the assimilation of Japanese was in process, such as the

United States, some did not register because this act was considered to be a symbol of political adherence to the old country. The consular registrations in 1940, for whatever they are worth, recorded a total of slightly less than half a million Japanese resident in all foreign countries, including 186,828 in the United States and its territories (Taeuber, 1958: 198–99).

In the schedule of each U.S. census, respondents are asked for the birthplaces of themselves and their father and mother. Those born abroad or of whom at least one parent had been born abroad are known collectively as the "foreign stock." Subsequent generations are not recorded, and in the census compilations they disappear into the general population except when —as in the case of the Japanese—the group is counted separately as a distinct race. Table 2-2 gives these data separately for native and foreign-born and for Hawaii and mainland United States. It was necessary to piece it together from a number of sources, for summary volumes do not furnish breakdowns for so small a unit of the national population. Yet it was this minuscule minority that was seen as a major threat to white America.

In sum, there are no satisfactory records of the movement of Japanese to Hawaii or the United States, but two main conclusions are possible from the data available. Since a very large proportion of those who left returned after a few years, one must clearly distinguish between departures-arrivals and genuine emigrants-immigrants. And the size of either category, but especially of the latter, was small—remarkably so in contrast with countries that had a far less urgent economic stimulus to seek better conditions elsewhere.

FIRST ADVANCES IN HAWAII

Under the convention that Irwin arranged, each Japanese signed a three-year contract with the Hawaiian government, which together with the employer furnished free steerage passage; guaranteed employment as an agricultural laborer at $9 a month (or $6 for a woman), plus a food allowance of $6 or $4, respectively; supplied free of cost suitable lodging, medical care

Table 2-2. Japanese Americans by Place of Birth, United States and Hawaii, 1870–1960

UNITED STATES (INCLUDING HAWAII)				MAINLAND UNITED STATES				HAWAII			
Date	Total	Foreign-born	Native-born	Date	Total	Foreign-born	Native-born	Date	Total	Foreign-born	Native-born
				1870	55	55	c	1884d	116	116	—
				1880	148	148	c	1890	12,610e	12,360f	250e
				1890	2,039	2,039	c	1896	24,407	22,329f	2,078
1900	85,437a	80,560a	4,877a	1900	24,326	24,326	c	1900	61,111	56,234f	4,877a
1910	151,832a	127,455a	24,377a	1910	72,157	67,655	4,502	1910	79,675	59,800f	19,875a
1920	220,284a	142,028a	78,256a	1920	111,010	81,338	29,672	1920	109,274	60,690f	48,584a
1930	278,465a	118,902a	159,563a	1930	138,834	70,477	68,357	1930	139,631	48,425f	91,206a
1940	284,852a	84,667a	200,185a	1940	126,947	47,305	79,642	1940	157,905	37,362f	120,543a
1950	326,366a	83,063a	243,303a	1950	141,768	52,255	b	1950	184,598	30,808f	153,790a
1960	464,332	101,656b	371,514b	1960	260,877	b	b	1960	203,455	16,699g	186,756a

a Calculated by addition or subtraction from other figures in the table.

b The numbers of native and foreign-born Japanese in the United States in 1960 are copied from Tables 7 and 8, "Nonwhite Population by Race," cited as one of the sources. The sum of these figures, 473,170, differs from the total shown in Table 2-2—namely, 464,332, which is the figure given in the general census volume (Vol. I, Part I, Table 44) and in subsequent editions of The Statistical Abstract of the United States. Presumably an error was made in the breakdown by nativity, and no breakdown has been calculated, therefore, for mainland United States.

c The numbers of persons listed as having been born in Japan were as follows: 1870, 73; 1880, 401; 1890, 2,202; and 1900, 24,788. Since in every case this figure slightly exceeded the count of ethnic Japanese in the United States, we can assume that there were virtually no native-born Japanese Americans.

d In three prior censuses, a small, indeterminate number of Japanese was included in the miscellaneous category of "other countries."

e The 1890 census lists 1,701 Hawaiian-born persons of either Chinese or Japanese parentage. Presumably more were of Chinese descent; Adams (1933:8) estimated that only 250 were of Japanese stock.

f Persons born in Japan, possibly including a small proportion of non-Japanese stock.

g Nonwhite persons born in Japan, possibly including a small proportion of non-Japanese stock.

SOURCES: Niles Carpenter, Immigrants and Their Children, 1920, Census Monograph No. 7 (Washington, D.C.: Government Printing Office, 1927), Table 43. Robert C. Schmitt, Demographic Statistics of Hawaii: 1778–1965 (Honolulu: University of Hawaii Press, 1968), Tables 17, 26, 27. Census of Population, 1940, Vol. II, Part I, Table 6. Census of Population, 1950, Vol. II, Part I, p. 1–88; Vol. II, Part I, Table 52, Tables 8, 18; Special Report P-E No. 38, "Nonwhite Population by Race." Census of Population, 1960, Vol. II, Part I, Table 6; Special Report PC(2) 1C, "Nonwhite Population by Race."

by Japanese physicians, and cooking fuel; and provided rice at not more than 5 cents a pound. A month's labor was defined as 26 ten-hour days (the vast majority agreed to work half an hour extra per day in return for a quarter-acre of land on which they could grow vegetables in their spare time).

The actual conditions, however, were more onerous even than these contractual arrangements. The inspector-interpreters that the Japanese government had demanded were often little concerned about the welfare of their charges. And at the insistence of the Hawaiian government, the financial burden of the whole operation was soon shifted. "Not only did the immigrant laborer come to pay his own 'importation' costs but most of the expenses of the Inspection Bureau and various unusual expenses as well" (Conroy, 1953: 70–76). In fact, within the framework of the plantation system, it was at first impossible to combat such abuses successfully. When the law was on the side of the worker, the law was not obeyed.

> It is perhaps inevitable that for a time the technical rights of laborers under American law will be disregarded. . . . It must be remembered that our legal codes were made for a country where social conditions prevail quite different from those in Hawaii.[7]

Those preparing the way for annexation by the United States were at best ambivalent about the rapid growth of still another Asian population, even one initially welcomed as a balance in the islands' ethnic structure. Yet until restrictions were imposed, the flow continued along the channel Irwin had set. In 1895–1896, the first full year after the system ended, 9,195 Japanese landed at Honolulu—or far more than the average over the previous eight years. In 1896, according to the last census of independent Hawaii, the Japanese constituted not quite 23 percent of the islands' population.

An economy grounded in plantation agriculture with social classes based largely on ethnic identification is generally far more rigid than Hawaiian society proved to be. How was it that this prototype of a European tropical colony transformed itself into a racially heterogeneous democracy? Several factors were relevant (Fuchs, 1961: 36–39).

1. Perhaps the most fundamental was public education, started under the influence of New England missionaries and made compulsory and universal by the time the Japanese started having children in the islands. The sons of coolies were thus prepared for other opportunities when they became available.

2. More generally, Congregational evangelism and, later, the American credo encouraged other democratizing institutions: a free press in various languages, including Japanese; universal suffrage for the native born.

3. The labor demands of the plantation system itself, with a new ethnic group brought in at the bottom of the social scale every two or three decades, repeatedly helped to push the earlier arrivals up one notch. Even so, the companies were under constant pressure to mechanize; eventually the cane was gathered with mechanical shovels, transported in trucks, and refined in mills operated exclusively by a handful of skilled technicians.

4. Most surprisingly, the ethnic stratification was gradually eroded by interracial breeding. Before annexation, the political link between Hawaiian royalty or nobility and their white advisers was often reinforced by marriage. Some of the proudest *haole* (or white) families have dusky Hawaiians among their legitimate ancestors, and in many cases their present power and wealth derive from the land acquired through such alliances. The *haoles* thus found it inexpedient to raise legal or even social barriers to the miscegenation of others; and in Hawaii, in contrast to other plantation societies or the rest of the United States, marriage across racial lines became both common and accepted.

Seen in retrospect, the advance of Japanese who began as coolie laborers was possible because of these factors. But this foreshortened view makes the process appear too easy, almost inevitable. The opportunities were there, but they were realized by dogged, unrelenting effort, and typically every half-step up was opposed by a more powerful group.

Although on the whole they were probably the most efficient

plantation workers, Japanese were generally paid less than any other nationality. According to official estimates, the monthly wages to contract field laborers in 1888–1890, including benefits paid by the planter, ranged from $19.53 for Portuguese down through successively lower rates for Hawaiians, Chinese, and South Sea Islanders to $15.58 for Japanese.[8] Such differential wages continued for decades, and as the demand for a larger white population grew, the increment offered to field workers of European (or part-European) stock went up. In his 1911 *Report*, the U.S. Commissioner of Labor commended the sugar planters for their willingness "to disregard the economic demand for cheap labor in consideration of what are at least partly civic motives in securing more costly labor" (quoted in Wakukawa, 1938: 187).

The product of a complex civilization, many Japanese had a manual dexterity and a ready adaptability that facilitated their rise from field labor to skilled jobs. Their training was often on the plantation itself. The process is vividly etched in remarks in two official reports, which though they have no connection might be successive paragraphs of a single commentary:

A [white] carpenter wants a board and tells a Japanese to get it; then he finds it convenient to have the man saw it, hold it in place, nail it; and so unconsciously he gradually begins . . . to associate an idea of degradation with the manual parts of his craft, and he becomes morally and physically unfit to ply his trade under the conditions surrounding him.[9]

Wherever a Japanese is given a position as assistant to a skilled worker or in a mechanical position, he becomes a marvel of industry, disregarding hours, working early and late, and displaying a peculiarly farsighted willingness to be imposed upon and do the work which properly belongs to the workman he is assisting.[10]

Once equipped with salable skills, plantation workers found it possible to get jobs in the general economy, but often not easy. A law passed in 1903 stipulated that only citizens or persons eligible to become citizens (that is, whites or Hawaiians among the adult population) were to be employed as mechanics or laborers on "any work carried on by this Territory, or by any political subdivision thereof, whether the work is done by contract or otherwise." Many other efforts were made to block the rise of Japanese into skilled occupations.[11]

A second route out of field labor, supplementing the development of Japanese artisans, was a shift to petty merchandising. The basic prerequisite was some capital, however tiny an amount. But was it possible to save anything out of the meager wages field laborers received? A typical budget of a single man in 1909–1916, reconstructed from historical data, is given in Table 2-3. The continuing link to Japan is indicated by the

Table 2-3. *Typical Monthly Budget of a Single Male Japanese Field Worker in the Sugar Plantations, Hawaii, ca. 1909–1916*

Monthly Wage			$18.00
Withheld by employer against contingencies			−3.40
Food		$ 7.00	
Clothing			
Work clothes	$0.75		
Rainwear	.50		
Oil for raincoat	.15		
Footwear	.60		
Cap	.08		
Laundry	.75	2.83	
Personal			
Cigarettes	$1.00		
Stationery	.30		
Baths	.25		
Lamp oil	.15		
Barber	.05	1.75	
Miscellaneous			
Contributions and gifts	$0.50		
Entertainment	.25		
Unknown	.17	0.92	
Total expenditures		$12.50	
Savings		2.10	
Net monthly wage		$14.60	$14.60

SOURCE: Ernest K. Wakukawa, *A History of the Japanese People in Hawaii* (Honolulu: Toyo Shoin, 1938), p. 177, as corrected in *The Hawaii Hochi*, Honolulu, June 15, 1968.

charges for stationery, lamp oil, and a portion of the contributions and gifts. Out of the monthly wage of $18, the companies withheld originally 25 percent, or at this time $3.40, as a deposit against possible future charges (this practice was abolished soon after the time of this schedule). Yet a frugal man could save $2.10 of the net monthly wage of $14.60.

As the size of the Japanese community increased, the demand for Japanese goods offered opportunities for importers and merchants (Conroy, 1953: 100). Retail groceries and dry-goods stores eventually became almost a Japanese monopoly, and other Japanese opened barber shops or restaurants, or became construction contractors. Some stayed in primary production with vegetable farms, coffee plantations, hog or poultry farms, or fishing. Of the Japanese who had immigrated from Oshima District in 1885–1899, Yataro Doi (1957) was able to find 29 still living in the islands in the 1950s. The range of occupations they followed is indicative—9 in dry-goods and/or grocery stores (usually combined; also some unspecified "business" or "store managers"), 3 in the hotel and/or restaurant business, 2 confectioners, 2 clerks, 1 watch repairman, 1 photographer, 1 tailor, 1 policeman, 1 contractor for railroad construction. Only 5 were skilled workers—3 carpenters and 2 metalworkers. A number of those surveyed had several occupations in strange combinations: a sugar-cane grower also owned a shop; one man doubled as proprietor of a dry-goods store and post-office clerk; a carpenter also raised poultry and hogs; a businessman was also a teacher. Manifestly, these men had not been able merely to step on an up escalator; they had patched together lives out of whatever was available to them, working twice as hard as most to achieve eventually a modestly comfortable middle-class level—but by routes they had to devise themselves.

Apparently the situation of field workers deteriorated after 1894, when government-assisted migration came to an end. The emigration companies that had been set up under the auspices of the Japanese government to protect the interests of its subjects abroad in fact joined with the plantation owners in exploiting the migrants, and because of the official link, the Japanese consul also often cooperated with the dual management (Kihara, 1935: 559–63). Only after a substantial Japanese community of skilled workers and small businessmen had come into existence did the plantation workers, responding to the assistance and even the initial stimulus of these more favored groups, begin to push for better conditions in agriculture.

> The Japanese . . . assert and enforce personal rights—as men, not as workingmen—by strikes. An unjust act to one of their number, or personal violence on the part of an overseer toward a laborer of their nationality, is resented with a vigor and directness that takes no account of economic results, either for the employer or for the strikers.[12]

More important, the policy of discrimination against workers as Japanese meant that many Japanese, businessmen as well as workers, felt their self-esteem to be under attack. The strike of 1909, "the most important labor conflict that ever occurred in Hawaii" up to that time,[13] was based on an interclass coalition led by intellectuals.

Motoyuki Negoro, who had just returned to Hawaii after studying law at the University of California, began the agitation with an article on plantation wages in a Japanese-language newspaper. (At that time Hawaii had eleven such newspapers, five radical and six conservative.) "The Japanese laborers," he declaimed, "who are placed in the position of slaves by reason of the prohibition of immigration to [mainland] America, do not have the courage to ask for higher wages." He petitioned the Japanese government to intervene, but it never encouraged him or the strike. With a number of like-minded intellectuals and businessmen, Negoro founded a Higher Wages Association, which was imitated throughout the islands. A letter that the "Chairman" of its "Executive Committee" (there had been fourteen at the founding conference) wrote to the Hawaiian Sugar Planters' Association set forth their demands. Prices had risen by 25 percent since the present wage scale had gone into effect (a true claim, according to a schedule of commodity prices the commissioner of labor submitted in his report), and they demanded an increase in wages in the same proportion, or from $18 to $22.50 per month. When the strikers were ousted from their plantation quarters, sympathizers housed them in the cities. But enough Hawaiians, Portuguese, Chinese, and Koreans were hired at $1.50 a day to break the strike.

Eventually 55 of the leaders, some of whom had tried violently to coerce other Japanese (though they carefully abstained from violence against those of other nationalities and even from destruction of property), were convicted of third-degree conspiracy and sentenced to a fine of $300 each and ten months' imprisonment. Because of the intervention of Rev. Takie Okumura, a Christian minister who was becoming prominent as a mediator between the two races (see pp. 59–60), they were pardoned after four months. Once the strike was lost, the planters raised the wages of the Japanese field laborers a bit, but they also fired or demoted some Japanese overseers and mechanics who had joined with their fellow countrymen. The planters suffered a loss estimated at $2 million, but they kept full control of wages and hiring policies.

In the succinct phrase of the commissioner of labor, the principal weakness of the strike movement was that "it was a plea for the Japanese as Japanese, and not for labor as a whole; and therefore the appeal did not inspire lively sympathy among workers of other nationalities, either on the plantations or in outside industries." In the context of a narrative on the Japanese Americans, it is this shift from class to ethnic conflict that makes the episode especially pertinent.[14]

Not surprisingly, a labor movement organized on a nationalist basis aggravated the nationalist sentiment on the other side. According to the Honolulu *Pacific Commercial Advertiser* (February 2, 1920), the purpose of the strike was to transfer to the Japanese "control of the sugar industry." The real issue, as given in an editorial of the Honolulu *Star-Bulletin* (February 5, 1920), was "whether Hawaii shall remain American or become Japanese." The material conditions of Japanese field laborers were improved somewhat, but at the cost of a considerable deterioration in Japanese-white relations.

THE ROUTE UP ON THE MAINLAND

In contrast to Hawaii, where almost all Japanese started as field laborers, mainland immigrants began in various places of the more diversified economy and shifted frequently from one occupation to another. The most detailed data come from surveys made in 1909 by the official Immigration Commission (U.S. Senate, 1911). During that summer, about 40 percent of the Japanese population was working as farm laborers, some 30,000 in California and between 700 and 3,000 in each of six or seven other Western states. Their employers were commercial growers of sugar beets, fruits, vegetables, and hops. Working hard for long hours on a piece basis, Japanese could make between $4 and $6 a day (compared with only $2 to $3 earned by those of other nationalities). The Japanese established themselves in many areas by underbidding not only white workers but even Chinese. Once their competitors were eliminated from most of the intensive crops, they became "less accommodating and [did] less work in a day; . . . by strikes and threats of strike and boycott they raised wages" (U.S. Senate, 1911, 23: 61–75).

Among nonagricultural employers of Japanese, the most important were the Western railroads. Some 6,000 to 7,000 worked as section hands and another 3,000 in the shops or as maintenance crews for bridges and buildings (U.S. Senate, 1911, 23: chap. 3). Other types of industrial employers—fish canneries, fruit and vegetable canneries, lumber mills, mines, and smelters—each employed only some hundreds of Japanese. Few generalizations are valid concerning the whole of this shifting industrial work force. "Seldom have other classes been discharged in large numbers to make room for the Japanese; on the contrary, Japanese have usually been employed to fill places vacated by others because of the more remunerative or agreeable employment to be found elsewhere." Japanese were typically paid less than other nationalities, except sometimes Chinese or Mexicans. Often they were hired in gangs through an agent, who for an additional fee also supplied the workers with Japanese food on the job.

Most Japanese wanted to acquire a plot of land, and many accomplished this piecemeal through a succession of different types of tenure. Contract labor was followed by "share tenantry," with the landlord's control dependent on how much money the tenant was able to furnish. This became "cash tenantry," under which the tenant put up most of the capital and was therefore fairly independent of the landlord. And, for the fortunate few, this was followed by purchase of the land, often in partnership with a white. Progress along this route was rapid. According to the 1900 census, in all of continental United States there were only 39 Japanese farmers, who held an aggregate of less than 5,000 acres. In 1909, according to the Immigration Commission's estimate, some 6,000 Japanese were farming under all forms of tenancy; the number of their holdings was perhaps in excess of 4,000 (of which 3,000 to 3,200 were in California), with a total area of more than 210,-000 acres.

> These farmers have practically all risen from the ranks of common laborers. . . . Of 490 for whom personal data were secured, 10 upon their arrival in this country engaged in business for themselves and 18 became farmers, while 259 found employment as farm laborers, 103 as railroad laborers, 4 as laborers in sawmills, 54 as domestic servants, and 42 in other occupations.

The success of Japanese farms derived in part from an extreme specialization. "Few of them keep cows unless they are conducting dairies, or pigs unless they are engaged primarily in raising livestock, or poultry unless they are conducting poultry yards." Japanese generally were willing and able to pay the highest rents for agricultural land—willing because of their strong desire to become independent farmers, able because of their extraordinary efficiency (U.S. Senate, 1911, 23: 75–89).

Another typical beginning employment was personal service. Many of the first Japanese immigrants, especially the so-called "schoolboys" (some of whom were actually students), were domestic servants, who worked four or five hours a day for $10 to $15 a month plus room and board. From this start many gravitated toward related service occupations, so that by 1909 between 12,000 and 15,000 were employed as servants, cooks, waiters, butlers, or the like (Ichihashi, 1932: chap. 8).

According to the same 1909 survey, Japanese owned a total of 3,000 to 3,500 small shops in many of the cities of Western states. As in Hawaii, many of these businesses catered more or less exclusively to a Japanese clientele, making specialty products like bean curd, running a Japanese-language printshop, acting as an employment agency for Japanese laborers, and so on. But the mainland Japanese were too few and too scattered to offer much of a market for such goods and services. Ambitious immigrants could do better introducing Japanese products to the general public, and so they became dealers in art goods and curios, florists, and especially restaurant owners, tailors, and purveyors of other personal services. The art shops or dyeing plants sometimes prospered, but the numbers engaged in most of these enterprises remained static or declined (Ichihashi, 1932: chap. 9).

In sum, the Japanese on the mainland began typically as laborers in agriculture, railroads, or industry. In spite of the low pay and uncertain tenure in these jobs, many were able to attain a greater stability at a higher return, either as tenant/owners of farms or as proprietors of small retail businesses. Several contrasts to Hawaii began to develop early, especially the more virulent animus that mainland whites felt toward the far smaller proportion of Japanese.

CALIFORNIA LEADS THE NATION

Though diffused over many sectors of the labor force, mainland Japanese have always been highly concentrated geographically. According to every census, by far the largest proportion have lived in California, sizable numbers in Oregon and Washington, a few scattered thousands in the Mountain States, and hardly any elsewhere in the country.[15] Even in California, one should note, Japanese were a tiny minority. The highest proportion ever was 2.1 percent of the state's population in 1920, and even figures for particular counties, though sometimes higher than this, were generally not significantly so. This concentration in the West was a fateful circumstance, for California led the rest of the nation in pushing, eventually successfully, for one anti-Japanese measure after another.

As in Hawaii so also in the United States, the welcome extended to the first Japanese had sometimes contrasted them with other, less desirable minorities. Even the Immigration Commission, not a body that indulged in empty praise of any group, commented that "their greater eagerness to learn has overcome more obstacles than have been encountered by most of the other races, obstacles of race prejudice, of segregation, and wide differences in language" (U.S. Senate, 1911, 23: 149). More generally, however, the Japanese were fitted into slots that had been fashioned for Negroes and Chinese. After they began to arrive, the national mood was to reverse the liberalization embodied in the civil-rights amendments to the Constitution, and a recurrent demand of anti-Japanese agitators was to extend to these other "Mongolians" the various measures that had already proved effective in putting down the Chinese. In a number of instances, these precedents proved to be more significant than anything the Japanese themselves did.

Following the discovery of gold in California, tens of thousands of Chinese coolies had been brought in, or had come as regular migrants, to work in the mines or on other mass projects. In 1869, to mark the completion of the transcontinental link, a golden spike was driven to hold the last rail— and some 10,000 Chinese were thrown out of work into an already depressed labor market. Anti-Chinese clubs already existed in every ward of San Francisco, and a new Workingmen's party thrived briefly on the basis of its single issue: "The Chinese must go!" In two cases that reached the Supreme Court, the only justice who argued for exclusion was from California, and he eventually convinced his colleagues of his position. A revised treaty with China gave the United States the new right to "regulate, limit, or suspend," but not "absolutely to prohibit," the immigration of laborers. In line with this stipulation, the Exclusion Act of 1882 suspended the immigration of Chinese laborers for ten years. The pressure that had been exerted to get the original bill through Congress was reapplied before the expiration date, so that the suspension was renewed in 1892 and in 1902 was made permanent (Konvitz, 1946: 4–12). Thus, for the half-century during which Japanese were first entering the United States, anti-Oriental agitation was a more or less constant factor in California politics.

The first large-scale protest specifically against Japanese took place in 1900, when in all mainland United States they numbered fewer than 25,000. Several of its features were to become characteristic. The site was San Francisco, the mecca of the anti-Oriental movement. The principal organizers and participants were trade unionists. The main speaker was James D. Phelan, then mayor of San Francisco and later United States Senator from California, who until his death in 1930 endlessly iterated the same theme: "The Japanese are starting the same tide of immigration which we thought we had checked twenty years ago. . . . The Chinese and Japanese are not bona fide citizens. They are not the stuff of which American citizens can be made" (quoted in Daniels, 1962: 21). In response to such propaganda, the Japanese government withheld passports from laborers who wanted to go to the United States, and the number entering the country fell by half from 1900 to 1901. However, the effect of this restriction was only to stimulate the California militants to greater demands.

In 1901, in the aftermath of a violent strike that the trade unions lost, they organized their own Union Labor party and elected a mayor backed by Abraham Ruef, "the most able and most crooked political boss San Francisco has ever seen" (Buell, 1922–23). The link to labor tied this unsavory administration closely to the anti-Asian movement, and particularly after the rampant boodling began to attract unfavorable attention from the bilked citizenry, Ruef was happy to divert public attention to the "yellow peril." The attack was renewed by a campaign in the *San Francisco Chronicle*, the most influential newspaper on the Pacific Coast. On February 23, 1905, a story appeared under a front-page banner, "THE JAPANESE INVASION, THE PROBLEM OF THE HOUR." For months similar stories appeared almost daily under menacing headlines, and the series continued intermittently for more than a year. In the middle of the campaign, the California legislature, by unanimous votes in both houses, passed an anti-

Japanese resolution repeating in detail the newspaper's charges; and for the next four decades, without exception, anti-Japanese bills were introduced in every biennial session.

Also in the spring of 1905, delegates from 67 organizations met in San Francisco and founded the Asiatic Exclusion League, which became the principal locus of anti-Japanese agitation. As its president, the league named Olaf Tveitmoe, an immigrant (possibly from Norway; his nationality is not established) who had served a term in prison for forgery (see Kawakami, 1912: 304–5). Most of the league's money seems to have come from the Building Trades Council, and of the 231 organizations affiliated with it in 1908, 195 were labor unions.

The antipathy that working-class and Socialist organizations expressed against Asians had an economic basis, but often this was no more than a rationalization for frankly racist opposition. AFL President Samuel Gompers frequently denounced Asians as scabs, but he also refused to accept them even into segregated locals.[16] From its center in San Francisco, this sentiment spread to national organizations. Together with the AFL representative in that city, Gompers authored a pamphlet picturesquely titled, *Some Reasons for Chinese Exclusion: Meat vs. Rice, American Manhood Against Asiatic Coolieism, Which Shall Survive?* If it was not possible to exclude the congenitally inferior Asians by law, the pamphlet called for doing it "by force of arms." When the Japanese poet and Socialist, Sen Katayama, visited the United States in 1904, Gompers welcomed him in *The Federationist* as "this presumptuous Jap," out of whose "leprous mouth" come "mongrel utterances." At the same year's AFL convention, delegates urged that Asian exclusion be broadened to include Japanese and Korean workers.

The racist virus infected also the ostensibly internationalist Socialist party. Its National Executive consisted in 1908 of two lawyers, two editors, one well-to-do merchant, one millionaire reformer, and one minister. These middle-class Socialist leaders issued a series of pronouncements on the immigration question that reflected, and helped increase, the xenophobia of the general public. Their stand did nothing to harm the cause: both in dues-paying membership and in votes polled, the party climbed during these years to the zenith of its prestige and influence.

> Between 1904 and 1907 the virulence of the attacks on Chinese and Japanese immigration in the West Coast socialist press had risen to such heights that the Japanese Socialist party appealed to American party leaders "to be true to the exhortation of Marx—'Workingmen of all countries, unite.'" There is no record of a reply being sent to Japan.[17]

Socialist opposition to contract labor or scabs was mixed with a generous dollop of racism. Victor Berger, one of the party's founders, asserted that the United States and Canada must be kept "white man's" countries; if the millions of Asians who wanted to invade the country every year were permitted to come in, "this country is absolutely sure to become a black-and-yellow country within a few generations." Ernest Untermann, whom many considered to be the country's leading Marxist theorist, asserted, "I am determined that my race shall be supreme in this country and in the world." Herman Titus, a leader of the party's left wing, noted that racial incompatibility is a fact and that "no amount of Proletarian Solidarity or International Unity can ignore it. We must face facts."[18] Jack London's essay "The Yellow Peril" voiced the general Socialist sentiment:

> Though we [whites] have strayed often and far from righteousness, the voices of the seers have always been raised, and we have harked back to the bidding of conscience. . . . We are a right-seeking race. . . . The Japanese . . . has developed national consciousness instead of moral consciousness. . . . The honor of the individual, *per se*, does not exist.[19]

In 1907 the party's National Executive Committee voted unanimously to exclude all Asians from the United States. A committee on immigration wrote a resolution calling for the "unconditional exclusion" of all "Mongolian races," in part because any other stand would place the party "in opposition to the most militant and intelligent portion of the organized workers of the United States, those whose assistance is indispensable to the purpose of elevating the Socialist party to political power." The resolution was vehemently opposed by a minority, and its wording was watered down. With its substance unchanged, an amended version passed, the authentic voice of American Socialism on immigration policy.[20]

In short, much of California's antidemocratic energy was generated by precisely those ostensibly most dedicated to democracy: the labor unions, the progressives, and the Socialists.[21]

Notes

[1] In 1968, on the occasion of the centenary of this pioneer immigration, thirteen children of the "first-year men" were still living in Hawaii, as well as many of their descendants (Goto, 1968).

[2] Quoted in Kuykendall, 1967: 179. "In many respects," according to Honolulu's *Pacific Commercial Advertiser* around the same time, "the Japanese are in advance of Western nations, and at all events they cannot be classed as 'Asiatics.'" In the future, therefore, Hawaii should "depend upon family immigration from Japan, Europe, and the United States" (*ibid.*: 174).

[3] One *rin* was the nominal equivalent of 0.05 U.S. cents. A better comparison is with the daily wage given in the text, for the income of 3.5 to 7.5 cents per day is obviously not a measure of the actual standard of living.

[4] Walter F. Willcox (ed.), *International Migrations* (New York: National Bureau of Economic Research, 1929), Vol. 1, "United States," Tables X, XIX. For a graph representing the same data over a longer period, see D. S. Thomas, 1950.

[5] Since 1898 Japan has classified "emigrants" and "nonemigrants" separately, but for someone accustomed to the jargon of the American immigration bureaus, the terms are confusing. An "emigrant" is a Japanese citizen "who goes abroad for the purpose of earning a living at some form of labor"—that is, for the period we are discussing, mostly contract laborers, many of whom later returned to their homeland. A "nonemigrant" is a Japanese citizen who travels as a tourist or student or government official—and also typically returns to Japan (Japanese National Commission, 1958: 163; Ichihashi, 1931).

[6] Jeremiah W. Jenks and W. Jett Lauck, *The Immigration Problem: A Study of American Immigration Conditions and Needs* (New York: Funk and Wagnalls, 1922), pp. 237–38.

[7] U.S. Bureau of Labor Statistics, *Report of the Commissioner of Labor on Hawaii, 1905* (Washington, D.C.: Government Printing Office, 1906), p. 142.

[8] Hawaii Board of Immigration, *Report, 1888–90;* cited in Katharine Coman, *The History of Contract Labor in the Hawaiian Islands,* Publications of the American Economic Association, 3rd Series, 4 (1903), 23.

[9] U.S. Bureau of Labor Statistics, *Report of the Commissioner of Labor on Hawaii, 1902* (Washington, D.C.: Government Printing Office, 1903), p. 103.

[10] U.S. Bureau of Labor Statistics, *1905 Report, op. cit.,* p. 31.

[11] *Ibid.,* pp. 45–46.

[12] *Ibid.,* p. 136.

[13] U.S. Bureau of Labor Statistics, *Report of the Commissioner of Labor on Hawaii,* Bulletin No. 94 (Washington, D.C.: Government Printing Office, 1911), p. 726. The following account is based mainly on *ibid.,* pp. 726–34, and for some details on Kurita, n.d.

[14] A strike in 1920 followed the same script with only minor variations. In the interim the Young Men's Buddhist Associations that had been organized on many of the plantations were federated into an association of Japanese laborers. One Japanese newspaper drew a parallel between the strike and Japan's victory over Russia, which had been due to "conviction of righteousness and enthusiasm born of honesty." Strikebreakers of other nationalities were hired again; and when the Filipinos, who had organized and struck separately, went back to work, the strike was broken with no gains. After their victory, the planters again made a number of concessions while retaining full control over their enterprises (*ibid.*).

[15] After the evacuation to camps during World War II, there was a slightly greater dispersion. The Japanese population of Illinois, as the prime example, increased from a few hundred in 1940 to 12,000 in 1950. But most evacuees returned to the West Coast and especially to California. The number of Japanese in that state, 93,717 in 1940, fell to 84,956 in 1950 but then increased sharply to 157,317 in 1960.

[16] For example, the AFL denied a charter to an agricultural workers' union in California's sugar-beet fields because its membership was principally Mexican or Japanese. See Herbert Hill, *The Racial*

Practices of Organized Labor—in the Age of Gompers and After (New York: NAACP, 1965), pp. 16–18.

17 Ira Kipnis, *The American Socialist Movement, 1897–1912* (New York: Columbia University Press, 1952), p. 277.

18 The quotations from Berger, Untermann, and Titus are from *ibid.,* pp. 278–79, 280, and 278.

19 Jack London, *Revolution and Other Essays* (New York: Macmillan, 1910), pp. 267–89.

20 Kipnis, *op. cit.,* chap. 13.

21 Each time a historian recounts one occasion when a Marxist or other Leftist organization followed a chauvinist policy, he is likely to note this as an exception to the presumed overall advocacy of international and interracial cooperation. Yet the ideology of solidarity across ethnic lines has always been mixed with the strong and sometimes vicious rejection of alien peoples. Marx's anti-Semitism is notorious. Two anonymous pamphlets that Engels wrote on how to resolve Europe's nationality problems—and that Marx fervently praised—were so pro-German that it was widely believed they had been written by a Prussian general. See Bertram D. Wolfe, *Marxism: One Hundred Years in the Life of a Doctrine* (New York: Dial Press, 1965), chap. 2. The Second International foundered because the internationalist protestations of the constituent parties proved in 1914 to be quite empty. Stalin's "socialism in one country" was a model for Hitler's "National Socialism." And such examples that might seem to warrant another judgment are often specious. If Communists have opposed the national aims of the countries of their residence, it has mainly been as Russian or Chinese patriots; when they have championed the causes of minority groups, it has largely been to make political capital out of social issues.

Chapter 3 ◉ Japanese Americans as Japanese

The Immigration Act of 1924, by excluding aliens ineligible for citizenship,[1] completed the succession of legal blocks to the entry of Asians that had been begun in 1882. Japan's reaction to the law was well expressed in a note by Ambassador Masanao Hanihara: "To Japan . . . the mere fact that a few hundreds or thousands of her nationals will or will not be admitted to domains of other countries is immaterial, [but] . . . the manifest object of the [exclusion clause] is to single out Japanese as a nation, stigmatizing them as unworthy and undesirable in the eyes of the American people" (quoted in Daniels, 1962: 101). When the bill passed, both Ambassador Hanihara and C. E. Woods, the American ambassador to Japan, resigned in protest.

One of the main underpinnings of the law had been an analysis by Dr. Harry H. Laughlin of the Carnegie Institution of Washington. Appointed "expert eugenics agent" to the House Committee on Immigration and Naturalization, he submitted a report entitled "Expert Analysis of the Metal and the Dross in America's Melting Pot":

> There has, thus far, been no suggestion in our law of any requirement except personal value in our sorting of would-be immigrants. [However,] the surest biological principle . . . to direct the future of America along safe and sound racial channels is to control the hereditary quality of the immigration stream.[2]

This analysis laid a pseudoscientific basis for favoring the immigration of Northwest Europeans, inhibiting that of Southern and Eastern Europeans, and—at least by strong implication—barring that of other races altogether.

The criterion that Laughlin used to rank the relative genetic quality of European nationalities was the proportion of each American subnation to be found in such institutions as prisons, insane asylums, and hospitals. If he had applied this logic to Japanese, he would have had to recommend that the United States encourage their immigration. But long before Congress was called on to consider the bill, the anti-Oriental sentiment once localized on the West Coast had spread over the entire nation. A seemingly routine decision of the San Francisco school board developed into an international crisis, and to avert what he feared might become a war, the President himself intervened. In arguing their case, the California militants thus got a nationwide audience.

FROM THE SCHOOL CRISIS TO THE GENTLEMEN'S AGREEMENT

The 1906 earthquake interrupted San Francisco's anti-Japanese campaign for only a few months. On October 11 of that year, the city's board of education directed school principals to send all Chinese, Japanese, and Korean children to the single Oriental public school, located in the Chinese quarter.[3] Almost half of the city's schools had been destroyed in the earthquake and subsequent fire, and the resultant overcrowding, the board later explained, was one of the main reasons for its decisions. Not that it had any choice, for—according to its second argument—segregation was mandatory under the law. Moreover, it found the mixture of races particularly distasteful because in the elementary classes Oriental immigrants just learning English, men in their mid-twenties, were sitting side by side with white girls and boys. A report of the segregation order was printed in Tokyo newspapers, and President Theodore Roosevelt received an official complaint from the Japanese government.

In private, Roosevelt half-agreed with the substance of the Californians' charges.[4] But the antics of Ruef and his gang could transform Japan, which had just completed its amazing victory over Russia, from a most friendly power into a hostile force. It was as the official mainly responsible for the nation's welfare that the President believed it necessary to involve himself in this parochial matter. He sent Victor Henry Metcalf, his Secretary of Commerce and Labor and the only Californian in the cabinet, to investigate the school crisis on the spot. The report Metcalf (1906) wrote is the best account of the affair (see also Daniels, 1962: chap. 3; Bailey, 1934, chaps. 2–3). A good half of it is devoted to background events. Only two months after the fire, the anti-Japanese campaign had been renewed with a boycott of all restaurants owned by Orientals. Windows were smashed, and a few Japanese proprietors and white customers were beaten. When Japanese restaurant owners agreed to pay $350 for "protection," the boycott came to a quick end.

But the pattern of violence was spreading. It was not safe for a Japanese to walk the streets of California towns. Metcalf gives vignettes on nineteen of the victims of assault; written in police-blotter style, they have a greater impact than would an emotional account, as these slightly paraphrased examples show:

> T. Kadono, a student, was attacked by a crowd of about 30 teenagers and young men on a Sunday morning while he was on his way to church. Treated at a local hospital for his injuries, he was incapacitated for about a week. The superintendent of the Japanese Presbyterian Mission, from whom he sought counsel, advised him not to report anything to the police.

> K. Kai was the owner of a provisions store, which about 20 young men entered for the purpose of starting trouble. When they started to steal some bananas, a Japanese clerk interfered and was beaten so badly that he had to stay in bed for several days. A thrown rock hit Mrs. Kai and hurt her leg. Mr. Kai lodged a complaint with the Japanese Association but did not dare approach the police.

> R. Koba, the secretary of the Japanese Association of San Francisco, was attacked one evening by three men, one of them holding a revolver. He was rescued by some friends who happened to be passing by. He reported the incident to the police, with no result.

Metcalf's conclusion from these incidents was that if the police power of San Francisco was not sufficient to give Japanese residents full protection, "it is clearly the duty of the Federal Government to afford such protection." No wonder Californians regarded Metcalf as a kind of traitor!

Nor was his report on the school crisis itself more satisfactory to the militants. The three reasons the school board had cited for its action all proved to have no substance.

1. The law supposedly forcing the school board's action read as follows:

> Trustees shall have the power to exclude children of filthy or vicious habits, or children suffering from contagious or infectious diseases, and also to establish separate schools for Indian children and for children of Mongolian or Chinese descent. When such separate schools are established, Indian, Chinese, or Mongolian children must not be admitted into any other school.[5]

Manifestly the board was under no legal compulsion to build a separate school, or to rebuild it after it had burnt down. Whether in a legal sense Japanese were "Mongolians" was a moot point. The courts had challenged the whole process of segregation, and the statute may not have been valid law even at the time. If it was, the school board did not enforce it either before its October 11 ruling or later, after the eventual settlement.

2. With newspaper accounts of "Mongol hordes" invading the schools, the precise number that Metcalf gave probably came as a surprise to most persons. Of the roughly 25,000 pupils in San Francisco, precisely 93 were Japanese, 68 born in Japan and 25 in the United States, distributed among twenty-three different schools.

3. The most unpleasant propaganda centered on the disparity in ages and the opportunity that grown Japanese were supposedly given to molest white children. Japanese males from advanced classes had been brought into kindergarten rooms, where they were photographed seated beside white children, and the school board had used these pictures to reinforce its case (Bailey, 1934:34*n*). But according to Metcalf's figures, the ages of the Japanese pupils ranged with an almost equal distribution from 7 to 20 years. More than a quarter of the total were girls, and no boy of any age sat in the same seat with a

white girl. No oral or written protest was ever made against a specific Japanese pupil (as contrasted with the vague category of "Mongolians"), and none was ever under the slightest suspicion of immoral or disorderly conduct.

"The labor unions," Roosevelt wrote, "bid fair to embroil us with Japan"; he instructed his Secretary of the Navy to compile a comparison of the two nations' warships (Bailey, 1934: 81). The President tried both to assuage Japan's resentment and to yield enough to the California radicals to satisfy them. To the Japanese ambassador, he termed the school board's action "a wicked absurdity." The Attorney-General brought suit (eventually two suits) against the school board on constitutional grounds, and under this threat its members rescinded their resolution ordering Japanese children to the Oriental school. The suits were dropped, and thus the constitutionality of the ruling was never tested. A considerable sector of California public opinion denounced the whole affair as an unwarranted intrusion of the national bureaucracy into state and municipal affairs.

Then Roosevelt carried out his part of the bargain. By an amendment attached to an immigration bill already before Congress, the President was empowered to prohibit aliens from migrating via an intermediate stopover (including even American territories) to the United States whenever he was satisfied that their passports had been issued "for the purpose of enabling holders to come to the continental territory of the United States to the detriment of labor conditions therein." Less than a month after the bill became law, Roosevelt issued an executive order (which remained in force until President Truman revoked it in 1948) barring immigration of Japanese from Mexico and Canada, as well as in-migration from Hawaii to the mainland. Had the last provision ever been tested in court, it was less likely to have been declared constitutional than the school board's ruling itself.

After more than eighteen months of detailed negotiations, Japan and the United States reached the famous Gentlemen's Agreement. The first publication of its terms was in the 1908 report of the U.S. Commissioner-General of Immigration:

An understanding has been reached with Japan that the existing policy of discouraging the emigration of its subjects should be continued, and should, by cooperation of the two governments, be made as effective as possible. This understanding contemplates that the Japanese Government shall issue passports to the continental United States only to such of its subjects as are non-laborers or are laborers who, in coming to the continent, seek to resume a formerly acquired domicile, to join a parent, wife, or children residing there, or to assume active control of an already possessed interest in a farming enterprise in this country. . . . The three classes of laborers entitled to receive passports have come to be designated as "relatives," "former residents," and "settled agriculturists." With respect to Hawaii, the Japanese Government, of its own volition, stated that . . . the issuance would be limited to "former residents" and "parents, wives, and children of residents." The said government has been also exercising a careful supervision over the emigration of the laboring classes to foreign contiguous territory.[6]

The bargain President Roosevelt struck was heavily weighted on the side of the California militants. In exchange for the rescinding of a minor ruling by a municipal board, they received what they took to be a virtual cessation of migration to the mainland not only from Japan and other foreign countries, but even from Hawaii. Moreover, "all the evidence indicates that the Japanese Government scrupulously kept the agreement" (Daniels, 1962: 44; cf. Bailey, 1934: 233–34, 278–79, 305ff). As the President wrote, "the whole object nominally desired by those who wish to prevent the incoming of Japanese laborers has been achieved." More Japanese were leaving the country than entering, and "by present indications in a very few years the number of Japanese here will be no greater than the number of Americans in Japan."[7]

The issue shifted from the immigration of Japanese laborers to that of "picture brides," from the exaggeration of immigration statistics to that of fertility rates. By Japanese tradition and law, a marriage was less a joining of two individuals than of two family lines. It was therefore arranged through a go-between by the families of the two persons to be wed, and when both of them could not be present, a proxy stood in for the absent partner (see pp. 197–198). The continued immigration of Japanese residents' wives, though in full accordance with the agreement, was seen by the California militants as another evidence of Asian perfidy. Roosevelt's seeming success in negotiating the Gentlemen's Agreement thus had an effect precisely the opposite of his goal; it stimulated the anti-Japanese extremists to demand a total victory.

NONCITIZEN PERMANENT RESIDENTS

It was necessary, by the logic of the California radicals, to define Japanese Americans not as a minority incompletely assimilated, but as Japanese incapable of ever becoming American. A key decision, that no Japanese may ever be naturalized, laid the foundation for much that was to follow.

One of the grievances against the English king that American colonists voiced in the Declaration of Independence was that he had "endeavored to prevent the population of these States, for that purpose obstructing the laws for naturalization of foreigners." Thus, when the new republic wrote its first naturalization act in 1790, citizenship was made a statutory right available under specified conditions to "any alien, being a free white person"—that is, not a Negro or an Indian.

An extension of the term "free white person" to exclude Asians was contrary to the apparent intent not only of the original law but of much subsequent legislation. The title on naturalization of the federal laws consolidated in 1873 began simply: "An alien may be admitted to become a citizen," followed by a list of such personal requirements as residence. A 1906 statute resulting from a general overhaul of the naturalization law once again used the general phrase, "An alien may be admitted," conditioned only by several personally attainable qualifications (McGovney, 1922–23). In 1918, Congress passed an act providing that "any alien" who had served in the country's armed forces during World War I could file for naturalization without the five years' residence ordinarily required (Konvitz, 1946: 93–94). The clearest legislative steps toward liberalization, finally, were two laws removing the original limitations; by acts of 1870 and 1940, respectively, foreign-born Negroes and Indians also became eligible for naturalization. In short, Congress's record suggests that it interpreted the phrase "free white person" to exclude from naturalization only Negroes and Indians, both of whom were eventually made eligible.

This was also the interpretation of the courts until 1878, when for the first time anyone of another race—a Chinese— was denied citizenship on that ground. But even that decision was not final, for later other Chinese were naturalized. More important was the Exclusion Act of 1882, by which Chinese residents became ineligible for citizenship; but nothing in that law or in the debates concerning it in Congress suggests that the intent was to bar naturalization to persons of any other nationality. The extension was made by the courts—less at the state or district level, where the record was inconsistent but generally liberal, than in the Supreme Court.

No one knows how this ambiguity would have been resolved if multiracial Hawaii had not been annexed to the United States in 1898. Once this happened, the possibility that Asians would be formally excluded from citizenship on the mainland was greatly reinforced.

By a new constitution that the Kingdom of Hawaii had promulgated in 1887,[8] all Asians were denied suffrage. The Japanese in the islands did not react until the monarchy had been overthrown and a provisional government was being installed. Then a group petitioned the Tokyo government for its assistance:

> The most influential element in these Islands is the Americans, [who] . . . run things to suit themselves. . . . We should be dominant as we are the most important element in these Islands. . . . It is not merely because of our numerical strength that we wish political suffrage, but to maintain the dignity of the 40 million Japanese in Japan (quoted in Wakukawa, 1938: 73–75).

Tokyo did intervene, but to no avail. At the constitutional convention of 1894, the principal issue was qualifications for suffrage in the Hawaiian Republic to be established. The Japanese consul general demanded that Japanese in the islands be given the vote, but the delegates (who had been chosen "without distinction of race"—6 native Hawaiians, 2 Germans, 3 Portuguese, 4 Americans, 6 British, and 14 Hawaiian-born Americans) found a means of rejecting the proposal while ostensibly postponing the decision. For to have acceded to the demand "would have hoisted automatically the Japanese flag over Hawaii" (Hatch, 1914).

Of the many weaknesses of the Hawaiian Republic, the greatest was that it had no substantial population behind it—not the native Hawaiians, certainly not the Asians, probably not even the British and other Europeans (see Table 3-1). Annexation was a prerequisite to survival, and it was arranged by a

Table 3-1. *Percentage Distribution of Population* by National Origin, Republic of Hawaii, 1896*

ORIGIN	FOREIGN-BORN	NATIVE-BORN	TOTAL
Native		36.2	36.2
Hawaiian		28.4	28.4
Part-Hawaiian		7.8	7.8
United States	2.1	0.8	2.9
Western Europe†	2.5	1.3	3.8
Portugal	7.5	6.4	13.9
China	17.8	2.1	19.9
Japan	20.5	1.9	22.4
Other countries	0.8	0.2	1.0
Total (rounded)	51.2	48.9	100.0
	(55,783)	(53,237)	(109,020)

* These percentages are of the total population, rather than of the adult population that might have exercised political power; but the intergroup differences are so large that a breakdown by age would not change the argument.
† Great Britain, Germany, France, and Norway.

SOURCE: Robert C. Schmitt, *Demographic Statistics of Hawaii: 1778–1965* (Honolulu: University of Hawaii Press, 1968), calculated from Tables 16–17.

series of deals that prompted President Cleveland to write to his Secretary of State, "I am ashamed of the whole affair" (Kuykendall, 1967: chap. 21). Tokyo formally protested that the annexation endangered the welfare of Japanese subjects in the islands, and eventually the United States paid an indemnity of $75,000. But in the Organic Act establishing Hawaii as a territory, all persons who had been citizens of the Republic were given citizenship, and no others. The annexation solved what had seemed to the American residents an insuperable problem. The 3,086 Americans (including Hawaiian-born children of American parents), even when augmented by perhaps twice as many whites from various European countries,[9] would have been overwhelmed by the 24,407 Japanese and the 21,616 Chinese. But once this mass of Asians was diluted into the general population of the United States, the proportions were reversed.

The key court case concerning the citizenship of Japanese Americans was a test of Takao Ozawa's naturalization. Ozawa, "a person of the Japanese race born in Japan," had applied for citizenship in 1914, against opposition by the federal district attorney in Hawaii. It took more than eight years before the final decision was made by the Supreme Court:

Including the period of his residence in Hawaii, applicant had continuously resided in the United States for twenty years. He was a graduate of the Berkeley, California, High School, had been nearly three years a student in the University of California, had educated his children in American schools; his family had attended American churches, and he had maintained the use of the English language in his home. That he was well qualified by character and education for citizenship is conceded. . . .

In all of the Naturalization Acts from 1790 to 1906, however, the privilege of naturalization was confined to white persons. . . . The appellant . . . is clearly of a race which is not Caucasian. . . . Of course, there is not implied—either in the legislation or in our interpretation of it —any suggestion of individual unworthiness or racial inferiority. These considerations are in no manner involved.[10]

Speaking for a unanimous court, Justice Sutherland interpreted the phrase "free white person" as narrowly as possible: "the provision is not that Negroes and Indians shall be excluded, but it is, in effect, that only free white persons shall be included." By *white* is meant not color (for this varies "even among Anglo-Saxons," not to say other European peoples), but inclusion in the Caucasian race. According to a decision handed down in the same year, however, the same justice speaking for the same court held that a high-caste Hindu of full "Indian blood," who had maintained successfully that he *was* a Caucasian by race, had nevertheless received his American citizenship illegally— in this instance, because of his color. As the court averred, "the words of the [1790] statute, it must be conceded, do not readily yield to exact interpretation." The test of what is a white person is not a scientific one (as it had supposedly been in the Ozawa case), but the understanding of the "common man" of 1790, as interpreted by the Supreme Court in 1922.[11]

The first law denying Asians citizenship had been the Chinese Exclusion Act of 1882. In the Immigration Act of 1924, vice versa, aliens ineligible for naturalization were not permitted to immigrate. In fact, however, the two policies are not parallel. It was inevitable that the United States should have set at least a numerical restriction to immigration, and those who advocated national quotas argued from the plausible thesis that the immigrants most similar to the native population were by that fact the most assimilable (see p. 225). There could be no good argument from the national interest, however, to denying full civil participation to persons given the legal right to live in the United States, work there, and bear their children there.[12]

DUAL NATIONALITY

Those few Issei who acquired temporary citizenship by decisions of lower courts, as well as all Nisei, who were citizens by reason of their native birth, were plagued by the conflict between Japanese and American laws defining their status. Some nations define their members by the principle of *jus soli*, others by that of *jus sanguinis;* nationality is acquired, respectively, by birth

within the territory of the state or by blood line. In many cases
a person may therefore have a dual nationality, but Western
law is not at all consistent on the point. In the Roman Empire,
nationality was generally defined by descent. Then in feudal
Europe children of alien parents acquired the nationality of
their place of birth. The disintegration of the feudal system
brought about on the European continent a reemphasis on the
blood line at the expense of territoriality. Under English common law, on the other hand, territoriality remained the dominant principle. And in the United States, nationality was con-
ceived as an application of *jus soli:* according to the Fourteenth
Amendment, which followed earlier American practice, "All
persons born or naturalized in the United States, and subject to
the jurisdiction thereof, are citizens of the United States. . . ."

What, then, should American agencies do to protect the interests of persons "born or naturalized in the United States," but
of forebears who came originally from a country that defines
nationality by the principle of descent? When the issue has
arisen, the United States has taken the stand that diplomatic
protection must be given to those who at maturity have indicated their adherence to American citizenship, and need not
be given to those who—for example, by permanent domicile
abroad—have evidently elected another nationality. "In 1897,
. . . the Department of State made great efforts to release from
military service in Switzerland a person born in the United
States of a naturalized father of Swiss origin," rejecting what
it termed that country's "exceptional doctrine of inherited allegiance." Two decades earlier it had intervened on behalf of
two brothers born in the United States of a German father; two
decades later, on behalf of the American-born son of an Italian
immigrant.[13] As these examples suggest, the United States has
consistently defended the position that native Americans of
dual nationality have the right to be protected against the second country's claims for military service or other supposed
duties. (The matter is more complex with respect to naturalized
American citizens, but this body of law is not relevant to the
Japanese case.)

Japan defined nationality in the same way as continental
Europe—possibly because after the Meiji Restoration it called

in jurists from those countries to codify its laws. But in this case, the United States cited this common conflict of law as a reason for excluding immigrants. Thus, according to the California State Board of Control:

> Every Japanese in the United States, whether American-born or not, is a citizen of Japan and as such is subject to military duty to Japan. . . . American-born Japanese would appear to be enjoying all the advantages of American citizenship [!] without assuming the most important responsibilities of such citizenship. Once a Japanese always a Japanese (quoted in Malcolm, 1921).

Indeed, Japan differed from continental European countries in one important respect: following petitions from Japanese Americans (see pp. 57–58), the rule of descent was successively relaxed to accommodate it to the American rule. In 1916, Japanese law was revised to permit Nisei (except for males between the ages of 17 and 28, who were eligible for military service) to renounce their allegiance to Japan. And according to a law passed in 1924, American Nisei automatically lost their dual nationality unless, within fourteen days of their birth, a parent or legal guardian took the initiative and registered the infant as a Japanese subject with a consulate.

Loyalty, allegiance to country—these are attitudes of the conscious mind. Dual citizenship, on the other hand, derives from factors over which no person has any control—his ancestry and place of birth (plus his parents' decision, in the case of Nisei, whether to register his birth). Even before the change in law, the registration of *honseki* was markedly incomplete (Buell, 1923; see above, pp. 18–19); and after 1924 only a minority of Japanese infants born in the United States acquired dual nationality. According to a survey that the War Relocation Authority made in 1943, only 15 to 25 percent of all Japanese Americans (very possibly something of an understatement) admitted to being dual citizens (tenBroek, 1968: 273).

THE ANTI-JAPANESE LAND LAWS

Prescribed noncitizenship bars permanent residents from the only legitimate route to political power. That in a heterogeneous population some public officials discriminate against ethnic minorities is hard to avoid; but in a democracy the remedy for this pathology, the revenge against such officials at the polls, is ordinarily effective. When groups are denied suffrage, as were most Negroes in the South and all foreign-born Asians anywhere, they are likely to become the butt of the continual denigration, often petty but sometimes not, that is seen as appropriate to their second-class status. The right to vote entails much more than making a choice on election day.

Citizenship, moreover, is often a prerequisite to certain upper-level economic activities. On the same day that the Ozawa decision was handed down, the Supreme Court heard another case: two Issei, Takuji Yamashita and Charles Hio Kono, had been naturalized but were denied permission, legally restricted to citizens, to incorporate a real-estate company. Since "the petitioners were not eligible to naturalization," the judgment of the lower court that had granted them citizenship was void. And since the naturalization was void, activities limited to citizens were denied them. So simple a route to economic discrimination was irresistible. It required only a law restricting land ownership to citizens or aliens eligible for naturalization to oust the Japanese from agriculture altogether. That at least was the intent; the reality was not so simple.

The first anti-Japanese land law was enacted by California in 1913. At that date, according to the state's own records, out of its 27 million acres of improved and unimproved land, Japanese owned 12,726 acres, much of which they had reclaimed themselves (Bailey, 1932). While the bill was being discussed, California newspapers reported that a mob of 20,000 had assembled in Tokyo to demand war against the United States, and once again the President felt it necessary to intervene. Wilson sent his Secretary of State, William Jennings Bryan, to Sacramento to confer; during the five days he was there, the bill was introduced, amended, and passed by 35 to 2 in the Senate and 72 to 3 in the House.

In its original version, the law denied to all persons ineligible for citizenship the right either to own or to lease agricultural land in California. In deference to the many white landowners who wanted to rent to Japanese tenants, it was amended to permit leasing for no more than three years. The law was a severe blow, but some Issei were able to circumvent its provisions by purchasing land in the names of their native-born offspring, and others paid white citizens to buy land and hold it for their children. During World War I, when many farm workers left agriculture for better paying factory jobs, Japanese were eagerly sought as agricultural tenants, and they made their most notable advances in California agriculture in the years immediately following 1913 (Iwata, 1962).

The end of the war, however, brought thousands of returning veterans, the beginning of an economic depression, and—predictably—the renewal of anti-Japanese agitation. The American Legion distributed a movie purportedly exposing the Japanese spy system, the abduction of white girls, and the manipulation of vegetable prices by Japanese growers. A mob of several hundred whites took 58 Japanese agricultural laborers from their beds, put them on a freight train out of town, and warned them never to return (Buell, 1922–23). In 1920, California tried to plug the loopholes that had made the 1913 land law more or less ineffective. Japanese lost the right to lease agricultural land altogether, and they were forbidden to act as guardians of native-born minors with respect to property that they themselves could not legally own. With some variations, the California law was imitated by Arizona in 1917, Louisiana in 1921, New Mexico in 1922, Idaho, Montana, and Oregon in 1923, Kansas in 1925, and Arkansas, Utah, and Wyoming (all of which had had Japanese shipped in to relocation camps) in 1943. As the dates suggest, most of this legislation was actually part of the campaign to prohibit Asian immigration, the goal that was realized in 1924, with the three stragglers in 1943 expressing wartime hostility. Only the Arkansas law referred to Japanese by name; all the others followed the California precedent of denying to aliens ineligible for naturalization the right to own land or to lease it except under specified conditions (McGovney, 1947). In 1923, the Supreme Court had heard three cases challenging the California law, which the plaintiffs held was in conflict with both the Fourteenth Amendment (which guarantees equal protection of the laws to all persons) and the Civil Rights Act of 1870 (which made it a criminal offense to deprive "any inhabitant of any state" of his rights). The Court upheld the law on the ground that, in the absence of a treaty stipulating aliens' rights, each state has the power to set its own legal structure (McGovney, 1947; Konvitz, 1946: 148–57; cf. Mears, 1928: chap. 7).

How much of an impediment the 1920 law was to Japanese agriculturists in California is a matter of dispute. Its enforcement was postponed until the Supreme Court found it to be constitutional. Thereafter, the pattern of enforcement depended on local officials, who in some instances ignored evasions. The structure of agriculture was changing in any case, and estimates differ on how much Japanese participation was altered for that reason. According to Iwata (1962), the law "did much to discourage the Japanese from entering farming or expanding their operation," while Daniels (1962: 88) termed the 1920 law "an empty gesture, an ineffective irritant; it caused much litigation, but in no wise significantly affected land tenure in the state." It is noteworthy that the argument is generally, as in this instance, between Nisei and white scholars. Agreeing with Iwata are Miyakawa (in a review of Daniels's book) and Kitano (1969: 26); and with Daniels are McWilliams (1945: 64–66) and Modell (1969a). Nisei emphasized such factors as personal badgering,[14] while the others countered with "hard" though possibly less pertinent data.

The life of the Japanese, particularly after the depression of the 1930s started, was in any case "tough, risky, and unglamorous." Around 1935 the median farm in Los Angeles County— 20 to 24 acres, with more than half the labor provided by the family—had an average net return of only $4,229. Even so, fewer than one farm in five showed a loss (Modell, 1969a). The legal harassment, in short, did not undermine the remarkable resilience of this people, but it did change their behavior in one respect. However law-abiding in every other way, they could continue to survive only by circumventing the purpose of the land laws, taking advantage of every quasilegal or plainly illegal deal that opportunity offered.

COMMUNITY ORGANIZATIONS

That in spite of all obstacles these small farmers could compete successfully against the large corporations that were starting to dominate California agriculture was due to their organization. "The Japanese," according to a standard sociological source of the 1920s, "are the most efficiently and completely organized among the immigrant groups."[15] Some of these organizations can be classified as social or religious or economic or political, but most were multifunctional. Since in all of them the Japanese were cut off from other Americans, even those established to assist in acculturation to some degree reinforced their differentiation from the white population.

Japanese farmers worked hard, and their skill in husbandry was of a high order, but these qualities were not sufficient. They also cooperated to meet common problems.

The early Japanese farm organizations . . . aided their members in finding ranches, served to limit the competition for land by fixing a maximum rental that a Japanese should pay, assisted in marketing the crops and obtaining supplies, interested themselves where disputes arose between a landlord and a tenant, and disseminated scientific knowledge of agriculture and horticulture through publications of their own. Many . . . served as mutualbenefit societies as well (Iwata, 1962; cf. U.S. Senate, 1911, 23:131–34).

An added strength of the producers was that in California the Japanese also dominated the retail distribution of fruits and vegetables. In 1941 the thousand or so Japanese-run "fruitstands" employed a total of about 5,000 persons (most of them Nisei) and enjoyed gross sales of $25 million.

In 1937, Local 770 of the Retail Food Clerks, AFL, tried to organize the fruitstand employees, who worked about twelve hours a day for low wages. The Nisei hurriedly organized a union of their own, thoroughly nonmilitant, which their employers promptly recognized. After its initial thrust failed, Local 770 reverted to the AFL norm and issued handbills calling on the public: "DON'T BUY JAPANESE. . . . Do not let us compete with un-American standards of living." Finally, in the spring of 1941, a Nisei was given an AFL charter to organize all the Japanese employees of retail produce outlets in southern California. The ethnic union voted unanimously to transfer, and the new local was granted the same contracts previously won by Local 770. When war broke out several months later, this precarious foothold in the Los Angeles labor movement was far too little to influence it on behalf of the Japanese (Modell, 1969b).

Outside the economic sphere, the organizational life was transferred in large part from the old country.[16] Japan was divided geographically by two systems, the formal administrative units of prefecture, county, city, town, and village, and the "natural" units established in tradition but with no legal existence. In their new setting overseas, emigrants did their best to duplicate the latter, especially the hamlet or *buraku*,[17] which to an outsider would look like a cluster of several dozen farm households. But through its informal pattern of cooperation, the hamlet was in fact the most important social unit intermediate between nation and household. Its functioning can be illustrated by one thoroughly studied village, Niiike, in southwestern Honshu. All its members met regularly for Buddhist services, rotating from one house to another. After the prayers and ceremonies, the oldest man would initiate discussions of general community interest, and after each side had had its say, a decision would be reached by consensus—affected, of course, by the landlords' influence over their tenants, but ostensibly the community's single voice (Beardsley, 1959: 352).

John Embree, whose analysis of a Japanese village (1939) is an ethnographic classic, did a study shortly thereafter of the Japanese in Kona, Hawaii (1941). Each Japanese farm family in the area cultivated an average of 5 acres of leased land, from which they wrested about 125 bags of coffee, then worth approximately $625—or scarcely enough to cover the year's living expenses. Other Japanese had taken over most of the small shops, and some of the second generation had become schoolteachers or even doctors or lawyers. A few Nisei had joined Christian churches, thus sacrificing status among the Buddhists for increased prestige among the whites. In short, fifty years after settlement, acculturation was well under way. The organizational structure transferred from Japan, however, was still important. The functional equivalent of the hamlet was the *kumi*, or neighborhood (in Japan, this would be an informal subunit of the *buraku*). "Perhaps the most important social group in Kona," the *kumi* consisted usually of fifteen to twenty households, including even Okinawans and Eta (see pp. 228–229), who were excluded from other organizations. Through the *kumi* the community engaged in all kinds of co-operation—helping in such emergencies as a house fire, participating in communal activities like road repair, assisting at weddings and funerals, and insuring its members for the cost of their burial. Such a utilitarian orientation was sufficient to retain the loyalty of the Issei; but "some of the second generation are opposed to the *kumi* system as uneconomical or troublesome, and younger men frequently do not belong to a *kumi* or do so rather passively" (Embree, 1941: 33–45).

An interesting variant of the local organization was the so-called *tanomoshi* (or *kō*), a combination of investment fund and credit service organized for one specific goal.

> *Tanomoshi* . . . vary somewhat as to the number of members, the size of the investments, [and the] purpose. An interesting *tanomoshi* was once started by several women who wanted wrist watches. They solicited friends and made up a group of ten members, each agreeing to pay $5 a month. In this way each received her watch eventually (Masuda, 1937).

Through such cooperation, some in the fund were able to procure the watch much sooner than if each had had to save up for it individually. The system is built, of course, on absolute trust; the word derives from *tanomu*, which means "dependable." Nothing bound a person to pay his share except honor, but to default was rare.

Both in Hawaii and on the mainland, the commonest organization among the Japanese was the *kenjin-kai,* an amorphous social association based on common prefectural origin. A *kai*'s convivial activities were climaxed each year with a lavish picnic, and in addition it served as an employment agency, legal aid, newspaper publisher, and focus of *tanomoshi* and other, more formal arrangements for the development of capital. According to the estimates that Modell (1969a) cites, the Los Angeles area had twelve *kai* in 1909, more than double that number in 1924, and forty in 1940. The *kai* were also the member organizations of the Japanese Associations, which until the mid-1920s were the Japanese Americans' principal spokesmen. There were two such organizations in Hawaii, one based on the prefectures of Japan proper and the other on those of Okinawa. On the mainland there were four large associations—located in Los Angeles, San Francisco, Portland, and Seattle, with a total of about eighty affiliated local branches—plus smaller independent groups elsewhere in the country. Their activities were similar to those of individual *kai* on a larger scale. Japanese Associations published various aids to Americanization (lessons in English or on American culture, pamphlets on child care), undertook to keep their members in line (for example, with antigambling campaigns), translated into Japanese all laws and regulations bearing on the life of their members, and presented in English booklets the Japanese American case on political issues.

On several occasions, the most important concerning dual citizenship, the Associations induced Japan to change its policy so as, in effect, to facilitate acculturation to American society. In 1914, their representatives memorialized the Japanese legislature to alter its nationality law and then went to Tokyo to persuade it to act on their petition. That the law was changed in 1916, and again in 1924, was "entirely through the activities of the Japanese Associations" (Fujita, 1929; see above, p. 50). On the other hand, the Associations also acted as quasi-official representatives of Tokyo.

Since the Japanese in America have been treated by their home country as colonists, . . . the Japanese Associations in America are practically a department of the Japanese

Government. They . . . register and regulate Japanese
subjects, . . . and advise the home government through
local Japanese consulates as to the problems arising in
this country (Fujita, 1929; cf. Daniels, 1962: 26).

Japanese consulates gave the Associations the right to endorse
the legal documents that virtually all their members needed
from time to time, and for this service they collected fees of
$1 to $4. After the Immigration Act of 1924 was passed and
this function lapsed, the Associations started to decline.

The *kai* reflected the ambivalence of Issei toward a country
that persistently rejected them. In 1930 there was founded an
organization of Nisei, the Japanese American Citizens League
(JACL), which grew slowly over the following decade. Its
stance was the obverse of the first generation's partial link to
Japan—an absolute and defensive American patriotism. The
"Japanese American Creed" that Mike Masaoka, national secretary of the JACL, composed in 1941 is a good example of its
politics:

> I am proud that I am an American citizen of Japanese
> ancestry, for my very background makes me appreciate
> more fully the wonderful advantages of this nation. I
> believe in her institutions, ideals, and traditions; I glory
> in her heritage; I boast in her history; I trust in her fu-
> ture. . . . Although some individuals may discriminate
> against me, I shall never become bitter or lose faith, for I
> know that such persons are not representative of the ma-
> jority of the American people. True, I shall do all in my
> power to discourage such practices, but I shall do it in the
> American way: above-board, in the open, through courts
> of law, by education, by proving myself to be worthy of
> equal treatment and consideration. . . . Because I believe
> in America, and I trust she believes in me, . . . I pledge
> myself to do honor to her at all times and in all places,
> . . . in the hope that I may become a better American in
> a greater America.[18]

JAPANESE-LANGUAGE SCHOOLS

Among the various types of Japanese American associations, the one challenged most often was the private school, established so that Nisei children could supplement their regular public education with something about the language, customs, and ethical norms of the old country. These were no more unique than dual citizenship; such other immigrant groups as the Chinese and the Jews set up similar institutions. In the case of the Japanese, however, the mere existence of the schools was repeatedly cited as proof of disloyalty to the United States —for example, by the Supreme Court in the Hirabayashi case and by General DeWitt to justify the evacuation (tenBroek, 1968: 268–69).

The main objective of the curriculum was to teach the Japanese language. The first textbooks were those used in the school system of Japan, but they were both too difficult for instruction in a second language and full of adulation of the emperor. During the two decades following World War I, this instruction was a principal issue in anti-Oriental agitation. In Hawaii, all foreign-language schools were forcibly incorporated into the public system and taxed $1 per pupil. After a protracted legal battle led by Honolulu's main Japanese newspaper, the law was finally held to be unconstitutional and all fees were returned. The aggravated antipathy between whites and Orientals, however, remained (K. G. Harada, 1934; Reinecke, 1969: 126–29).

The controversy also split Hawaii's Japanese community into bitterly opposed factions, conciliatory versus oppositionist. Rev. Takie Okumura, a Christian clergyman, became the spokesman for assimilationists. The New Americans Conference that he founded agonized endlessly over which Japanese customs should be discarded, which retained, in order to facilitate Americanization. What might be taken to be the crux of the American credo, the desire to advance oneself, was paradoxically excluded: "We encourage the Japanese to induce their children to remain permanently on the plantation and to make farming a life profession" (Okumura and Okumura, 1927: 10;

Sanjume, 1939). During the same period the language teachers themselves wrote new texts that combined the elements of Japanese with instruction in American democracy. Whether the inculcation of Japanese patriotism was completely removed, however, continued to be an issue even among Japanese. Some held that since the curriculum had been "revised to meet American ideals and customs, . . . the schools were helping to promote good will and to better relations between Japan and the United States," others that "Americanization was hindered and Japanese nationalism and culture were taught and perpetuated" (Onishi, 1943: 27–28).[19] Daniel Inouye, later a United States Senator from Hawaii, tells of an incident in 1939, when he was a high school student attending Japanese classes.

> Day after day, the [Buddhist] priest who taught us ethics and Japanese history hammered away at the divine prerogatives of the Emperor. . . . He would tilt his menacing crew-cut skull at us and solemnly proclaim, "You must remember that only a trick of fate has brought you so far from your homeland, but there must be no question of your loyalty. When Japan calls, you must know that it is Japanese blood that flows in your veins."

One day, when the priest was mocking Christianity, Inouye demanded that he respect his Christian faith in the same way that the boy respected his teacher's Buddhism. Inouye was thrown bodily out of the school, and he never went back (Inouye, 1967: 36–37). That Daniel Inouye is an American patriot he has proved by his whole mature life, but he certainly did not acquire this ethical norm in his Japanese school.

The most important fact about the schools was their diversity. The proportion of Nisei children enrolled varied from almost all in Honolulu down to none in some areas of the mainland.[20] Some taught one political line, some another; some were efficient, others far from it; some students absorbed, others rejected, what they were taught. As extensions of the control that Issei parents tried to exert within their families, the schools were similarly ambivalent in their overall effect, passing on a bit of the Japanese language and Confucian ethics, but also thereby strengthening the generational revolt of many of their young charges (see pp. 203–204).

In sum, the Japanese in the United States were in various ways defined as anomalous sojourners, intrinsically incapable of ever fitting into a normal, legitimate place in American society. In part because of this rejection, many of them sought political and psychological support from a continued relation with their native country. And from its side, the Japanese state very often made the arrangements under which Japanese emigrated, tried to maintain control over all ethnic Japanese wherever they resided, and, in fact, perceived the Japanese abroad to be "permanent" residents of the places denoted as their *honseki*.

According to an account sympathetic to the Japanese in Hawaii, they long maintained a strong attachment to the homeland. They were "literally frantic with joy" at Japan's defeat of China in 1895; and when news came in 1905 of an important victory over Russia, "thousands of cheerful, enthusiastic sons and daughters of triumphant Nippon gathered bearing lanterns" (Wakukawa, 1938: 161–67). Eventually, as more and more of the Issei accepted the fact that they would die where they were living, the stage was set for eventual acculturation. Like all international migrants, they would retain something of their native culture, but these partial vestiges might have merged into composites more or less unobjectionable to their adopted country. Nothing in their behavior, however, could break through the exclusionists' slogan, "Once a Jap, always a Jap." Not only was the rejection total, but often it was expressed on substantive issues of such pettiness that the intent could only be to wound, to degrade.

Over the whole period up to the Immigration Act of 1924, Japan repeatedly adjusted its code on nationality to American norms, signed and rigorously maintained the Gentlemen's Agreement, and in general accepted with dignified good will the demands that Washington or circumstances set. During the same years American laws became increasingly harsh in ejecting Japanese from the polity, the economy, and—by intent—from the society altogether. After the 1924 act was passed, the Japanese Exclusion League was dissolved. The efforts of its supporters to get a constitutional amendment barring Nisei from citizenship never got off the ground. "Only after Pearl Harbor did the exclusionists again influence public policy: . . . the relocation camps are the last monuments to their patriotic zeal" (Daniels, 1962: 105).

Notes

[1] The application of the law was full of anomalies. For example, if the immediate family of a Chinese or Japanese man born in the United States (and thus a citizen) came to join him, his wife was barred as inadmissible, but his children were permitted to enter. As another example, though a child born of alien parents temporarily visiting the United States was a citizen, one born to a citizen of Asian stock who temporarily resided abroad was not and, moreover, could never be naturalized (McKenzie, 1928: chap. 6).

[2] U.S. House of Representatives, *Hearings Before the Committee on Immigration and Naturalization,* 67th Congress, 3rd Session, Serial 7–C, November 21, 1922 (Washington, D.C.: Government Printing Office, 1923). See also William Petersen, "The 'Scientific' Basis of Our Immigration Policy," in *The Politics of Population* (Garden City, N.Y.: Doubleday, 1964), pp. 195–215.

[3] Some decades earlier the Chinese had been provided with no public education at all. In a series of decisions, the state's supreme court held that those born in the city and permanently residing there had to be given schooling between the ages of 6 and 21, and in response the city built the Oriental Public School. By the court decisions, Chinese children were still admissible to any school in the city, but all except a handful were segregated into this one building. See Lee S. Dolson, Jr., "The Administration of the San Francisco Public Schools, 1847 to 1947" (Unpublished Ph.D. dissertation, University of California, Berkeley, 1964).

[4] In a personal letter, he wrote that they were right "to protest as vigorously as possible against the admission of Japanese laborers, for their very frugality, abstemiousness, and clannishness make them formidable to our laboring class. . . . I would not have objected at all to the California legislature passing a resolution, courteous and proper in its terms, which would really have achieved the object they were after" (letter to George Kennan, May 6, 1905; quoted in Daniels, 1962: 34–35).

5 *School Law of California* (Sacramento, 1902), p. 37; quoted in Bailey, 1934: 32.

6 Quoted in Ichihashi, 1932: 245–46. The notes exchanged between the two governments were not published until fifteen years later; see U.S. Department of State, *Foreign Relations of the United States, 1924* (Washington, D.C.: U.S. Government Printing Office, 1939), pp. 339–69.

7 Letter to Governor James M. Gillett, January 16, 1909; quoted in Bailey, 1934: 305–6.

8 By that date it was becoming obvious that the islands were too weak and too valuable to remain independent; the only question was which country would annex them. The Hawaiian royal house favored Japan, which had extended King Kalakaua a magnificent welcome when he visited that country. In a private conversation with the Japanese emperor, Kalakaua proposed the formation of a "Union and Federation of Asiatic Nations and Sovereigns" (the first version of the Co-Prosperity Sphere?). In a letter still extant, the emperor expressed cordial interest, but for some time in the future (Kuykendall, 1967: 228–31). Japan's first priority at that time was to secure a revision of the treaties that had been imposed by Western powers, and this could be done only with America's help.

9 The precise number is impossible to calculate from the published data, for the largest component among Caucasians in the 1896 census was "Portuguese," many of whom were Negro or part-Negro immigrants from the Cape Verde Islands and other Portuguese colonies (cf. Petersen, 1969).

10 *Takao Ozawa* v. *United States*, 260 U.S. 178 (1922). Cf. Konvitz, 1946: 80–97.

11 *United States* v. *Thind*, 261 U.S. 204 (1922). The Court refused to specify which other peoples are ineligible for naturalization, holding, of course, that this question would be answered through further litigation. The situation left many questions. The most clearly ineligible, so specified in the Exclusion Act of 1882, were Chinese. In various decisions the same interpretation was applied to Japanese, Koreans, Burmese, and Malays—excluding, however, Filipinos. For under a 1906 act, native inhabitants of the Philippines and Puerto Rico were described as "persons, not citizens, who owe permanent allegiance to the United States" (a new category in American law) and who might become citizens by naturalization. Somewhat similarly, the Supreme Court denoted American Indians "domestic, dependent nations," so that even those born within the boundaries of the United States were deemed

to be aliens and, under legislation beginning in 1887, eligible for naturalization. In most decisions by lower courts before 1922, natives of India had been adjudged admissible; the 1920 census listed 2,507 "Hindus" who were American citizens as of that date. And even after the Thind case, "white" persons included such marginal groups as Parsees, Armenians, Syrians (though in two instances only on appeal), and Mexicans (but on an especially weak basis). What the courts did with persons of mixed antecedents was even more inconsistent. One appellant, the legitimate son of an English father and a Chinese-Japanese mother, who had served with bravery and honor in the U.S. Navy for 27 years, whose character and intelligence were not challenged by the federal judge, was denied citizenship (McGovney, 1922–23).

12 It is true that eventually, after World War II and the internment of Japanese, these provisions were changed by new legislation. Under the current law, "the right of a person to become a naturalized citizen of the United States shall not be denied or abridged because of race," and even the citizens of a country with which the United States is at war may, under specified conditions and after due investigation, be naturalized. See *Immigration and Nationality Act*, 5th ed., revised through December 31, 1965 (Washington, D.C.: U.S. Government Printing Office, 1966), Title III, Sections 311, 331.

13 Nassim Bar-Yaacov, *Dual Nationality* (New York: Praeger, 1961), pp. 64–66.

14 Some notion of the degree and kinds of legal harassment to which Japanese agriculturists were subjected can be had from the "documental" history of cases published by the San Francisco consulate general (Japan, 1925). The second of the two volumes, with 1,051 pages, gives briefs and decisions from 32 cases involving land tenure. Even at this considerable distance in time, the composite picture is dreary.

15 Robert E. Park and Herbert A. Miller, *Old World Traits Transplanted* (New York: Harper, 1921), p. 168.

16 The following account is based on Fukutake, 1967: chap. 6; Beardsley, 1959: chap. 12; and Embree, 1939: chap. 2. The description is deliberately less complicated than the reality, for it would be out of place here to note local variations or the alternative Japanese words to designate the same institution.

17 In fact, the *buraku* is a formal subunit of the *mura*, or administrative village. "There is an infinite variety of complications where the *buraku* and the actual settlement do not coincide. However, in most cases they do, . . . [and] we shall not go very far wrong if we

assume that the hamlet as a physical settlement and the *buraku* as an administrative subunit of the *mura* or *machi* [town] governments are by and large identical" (Fukutake, 1967: 88–89). In 1934 the national government attempted to link the *buraku* more closely to itself through an agricultural association, and thereafter the character of these informal associations changed somewhat. But since this took place well after the main emigration to the United States, it had no effect on Japanese Americans.

[18] Mike Masaoka, "The Japanese American Creed," *Common Ground*, 2 (1942), 11; also printed in the *Congressional Record*, May 9, 1941.

[19] The survey from which these data come was made just before the war and not yet published when it started. The author then conducted a second survey to compare attitudes before and after Pearl Harbor. In both instances, the overall stance toward the language schools was positive, with the following group differences: Issei more favorable than Nisei; among Issei, Buddhists more favorable than Christians; women slightly more favorable than men; prewar responses significantly more favorable than those in 1942 (Onishi, 1943: 222–26).

[20] Of the 12,517 Japanese pupils in the first twelve grades of Honolulu schools in 1930, 12,060 were enrolled in a Japanese school in that year (Shichiro Miyamoto, 1937). Around 1920, California had a total of 54 Japanese schools with an average enrollment of only 37 (Kawakami, 1921: 150). In other Western states, particularly in some of the rural areas with a sparse Japanese population, there were no schools at all where Nisei could learn Japanese.

Chapter 4 ● The Camps

The devastating attack on Pearl Harbor on December 7, 1941, was only one of a long series of Allied defeats. Nazi armies, having conquered Denmark, Norway, the Low Countries, and France in record time, had continued their *Blitzkrieg* eastward, moving deep into Soviet territory along a 2,000-mile front. In the Pacific, Guam fell to the Japanese on December 11, Wake Island on December 23, Hong Kong on Christmas Day. Thailand was induced in December to ally herself with Japan and, a month later, to declare war on the United States. On February 15, 1942, "impregnable" Singapore surrendered unconditionally. The fall of Sumatra, Borneo, and the Celebes forecast the loss of resources-rich Java. Japanese invasions of the Philippines were climaxed by the surrender of Bataan on April 9, of Corregidor on May 6. Not until June was the United States able even to begin a counteroffensive, with the naval battle off Midway Island. The first Allied victories came late in 1942 and were still at the peripheries of the two theaters—an end to Rommel's romp through North Africa and the initial successes of American task forces in Guadalcanal.

During the first year the United States was in the war, the typical American, especially along the Pacific Coast, felt angry, frustrated, and fearful. The repeated rumors of Japanese submarines gained some substance when, on February 23, 1942, one actually surfaced off Goleta, California, and lobbed thirteen rounds into a complex of oil tanks. One week after the attack on Pearl Harbor, Secretary of the Navy Frank Knox remarked that the Japanese Americans in Hawaii had carried out "the most effective fifth-column work that's come out of this war, except in Norway" (tenBroek, 1968: 70). The press gave far less coverage to the facts that in his subsequent official report Knox failed even to mention fifth-columnists, that

authoritative denials of Japanese American sabotage started
to appear as early as January 1942, and that eventually these
were fully documented.[1] Fact was less potent than rumor in
shaping public opinion.

Beginning the very day that war started, the FBI began a
planned arrest of all enemy aliens it had any reason to suspect.
The net was cast wide, on the theory that it was better to be
safe than sorry; and of the 12,000 apprehended, more than
two-thirds were released or paroled after questioning. The Japanese arrested included Issei businessmen; such community
leaders as Shinto and Buddhist priests, officers of the Japanese
Associations; most teachers at Japanese-language schools and
many editors of Japanese newspapers; all fishermen operating
out of Terminal Island in Los Angeles Harbor.[2] More than
half of the 3,600 enemy aliens interned during these first weeks
of the war were Japanese; but after all were thoroughly investigated, only one was convicted of any wrongdoing. Tsutomo
Obana, a businessman, had been required to register as a foreign agent because one of his customers was the Japanese
government. He tried to do so, was held up by the red tape of
Japanese officialdom, and eventually was sentenced to a term
of two to six months for his neglect (Bosworth, 1967: 46).
That was the sum total of Japanese American "sabotage" on
the mainland. But the rounding up of thousands of Japanese,
the confiscating of such "contraband" as cameras, flashlights,
and hunting rifles, were given more prominent notice in the
news media than the fact that none of those apprehended had
done anything at all to harm the national interest. These events
during 1942 set the scene for revivifying the anti-Japanese sentiment that for a decade had been more or less quiescent.

INCARCERATION

The bare facts are simple. In the major portion of the West,
all persons of any degree of Japanese descent—a total of more
than 110,000 citizens and aliens, men and women, grandmoth-
ers and babes in arms, simple gardeners and professionals—
were transferred en masse to "relocation camps," where they

were kept behind barbed wire and guarded by armed white or Negro soldiers. No charge of disloyalty was brought against any individual; the basis for the evacuation of a whole subnation was a loosely specified "military necessity."

The process by which this end state was reached, however, was tortuous. Official assurances ignored after some weeks and strict orders soon to be countermanded added inordinate confusion to the distress. Today, after the confidential records have been opened, we know that the various government agencies differed fundamentally on whether a mass evacuation was in the national interest. According to Allan Bosworth (1967: 45–46), who at the time was a captain in Naval Intelligence, that service and the FBI had long cooperated in a program to identify enemy sympathizers, while Army Intelligence concentrated on policing its own personnel. In Los Angeles, Lieutenant-Commander Kenneth D. Ringle (1942) of the Eleventh Naval District of Naval Intelligence reported that the problem of Japanese Americans had been "magnified out of its true proportion" on racial grounds. He advocated that suspects be reviewed on an individual basis, precisely the policy that the FBI followed.

The most significant interagency dispute was between Attorney-General Francis Biddle and Lieutenant-General John L. DeWitt, commanding general of the Western Defense Command, both of whom vacillated in their jockeying to avoid responsibility for the evacuation that, eventually, both justified as in the national interest. Biddle's first directive concerning the arrest and, "where necessary," evacuation of alien enemies did not, "of course, include American citizens of Japanese race." If they were to be evacuated, he stated, that action "should, in my opinion, be taken by the War Department and not by the Department of Justice" (tenBroek, 1968: 108). According to DeWitt, on the other hand, the Army would accept this task only "with the greatest reluctance. Its desire is only that the Department of Justice act with expedition and effectiveness in the discharge of its responsibilities" (Bosworth, 1967: 62). In the end Biddle simply defaulted on his oath to provide all citizens equal protection under the law; the evacuation was carried out by the Army under DeWitt's orders; and the camps were administered by a civilian agency, the War Relocation Authority (WRA), specially created for that purpose.

The first steps in the evacuation were Biddle's five successive directives excluding "all German, Italian, and Japanese alien enemies" from 146 designated zones. While this first stage was in process, a group of West Coast congressmen wrote to President Roosevelt recommending the "immediate evacuation of all persons of Japanese lineage, . . . aliens and citizens alike," from the "entire strategic area" of the three coastal states. A few days later, on February 19, the President signed Executive Order 9066, authorizing the Secretary of War or any military commander he designated to establish military areas and to exclude therefrom "any or all persons"; and the very next day General DeWitt was empowered to carry out this directive. Then, as a cruel anticlimax, the Select Committee Investigating National Defense Migration convened in San Francisco under Congressman John H. Tolan to determine whether the evacuation already authorized was necessary. As though to make its hearings doubly farcical, after only perfunctory discussions Congress passed Public Law 503, giving military commanders the power they already had under the President's order.

General DeWitt's first act under the power given him by Executive Order 9066 was to direct all Japanese, aliens and citizens both (but not German or Italian aliens), to leave the coastal area and find other homes outside the proscribed region. Between three and four thousand moved to inland California counties, depending on assurances from both DeWitt and Tom C. Clark (acting as liaison of the Justice Department to the Western Defense Command) that they would not be told to move again. Less than a month later, it was decided to intern all persons of Japanese ancestry in camps for the duration. Within weeks, Japanese American businessmen had to liquidate their interests and properties. Obviously, a group the Army itself was defining as a military risk was fair game. Federal agencies were supposed to assist evacuees in preserving their property, but "at the sole risk" of the owner, with no insurance, and in accordance with a disclaimer of the agency's responsibility signed in advance.³ Understandably, few took advantage of these facilities, preferring to sell for the price offered or to store their goods and furniture themselves.

Evacuation was started in March and was not completed until November. In every community with Japanese residents, notices were posted instructing them to report to a designated civil control station, where each was given a family number. One of them was Miné Okubo, No. 13660, who later wrote a report of her experiences (Okubo, 1946).

Together with her brother, a senior at the University of California, Miss Okubo was dispatched to the "Tanforan Assembly Center," a slightly converted racetrack a few miles south of San Francisco. (The conditions she describes were typical, for the assembly centers were intended to house the evacuees only for a short time, while what the official documents term the "permanent" relocation centers were being constructed. In fact, most stayed in one of the twelve temporary centers—fair grounds or livestock exhibit halls, as well as racetracks—for an average of about seven months.) The evacuees could take with them only the baggage they could carry; both it and each person were tagged with a family number for the trip. To live in, the Okubos were given one stall divided into two small areas, one of which had housed a horse, the other its fodder. They were given two folding cots and two bags, which they filled with straw for mattresses. New evacuees arrived at the rate of 300 a day, until eventually the camp was full. The first weeks were spent building furniture out of scrap wood, trying to make the place habitable.

> There was a lack of privacy everywhere. The incomplete partitions in the stalls and the barracks made a single symphony of yours and your neighbors' loves, hates, and joys. One had to get used to snores, baby-crying, family troubles, and even to the jitterbugs. . . . The flush toilets were always out of commission. . . . Many of the women could not get used to the community toilets. They sought privacy by pinning up curtains and setting up boards. . . . The sewage system was poor, [and] the stench from the stagnant sewage was terrible. . . .
>
> We lined up for mail, for checks, for meals, for show-

ers, for laundry tubs, for toilets, for clinic service, for movies. We lined up for everything.

The inmates were on the edge of a large city; through the barbed wire on one side was the main highway, on the other side the San Bruno streetcar line. But they were isolated by restrictions on visits and periodic inspections of all quarters and baggage. Months later, after professional gardeners among the evacuees had converted the camp into a garden complete with lake and Japanese bridges, the move was started to the "permanent" camps (Okubo, 1946: 19–111).

One Nisei, Gordon Hirabayashi, tested the evacuation order and one imposing a curfew on Japanese Americans by deliberately disobeying both. He was a Quaker, a product of American schools, a senior at the University of Washington at the time. Nothing can represent better the Kafkaesque world in which he and his fellows were forced to live than his own account:

At the U.S. District Court, I was given a sentence of 30 days for curfew violation and 30 days for refusing to evacuate, the two sentences to be served [concurrently] in the federal tank of the county jail. When I requested a sentence to the prison camp, the judge changed the sentence to three months for each charge. . . .

My case was appealed, and I remained confined in Seattle for five months in addition to the original 30 days. At the end of the fifth month a compromise arrangement was made that, on my own recognizance, I could be released in Spokane rather than to an evacuation camp, as was the judge's previous stipulation. . . . In Spokane, I worked with the Quakers, assisting with the relocation of Japanese families. . . .

A couple of months after the Supreme Court ruled against me [see pp. 88–89], the FBI looked me up and informed me that I should report to the federal tank of the Spokane County jail, to serve my sentence. When I reminded them that I was given this particular sentence in order that I might serve it in a camp, the district attorney had to be brought in for a ruling. It was ruled . . . that I could report to the nearest federal prison camp. The nearest one was located near Tacoma, which was in the excluded area; therefore my only other option was the federal prison camp near Tucson. Having given me the option, he said that I would have to get there at my own expense if I wished to go there. . . .

I decided to hitchhike. In those gas-ration days rides were not too plentiful, and it took me approximately two weeks. When I finally got to Tucson, they could not locate the papers by which I could be placed in camp. I was invited to leave, but feeling that, sooner or later, the papers would be found and I would be interrupted later on, I insisted that they find something that would allow me to begin serving my sentence, so that I could get it over with. It took several hours and, in the meantime, I roamed around Tucson without enjoying the fact that it was also an excluded area, because neither the officials nor I realized it. . . .

In the prison camp my first assignment was on the recreation committee. Then followed my stint on the baking crew. It was not a school, but actually baking for the inmates. I had worked through bread, various types of cookies and pies, and was just beginning to learn the intricacies of cake-baking when my sentence expired. They gave me a bus ticket home.[4]

WHO WAS RESPONSIBLE?

All of the several dozen books on the relocation centers touch on this question, and two of them focus on it. To lay the responsibility with "the people of the nation in general, the people of the West Coast in particular" (tenBroek, 1968: 327), merely evades the moral issue. Blame that is not differentially distributed is in fact not assigned: the thesis of collective guilt means really that no one is guilty. Most commentators accuse California reactionaries—"certain agricultural and business groups," in the euphemism that Grodzins uses (1949: 21)—and the military, or specifically General DeWitt. But the Army acted under civilian directives, and the reactionaries (however much noise they made) were in control of nothing.

This was an era dominated by liberals, among whom one counts virtually every civilian significantly involved in the action against Japanese Americans. At the federal level were President Roosevelt; Attorney-General Francis Biddle; the Supreme Court, which since its chastening in the mid-1930s had consistently favored New Deal legislation; and even such relatively minor figures as Tom Clark. In California, the mainland state with most Japanese, the governor was a Progressive, Culbert Olson; the attorney-general, the official guardian of the law, was Earl Warren; Fletcher Bowron, the reform mayor of Los Angeles, had been elected with wide support from the Japanese community. It was men of this political stamp who engineered the evacuation. True, they moved into this unknown territory slowly, probing for public reaction at each stage of an unprecedented act. According to tenBroek (1968), the incarceration was achieved in "successive stages" (p. 3); early on, even DeWitt termed the proposed mass evacuation "damned nonsense" (p. 105). And at each stage the officials were encouraged to go forward not only by the anti-Japanese clamor but—more significantly—by the absence of meaningful resistance to incarceration of thousands of Americans whose only crime was their race.[5] The most interesting clue to the influence of pressure groups, as in the Sherlock Holmes story, is the dog that did not bark.

In a review of any position held by the Left, it is convenient to begin with the Communist Party, then at the far end of the political spectrum. On June 22, 1941, the day that Nazi Germany broke the Stalin-Hitler Pact and invaded Soviet territory, the American Communist Party had shifted abruptly from vociferous isolationism to all-out support of the war.[6] Except for demanding that the Western powers open a second front on the European continent in order to relieve the pressure on the Red Army and that Earl Browder (who was serving a sentence for swearing falsely on a passport application) be released from prison, on all other issues the Party was superpatriotic. In the *Daily Worker,* the popular *New Masses,* and the more pretentious *Communist,* the Party fought tirelessly against all who might be impeding the war effort in any way. It did its utmost to see that labor unions maintained their moratorium on militancy[7] and that racial minorities postponed any struggle for civil rights.[8]

Both types of wartime agitation, the abusive assault on those defined as unpatriotic and the indifference to civil rights, were relevant to the Party's position on Japanese Americans. According to an editorial on "the lessons of Pearl Harbor," "Japanese espionage and Fifth Column activities were rife in Hawaii." Dispatches from the West Coast, however nonsensical, were printed with their full bias—on contraband collected, on eight "Japanese agents" arrested, on an allegation that three planes launched from a Japanese submarine had flown over Los Angeles, and so on.[9] On the evacuation of Japanese Americans and their incarceration in camps, on the other hand, the publications of the Communist Party printed not a word,[10] presumably because its position was judged to be too unsavory for general dissemination. The Party's line was publicized only by the small Communist fronts in this field, of which the most important was the Japanese-American Committee for Democracy, with headquarters in New York City. According to an editorial in the August 1942 issue of its *News Letter*,

> The evacuation . . . may have seemed harsh. But we of the Japanese community must realize once and for all that this is a total war. . . . Surely it is not too much to ask the Japanese community to sacrifice, for the duration, some small portion of their civil rights. . . . We realize that the evacuation is not foolproof or perfect, nor is it the complete solution to the Japanese problem.

But for the duration, it was recommended as the best "solution" available.

In northern California, the Nisei Democratic Club was also a joint organization of liberals and Communists. Mrs. Edward Howden, who was then a Nisei student at Berkeley, told me later that the most devastating experience of the whole evacuation was the support given to it by her Leftist white friends. Michio Kunitani, who as one of the club's leaders testified on its behalf before the Tolan Committee, made a statement he later described as "rather flabby." The reason was that his liberal faction had compromised with those in the organization

who were following the Communist line supporting the evacuation.[11]

The Communist position on the relocation centers spread
widely throughout the population, especially throughout the
sector one might have expected to oppose the evacuation in the
strongest terms. For these years were the heyday of Communist-
liberal collaboration. The Popular Front of the 1930s, which
had been painfully interrupted by the Stalin-Hitler Pact, was
now realizing its consummation. The counterpart to the Party's
superpatriotism was a ritualistic obeisance to the Soviet Union;
almost every liberal and not a few conservatives felt obliged
to express personal appreciation of "our great and glorious
ally" in the war against totalitarianism. And as part of their
accommodation to Communism, most liberals accepted, or half-
accepted, the Party's line on Japanese Americans.

Norman Thomas stood apart from this strange association
because of his vehement and informed anti-Communism, his
pacifist opposition to the war, and his personal integrity. In a
short article on the evacuation, "a horrible indictment of our
democracy," he lamented the fact that so few liberals fought
against it.

> It is the "liberals" who lead in demanding more aggres-
> sive action from the administration against those whose
> opinions they do not like. If a future dictator of an Ameri-
> can totalitarian state is keeping files of *PM*, the *New York
> Post*, the *Nation*, the *New Republic*, and the releases of
> certain committees, ostensibly and stridently devoted to
> freedom or democracy, he can find quotations to justify
> almost all the repressions he may find advisable. . . .
> In an experience of nearly three decades I have never
> found it harder to arouse the American public on any im-
> portant issue than on this. Men and women who know
> nothing of the facts . . . hotly deny that there are con-
> centration camps. Apparently that is a term to be used
> only if the guards speak German and carry a whip as well
> as a rifle (N. Thomas, 1942; see also N. Thomas, 1943).[12]

One important locus of Communist influence was Carey Mc-
Williams, who was a member of the advisory board of the Jap-

anese-American Committee for Democracy[13] and, on the other hand, an official of the California government whose duties involved him in the fate of the Japanese. Two days after De-Witt issued his first proclamation, defining the area from which persons might be excluded (and the official press release made it clear that the Japanese were likely to be evacuated), Mc-Williams wrote to Congressman Tolan that the General's statement "should be highly commended for its courage, clarity, comprehensiveness, and insight into some of the social and economic problems involved."[14] McWilliams also wrote to various influential Leftists in California, trying to organize a group that would endorse the evacuation. He set out his views in a draft paper, "Evacuation—A Military Necessity," which was never published; the "primary reasons" for the evacuation were "military necessity and the security of the commonwealth" and the safety of the Japanese themselves.[15] The fullest public statement of his position at the time of the evacuation was in an article published in September 1942:

Wholly without precedent, this largest mass evacuation in American history has been accomplished by the Army on time, without mishap, and with virtually no friction . . . a miracle of effective organization. . . . Even the hospitalized cases have been concentrated in a few institutions and plans are now under way to evacuate the orphans. . . . The conduct of the Army has been wholly admirable. Both officers and troops behaved, at all times, with the utmost tact, good judgment, and consideration. . . . It must be credited as a major feat for the Army. . . .

It would certainly not be accurate to characterize Santa Anita [an assembly center near Los Angeles] as a "concentration camp." To be sure, the camp is surrounded by barbed wire; it is guarded by a small detail of soldiers; searchlights play around the camp and up and down the streets at night; and the residents [the residents!] cannot leave the grounds. Their automobiles are all impounded; two roll calls are taken each day; and . . . there is a military censorship on outgoing and incoming mail. . . . At the Manzanar camp, Hikaji Takeuchi, a 22-year-old Nisei, was shot by a guard, but the incident seems to have been the result of a misunderstanding on the part of both the victim and the guard. . . . There is undeniably a serious morale problem; there is also an undercurrent of resentment. . . .

Is what we have done actually at variance with our war aims? Is it consistent with our democratic ideals? What . . . were the alternatives? . . . There was always the danger of mob violence. . . . Can it be said that self-seeking groups were responsible for the evacuation program? A careful study of the Tolan Committee hearings has convinced me that such was not the case. . . .

Most of the relocation projects are, I believe, permanent in character. . . . Vast improvements are being made in the relocation projects, . . . and it is at least foreseeable that the government will eventually work out some scheme by which [the Japanese Americans] can acquire ownership of these projects. . . . In the long run the Japanese will probably profit by this painful and distressing experience. . . . There is no reason why the relocation projects cannot be successful, cannot in fact reflect great credit upon us as a nation—provided a majority of the American people will insist upon fair treatment of the Japanese and not succumb to demagogues and race-baiters (McWilliams, 1942b).[16]

Among organizations, the most significant counterpart to such an individual as McWilliams was the American Civil Liberties Union, which one would have expected to take a strong and unambivalent stand against the evacuation. Like every other liberal organization, it had been infiltrated by Communists during the 1930s; and a few years before the war, a fight over the ousting of Elizabeth Gurley Flynn from the ACLU board of directors split the organization. A few branches, including the one in northern California, held that it was impermissible to deny membership and leadership to such an avowed Communist and therefore severed formal relations with the national office. By this criterion, then, the northern California branch was the farthest Left of America's civil libertarians; and the attitude of its members toward the evacuation is symptomatic. Only 275 of this highly select group replied to a mail questionnaire on an issue of prime significance to civil liberties, and their replies hardly reflected a fanatic devotion to human freedom (Table 4-1). Among the members' comments

Table 4-1. *Opinion Poll on the Evacuation of Japanese Americans, Members of the Northern California Civil Liberties Union, Spring 1942*

QUERY	YES	NO	NO ANSWER
Do you favor the President's order?	144	84	47
Do you favor General DeWitt's order?	110	113	52
Should the ACLU test the constitutionality of the orders insofar as they apply to citizens?	117	120	38
Should the ACLU seek modification of both orders to provide hearing boards for citizens affected?	188	67	20
Should the ACLU seek to have both orders modified by having them apply only to regions in the immediate vicinity of the coast and near defense plants and military establishments?	110	120	45

SOURCE: *ACLU News*, San Francisco, April 1942. Reprinted by permission of the American Civil Liberties Union of Northern California.

printed in the same issue of the *ACLU News*, one upbraided the ACLU office for so much as posing the questions:

> The very fact that you make such an inquiry shows that the Union has completely lost its head. The question you raise is one of military strategy, and the decision of the President and of the Army is definitely none of your business as an organization.

In short, " 'freedom as usual' is part of the 'business as usual' attitude, which is dangerous in our times."

Disunity hampered the ACLU also at the national level. The national board accepted as constitutional and legitimate Order 9066, which in the absence of martial law gave military authorities unrestricted control over "any and all persons." "Immediately after the Presidential order, the Southern and Northern California offices met in response to a request from [the national office] for their advice. They were unable to agree and sent us a divided report."[17] After the evacuation was in process, the national office sent a letter of protest to the President, recommending that citizens and aliens be judged, "before or after removal," on the basis of their conduct and records, in order to "minimize injustice."[18] Presumably full justice was not to be considered even a goal the ACLU should strive for.

On the other hand, it must be stated with all possible emphasis that much of whatever legal aid the Japanese got from other Americans was provided by various ACLU units. Wayne Collins, of the northern California branch; A. L. Wirin, his counterpart in Los Angeles; and ACLU lawyers in other cities took on the burden of opposing the evacuation in the courts, with legal and especially financial assistance from the national office. Important as this aid was, however, it was far less than this same organization would have provided if Nazi Germany had not invaded the Soviet Union in June 1941.

That individuals like Carey McWilliams and organizations like the ACLU were greatly influenced by the Communist approbation of the camps is both true and, of itself, of limited importance. What of liberals not subject to direct pressure from the Communist Party? A good test is Earl Warren. When he ran for attorney-general of California in 1938, the liberal wings of both parties supported him, in part because of his stand on civil rights.[19] Then and later, the Communists opposed him, and with good reason.[20] Were Warren's actions against the Japanese Americans the consequence more of his own values or of imbalanced political pressures? The evidence strongly suggests the latter.

Some of Warren's early decisions concerning Japanese Americans were in sharp contrast to his dominant role. When a state bureau revoked the food-handler licenses that Issei needed to market farm produce and this decision was sanctioned by Governor Olson, Warren told him publicly that the action was illegal. Or when the state personnel board barred from the civil service all citizens descended from enemy aliens (that is, in effect, Nisei), Warren protested on grounds of both law and national morale (Bosworth, 1967: 70–72). The self-contradictory pattern is not so strange that Americans cannot identify the ambitious young politician, sending up trial balloons and opting for a principled position only after it seemed likely to pay off. For such a man, it was decisive that the usual Left-liberal support of civil rights was weak or absent. Warren's move to lead the campaign for the evacuation of Japanese Americans was a weathervane, accurately indicating the dominant direction of vocal opinion.

The attorney-general began his anti-Japanese statements early, and over the weeks his influence reverberated in all directions. On January 30, he termed the Japanese "the Achilles' heel of the entire civilian defense effort." On February 2, he detailed his activities to a convention of California law-enforcement officers:

> I have talked to General DeWitt. I have talked to subordinate officers, I have talked to the Army, I have talked to the Intelligence Unit of the Navy, I have talked to the FBI, I have talked to every federal agency that there is in this part of the country, trying to get some relief from this situation (Bosworth, 1967: 70–71).

Five days later (thus, almost two weeks before the President signed Order 9066), Warren concluded from this search that since action by any civil agency was "too cumbersome, . . . there is only one group in the last analysis that can protect this State from the Japanese situation and that is the armed forces" (Bosworth, 1967: 72).

The same day that General DeWitt was appointed to carry out the President's vague directive, when the whole operation was still fluid, the attorney-general testified before the Tolan Committee. Warren had gathered information on exactly where in each county the Japanese resided, and he came armed with maps to demonstrate that they lived close to airports, railroads, transmission lines, and other likely sabotage targets. True, there had not been a single act of sabotage in the more than six weeks since the war had started; and the attorney-general, in one of the most remarkable feats of logic ever performed by a lawyer, used this very innocence as evidence of guilt:

> Many of our people in other parts of the country are of the opinion that because we have had no sabotage and no fifth-column activities in this State since the beginning of the war, that means that none have been planned for us. But I take the view that that is the most ominous sign in our whole situation. It convinces me more than perhaps any other factor that the sabotage that we are to get, the fifth-column activities that we are to get, are timed just like Pearl Harbor was timed. . . . If there were sporadic sabotage at this time or if there had been for the last two months, the people of California or the Federal authorities would be on the alert to such an extent that they could not possibly have any real fifth-column activities when the M-day comes.[21]

Meanwhile, Warren had also been doing something to combat the ignorance of "our people in other parts of the country." On February 10 he conferred with Tom Clark, the Justice Department representative, on legal issues involved in an evacuation of both aliens and citizens. The following day he discussed the same matter with General DeWitt, who then wrote to Washington recommending the removal of all Japanese (Grodzins, 1949: 100). On February 12, after having discussed the question with California's chief legal officer, Walter Lippmann (perhaps the country's most influential liberal columnist) wrote vigorously in favor of mass evacuation; and his presentation inspired Westbrook Pegler (a powerful voice among conservatives) to make the same argument four days later. When the district attorney of a California county later commended Warren, "I have no doubt that the Presidential order stems back to the article written by Lippmann following the talk with you," this probable exaggeration had a germ of truth (Grodzins, 1949: 99–100).[22]

LIFE IN THE RELOCATION CENTERS

While the evacuees lived in temporary quarters at converted racetracks and similar facilities, ten relocation centers had been constructed at isolated sites in several states: Manzanar and Tule Lake in eastern California, Poston (or Colorado River Project, or Parker) and Gila River in Arizona, Minidoka in Idaho, Heart Mountain in Wyoming, Granada in Colorado, Topaz (or Central Utah Project) in Utah, and Rohwer and Jerome in Arkansas. The largest was Poston, with a capacity of 20,000 inmates; the smallest Granada, with one of 8,000. All together, they could accommodate 119,000 Japanese Americans. Most were situated in desert country, depressingly hot in summer and bitterly cold in winter and afflicted with wind-borne sand in all seasons.

In their function and mode of operation, these were essentially prison camps, but overlaid with a thick patina of official euphemism. In part with the professional help of social scientists (cf. Spicer, 1946), everything was prettified, beginning with "relocation center" or "project" for camp.[23] The inmates were called "colonists" or sometimes "residents." The wages they were paid—according to the level of skill, $12, $16, or $19 per month for 48-hour weeks—were called "cash advances." Fraternization was discouraged between the colonists and the appointed personnel, all of whom were Caucasians; "for administrative purposes even Negroes were classified as Caucasions" (D. Kitagawa, 1967: 75). The reason for the evacuation, military necessity, was displaced by a professed policy of shielding the Japanese from the wrath of the populace; and this rationalization was repeated often enough to generate hostility[24] and even to convince some of the evacuees of "the soundness of 'protective custody' " (D. Kitagawa, 1967: 81).

An important component of the camp background was the Army, which had constructed the barracks in the dreariest of its several functional styles. The operation by a civilian administration, the War Relocation Authority, imitated military routine in adapting daily activities to an institutionalized pattern suitable for large, undifferentiated numbers. The facts, for example, that meals were neither prepared by the wife-mother nor usually eaten in family groups contributed much to the loosening of family bonds. No ex-soldier can fail to recognize that old friend, SNAFU—the rigid adherence to innumerable rules that underwent continual, great, and seemingly pointless or in fact capricious alteration. That authorities did not divulge their plans—or, when they did, often equivocated or lied—set an ideal environment for the partial displacement of normal channels of communication by rumors, which were never too wild to gain acceptance.[25]

Under Milton S. Eisenhower, the first director of WRA, the policy was to retain the evacuees in camps for the duration of the war (D. S. Thomas and Nishimoto, 1946: 53), and a number of long-term activities (the "Work Corps," the "Producers' Cooperatives") were instituted. Eisenhower resigned after only two months and was replaced by Dillon S. Myer, who tried on the contrary to resettle evacuees outside the camps as quickly as possible. Thus, well before November 1942, when the last of the inmates were incarcerated, outward movements of various types were under way. Escape was attractive, of course, but it meant also that attempts to build an acceptable personal environment even under these onerous circumstances were often futile.

The first resettlement out of the camps was of students. While the initial evacuation was still under way, several professors had tried to arrange an exemption for Nisei students, but their various schemes came to nothing. Later, a student-relocation council raised funds to enable young Japanese to attend colleges in the Midwest or East. Government agencies contributed nothing. Most of the money came from Christian churches, each of which administered its own funds mainly to facilitate the education of a few Nisei at colleges associated with that denomination. A total of slightly more than $90,000 was distributed in scholarships to almost 4,300 at an annual rate of $150 to $200 per student. In a few instances hoodlums tried to prevent a half-dozen Nisei from attending a college, but in the main the students themselves were amazed at how cordially they were received. Their overall scholastic record was good and in a few instances outstanding (O'Brien, 1949).

The next group permitted to leave the camps was field laborers. Seasonal furloughs for agricultural work had been encouraged as early as the spring of 1942, but the evacuees still remained under military custody. Later, whenever the demand for field workers warranted it, stipulated persons were permitted to leave the camps permanently and relocate anywhere outside the militarily restricted areas, having first undergone an elaborate investigation of their character and loyalty.

Meanwhile, the Army's policy toward Japanese Americans was changing. When war was declared, those inducted before Pearl Harbor had been honorably discharged with no specification of the reason. Thereafter, Japanese Americans subject to the draft were arbitrarily classified IV-F (ineligible because of physical defects) until September 1, 1942, when the classification was changed to IV-C (enemy alien). A minority of the camp inmates under the leadership of the JACL agitated for the right of American citizens to serve in the United States Army. As a first step toward acceding to this extraordinary demand, Nisei of draft age were recruited to serve as instructors in the language school of the Army's Military Intelligence Service. An amazingly large number volunteered. Then, on January 28, 1943, Secretary of War Henry L. Stimson announced a new policy: "It is the inherent right of every faithful citizen, regardless of ancestry, to bear arms in the Nation's battle." Ten days later the Army began to recruit Nisei. As with the applications for extramural agricultural work, the registration for selective service involved clearances for loyalty, and the two agencies processed the camp populations jointly.

It is difficult to imagine how the procedure could have been more inept. Each of the two forms had about thirty questions, some routine, some more or less objectionable, and two, numbers 27 and 28, designed to test the respondents' loyalty. Washington officials had anticipated that the recruitment of volunteers might not be received enthusiastically, and they prepared a propaganda speech pointing out, for instance, that camp life "is not freedom" and that "the circumstances were not of your own choosing." Whatever effect this may have had was not tested with many of the Issei, for the Japanese version arrived too late at most camps to be used, and in two of them it was rejected as a poor translation. In any case, judging from the recorded colloquies, most of the registrars did not really expect such hostile replies as this, from a 22-year-old girl:

> I'm going to say "no" to anything as long as they treat me like an alien. When they treat me like a citizen, they can ask me questions that a citizen should answer (D. S. Thomas and Nishimoto, 1946: 98).

Some of the male Nisei in the Topaz camp petitioned the War Department to grant them, as a precondition to registration, full restoration of their civil rights and assurance that their families would be protected.

Males of draft age were asked whether they would be willing "to serve in the armed forces of the United States on combat duty, wherever ordered." All others, including aged Issei males, were asked whether they would be willing "to volunteer for the Army Nurse Corps or the WAAC." In substantially the same wording, both forms included the question:

> Will you swear unqualified allegiance to the United States of America and forswear any form of allegiance or obedience to the Japanese emperor, or any other foreign government, power, or organization?

Put to a Japanese immigrant, who under American law could not become an American citizen, this question was, in effect, a request that he declare himself stateless. After the registration was well under way, in order to avoid this implication, the wording was changed:

> Will you swear to abide by the laws of the United States and to take no action which would in any way interfere with the war effort of the United States?[26]

The instructions accompanying the questionnaire were often imprecise and vague, and some respondents were not sure what they were supposed to do. They tried to hold meetings to consult with each other, but these were forbidden on the ground that "registration is a matter of individual judgment and the final decision should be left up to each person." Many refused to register for the simple reason that they took the rationalization of "protective custody" seriously enough to want to stay in the camps (D. S. Thomas and Nishimoto, 1946: 76, 91).

At the outbreak of the war, when concern was expressed about possible fifth-columnists, the FBI and Naval Intelligence had proposed, it will be recalled, the internment of those judged after a full investigation to be potentially dangerous. Instead, the whole subnation was put in camps. Then, a year later, when the first effort was made to distinguish "loyal" from "disloyal," the procedure was so inefficient that the latter were almost as heterogeneous politically as the original camp population. Any who for whatever reason wanted to sit out the war were classified as "disloyal," and they were encouraged to believe that they could change their designation to "loyal" as soon as it became convenient (D. S. Thomas and Nishimoto, 1946: chaps. 11–12).

Divisions among the Japanese in the relocation centers had sometimes been regional (Californians against those from the Northwest; urban against rural), sometimes religious or political, but mainly generational. Issei fathers, proud of having wrested a living for their wives and children against all odds, were deprived of any familial role; and they watched their sons, hardly more than boys, being given quasi-administrative functions by camp officials who would not deal with noncitizens. During the crisis over the loyalty registration, this antipathy between father and son often became irreconcilably bitter. The "notorious questionnaire," as Kitagawa terms it, broke the camp population in two. Those who answered Questions 27 and 28 in the affirmative, the "Yes-yeses," opted for integration with the general American society in spite of every injustice, every evidence of official hostility. Most of the Nisei, led by the JACL, classified themselves as "loyal." Many of the Issei and Kibei were "No-noes," accepting the designation of "disloyal" that in fact they had been given by the evacuation and internment.[27] The Japanese nationalists denounced the JACL supporters as *inu* ("dogs") or, in English, from the organization's acronym, "jackals." Assimilationist leaders were listed (as by the FBI) as "Public Inu Number One"; several dozen were severely beaten and one, Takeo Noma, was murdered.

Eventually, most of the Yes-yes males of suitable age served in the Army. A total of some 33,000 Japanese Americans, about half each from Hawaii and the mainland, fought during World War II. In the Pacific theater, Nisei worked as interpreters or in combat intelligence; and in Europe two segregated units (except, of course, for the white officers), the 100th Infantry Battalion and the 442nd Regimental Combat Team, established records of peerless heroism. In Italy the famous 442nd was at the front four weeks without a break, getting only two hours' sleep a night and spending the rest of each day defeating battle-hardened elite German troops. Then the 442nd was sent to France, where in 35 minutes it smashed a Nazi stronghold that had defied other Allied forces for five weeks. By the end of the war, the unit had been engaged in seven major campaigns and won seven Presidential citations at a cost of 9,486 casualties. Individual members of the 442nd won a total of 18,143 decorations, including one Congressional Medal of Honor and 52 Distinguished Service Crosses. No other unit of the armed forces established a comparable war record (Bosworth, 1967: 13–20).

Of all inmates of the camps aged 17 years or older, 84 percent had replied in the affirmative to Question 28 (or 90 percent of all projects apart from Tule Lake). The registration at that camp was anomalous, apparently more because of a particularly incompetent administration than of any special characteristics of the evacuees. At Tule Lake, 42 percent either refused to register or answered "No" on the test of "loyalty." The project was then designated as a segregation center for all who by their No-no answers were defined as "disloyal" to the United States, and these were transferred there from other camps. Soon after all the "segregants" were gathered at Tule Lake, conditions there deteriorated seriously. When a truck overturned on a soft shoulder, a number of the workers riding in it were injured, and one of them died soon afterward. This incident brought to a head all the hatreds and frustrations festering since the first evacuation order. A strike reinforced by passive resistance developed into active revolt; and the civilian director, no longer able to cope, called in Army units to reestablish order. Tule Lake was put under martial law; a stockade was built in which the more active rebels and their alleged supporters were imprisoned. After the troops were withdrawn, the inmates achieved an uneasy accommodation with the administration, but it was not to last. When a soldier shot and killed a Japanese, the camp was again in a turmoil. Little of what was happening leaked out to the rest of the United States, but at one point the San Francisco ACLU was asked to intervene. It threatened to institute *habeas corpus* suits against the WRA in order to effect the release of the American citizens it had imprisoned for more than eight months without formal charges or hearings. The camp director retreated, and again a compromise was achieved, this one to last until the crisis during the final months of the camp's existence.

DISSOLUTION OF THE CAMPS

That wartime hysteria contributed to the establishment of the camps is obvious, but one can easily exaggerate the importance of this alibi. In the last year of the war, when the Allies were winning on every front, and *a fortiori* in the postwar period, the government had a number of opportunities to repair some of the damage it had wrongfully, and presumably hysterically, inflicted. But official behavior improved little—in some respects, even deteriorated.

Each step toward terminating the camp system was taken slowly, at the cost of long and expensive litigation. The most important cases were three that reached the Supreme Court, involving Hirabayashi, Korematsu, and Endo, and testing the legality, respectively, of the curfew, the evacuation, and the detention.[28] In fact, all three cases pertained to the same issues, which the Court chose quite arbitrarily to consider seriatim (tenBroek, 1968: chap. 5). Hirabayashi, it will be recalled, was convicted of disobeying the orders concerning both the curfew and the evacuation, but the Court took advantage of the fact that his sentences ran concurrently to consider only the first. It decided that Congress and the President, "acting in cooperation," did not offend the constitutional guarantee of due process in granting the power to impose a curfew. The only substantive issue was whether there had been discrimination against citizens of Japanese ancestry. But the military authorities, the

Court held, had "grounds for believing" the "facts and circumstances" by which they justified the curfew; and this was considered to be enough of a civilian review of the powers delegated to the Army. The opinion was unanimous, but Justices Murphy and Rutledge qualified their concurrence with statements that a state of war did not suspend the constitutional protection of "essential liberties," that "distinctions based on color or ancestry" were "inconsistent with our traditions and ideals," and—at least by implication—that the legitimate abridgment of constitutional rights beyond a certain point could only be under martial law and in circumstances warranting it. In short, a division of the Court was barely avoided, and only by restricting the substantive issue to the least significant among several raised by the case. The split came a year and a half later, when the alleged danger on the West Coast had waned considerably.

Fred Korematsu was unambiguously American. Born in Oakland, he was educated in American schools, knew no Japanese, had never been out of the country, was not a dual citizen. As with the other principals in the Supreme Court cases, his loyalty to the United States was never at issue. He intended to marry a white girl and, when the evacuation order disrupted his plans, hoped to evade detection by changing his name and appearance.[29] Apprehended by the FBI, Korematsu was convicted on two charges: he had violated an order excluding Japanese Americans from a defined area, and he had failed to report to an assembly center. Given a suspended sentence, he was placed on probation for five years. He was thus the one Japanese American legally at large in the prohibited area, with the order of a federal court to back his unique status. The commanding general had him picked up again, this time by military police, and lodged in an assembly center. At this point the JACL began to move his case through the courts as another test of the evacuation order.

The Supreme Court's review of the Korematsu case could hardly have been more perfunctory. Speaking for the majority, Justice Black evaded the main constitutional issue with the incredible assertion that Korematsu had not been "excluded from the Military Area because of hostility to him or his race." Essentially the decision followed the precedent supposedly set a year and a half earlier: "The Hirabayashi conviction and this one rest on the same 1942 Congressional Act and the same basic and military orders." But as Justice Jackson pointed out in his dissent, "The Court is now saying that in Hirabayashi we did decide the very thing we were not deciding." Two other members of the Court also dissented, Justice Roberts on relatively minor and technical points and Justice Murphy with an eloquent condemnation of the evacuation, which he placed in "the ugly abyss of racism."

If the logic of the Korematsu case is hard for a layman to follow, it does not help that on the very same day the Court handed down the Endo decision. Mitsuye Endo had been handpicked by James Purcell, a San Francisco lawyer, as a test case. A native-born citizen who knew no Japanese, Miss Endo had been an employee of California until, with all other Japanese, she was dismissed from the civil service; her brother was serving in the Army. By a unanimous decision, the Court held that the WRA, as a civil agency, had no right to detain persons in relocation centers whose loyalty to the United States was not at issue. Such detention, in the words of Justice Murphy's concurring opinion, exemplified the "racism inherent in the entire evacuation program," and this kind of discrimination "bears no reasonable relation to military necessity and is utterly foreign to the ideals and traditions of the American people." Until the decision was handed down on December 18, 1944, it took about two and a half years from the day Miss Endo filed her first petition; and it was during this period that the camps were built and peopled. By dividing the issue of constitutionality into meaningless parts, the Court had both sanctioned the evacuation and, after the fact, salved its conscience. Thus, the Court assisted in perpetrating what a leading scholar of constitutional law has termed—to repeat—"the most drastic invasion of the rights of citizens of the United States by their own government that has thus far occurred in the history of our nation."[30]

In principle, the Endo decision brought an end to the camps; in fact, it marked the beginning of a new series of cases. On December 17, 1944 (thus, the day before the Supreme Court declared its activities to be unconstitutional), the director of

WRA announced that all relocation projects would be closed within a year, and on the same day the Western Defense Command rescinded the order excluding Japanese Americans from the West Coast. At Tule Lake an Army team of some twenty officers, working at the rate of 400 to 500 interviews a day, began immediately to check once again the segregants' "loyalty." The inmates were fearful that they might now lose the protective custody they had so cleverly bought by their first No-no declaration, and the young males viewed permission to leave the camp as the first step toward induction into the armed forces.

In order to maintain their status quo, inmates at Tule Lake now renounced their American citizenship, which was possible for Nisei under a special law that Congress had passed six months earlier. Several associations of Japanese nationalists at Tule Lake, which had been trying with indifferent success to organize the camp in support of their political views, had set mass renunciation as their principal goal. During the first six months, however, the Department of Justice received only about 600 applications, or far fewer than the number of persons enthusiastically advocating renunciation for others. The breakthrough came in mid-December: One paradoxical consequence of the Court's belated condemnation of the camps was to stimulate some hundreds of harassed and befuddled inmates to adopt General DeWitt's famous aphorism, "A Jap's a Jap," in the literal sense.

Only Nisei and Kibei had citizenship that they could renounce, of course, but Issei believed that security for the whole family could be achieved by having their children apply, and often they did it for them. "We're going to have [our children] renounce citizenship just to stay here," one informant at Tule Lake declared. "If you set a deadline, I will renounce my citizenship due to the fact that I have no place to go." "What do they want us to do? Go back to California and get filled full of lead? I'm going to sit here and watch" (D. S. Thomas and Nishimoto, 1946: 339, 344, 347). As a consequence of such pressures, 5,371 American-born Japanese signed applications renouncing their citizenship. A small number were truly Japanese nationalists; they moved to their forebears' homeland and there assimilated.[31] Most took this drastic step only in order to keep their families together, to avoid going out into a world believed to be overwhelmingly hostile (the WRA refused to maintain Tule Lake as a "refuge camp"), or to avoid the draft. Many applications were by minors, which the government illegally accepted as valid. After five years of litigation,[32] most of the renunciations were voided by the U.S. District Court in San Francisco. A few cases were pending more than twenty years after the event.

When the Army reexamined the "loyalty" of the Tule Lake segregants, a vast majority—108,545 persons—were cleared and given permission to return to the West Coast. "Recommended for detention" at Tule Lake were 4,851 American citizens (some of whom had signed applications to renounce their citizenship) and 112 aliens on parole from internment in Department of Justice camps. By mid-August, 1945, some 1,600 of those excluded had appealed for reconsideration, 800 cases had been heard, and the exclusion of about 400 canceled. Most of the five thousand had to wait until after the end of the war: even a month or two before V-J Day, the Western Defense Command was still fearful of the sabotage for which it had yet to find a scintilla of evidence (Barnhart, 1960).

A parallel series of court cases opposed official acts that, even in the context of the whole evacuation, must be termed surrealist. In 1942, the State Department had arranged for the deportation to the United States of more than 2,100 persons of Japanese descent, most from Peru and the rest from other South American nations. General George C. Marshall had requested them in order to have bodies to exchange for American citizens interned in countries overrun by Japanese armies, but actually none was ever so used. In mid-1944 the Department of Justice investigated these internees and found no evidence whatever that a single one of them was politically dangerous. The transfer of Latin Americans was stopped, and those already in the United States were shifted from camp to camp, thus evading the attention of even the organizations supporting the litigation by Japanese Americans.

After the end of the war, the federal government began proceedings to deport the Latin American internees to occupied Japan, the charge against them being that they had entered the country without proper papers, though indeed under the escort of U.S. military police. A representative of some Japanese Peruvians in Crystal City, Texas, asked for and received assistance from the ACLU. In a seemingly endless series of legal moves, for many of which there were no precedents, this organization won their right not to go to Japan but back to Peru—and then not to go to Peru (which for years refused to permit their reentry), but to stay in the United States. After years in constant litigation and physically in and out of various camps, in 1954 the South American deportees were permitted to apply for permanent residence in the United States. Many became citizens (Barnhart, 1962).

In short, the end of the relocation centers was brought about by a process no less shameful than their establishment. The unprecedented act of imprisoning a whole subnation, no individual of which was charged with any crime or guilty of any, climaxed the long history of discrimination. But it was not the inevitable consequence of this preparation, even when anti-Japanese sentiment was aggravated by war hysteria. Politicians responded to this hysteria in part because liberal opposition to the evacuation was strangely silent. Again, one reason was that liberals were also confused, but the decisive factor was that for a full decade virtually every liberal organization had been infested with totalitarians. When for its own reason the Communist Party decided to sanction the incarceration of Japanese Americans, many who by their moral and political principles would have fought it were trapped into shamefaced approval or, at best, silent acquiescence. And once the fateful decision was made, the camps acquired a certain legitimacy, to be maintained and defended by official personages and institutions from the President and the Supreme Court down.

The Japanese Americans were the victims of a pointless, cruel injustice. Aided in their rehabilitation by only a few individuals and impecunious organizations, they had in fact to depend essentially on themselves to survive through the camp period, to establish a record of unmistakable loyalty to the

United States, and to find their way back to normal life. That they succeeded against such odds is a tribute to this people, though not to the country that made it necessary.

Notes

[1] See the report of Samuel W. King, Hawaii's delegate to Congress, in the *San Francisco Chronicle,* January 26, 1942. Hawaii had precisely one Nisei fifth-columnist, Yoshio Harada, who lived on the isolated island of Niihau, which is a private ranch of the Robinson family. On December 7, a Japanese pilot crash-landed there and induced Harada to help him. Later, when the islanders killed the pilot, Harada shot himself (Bosworth, 1967: 122–23).

[2] Carey McWilliams (1942a) gave a quite favorable report on this first evacuation to the *New Republic:* "There is no question that the Japanese colony should never have been tolerated on Terminal Island. . . . Within the last few weeks, the Department of Justice has wisely ordered all Japanese out of the district and, by a series of decrees, has limited the areas within which Japanese aliens may reside. With these regulations, I think, no one can quarrel." For his subsequent alibi, see Girdner and Loftis, 1969: 111.

[3] Even so, an evacuee who subsequently described her experiences took these assurances seriously: "The Federal Reserve Banks took charge of property owned by the evacuees, while the Farm Security Administration took over the agricultural property. This was necessary because of the social and economic vultures preying upon the unfortunates expecting to be evacuated" (Okubo, 1946: 14; cf. below, p. 104 ff).

[4] Personal communication from Gordon Hirabayashi, December 2, 1965.

[5] The analysis that Grodzins gives of the "Opposition to the Evacuation" (1949: chap. 6) is rather thin, though not for lack of diligent research on his part. The organizations expressing disapproval represented mostly the victims themselves or, if not, various types easily dismissed as either impractical do-gooders or selfish businessmen. The religious organizations voicing concern were mainly "church groups" rather than the churches themselves— that is, service-oriented adjuncts that had earned the reputation of defending every underdog. And any group that espoused pacifism, such as the Quakers with whom Hirabayashi worked, was by definition incapable of appreciating a policy that derived from "military necessity." The Postwar World Council, which Grodzins cites

(p. 197), had just changed its name from the Keep America Out of War Committee; in any case, it was hardly the "national group" he calls it, but rather a platform for Norman Thomas and his small personal coterie, a minority even within the tiny Socialist party. Some of the business groups dependent on Japanese labor expressed initial opposition to the evacuation, but their contingent stance could not stand up to the patriotic arguments of their more zealous fellows.

6 During the period of the Stalin-Hitler Pact, some of the Party's isolationist propaganda had been disseminated through its front organization, the American Peace Mobilization (APM), which fought against Lend-Lease and any other aid to the Western allies. Immediately after June 22, this organization was converted into the American People's Mobilization (still APM), which called for maximum aid to the Soviet Union, Britain, and all others fighting in what had suddenly become "the war against fascism."

7 The Communist Party far outdid the AFL-CIO in its effort to increase industrial production irrespective of the position of the workers. "Any strike hurts the war effort" (editorial, *Daily Worker*, April 3, 1942). The United Electrical, Radio, and Machine Workers, the most important of the unions dominated by Communists, voted to forgo extra pay for overtime and Sunday work (*ibid.*, March 26, 1942). William Z. Foster, the Party's top expert on trade unions, called for "the total mobilization of labor" (*ibid.*, May 2, 1942).

8 The report in a three-part series on the status of Negroes in war industry was altogether favorable, and this positive view was documented by such evidence (however bizarre in this newspaper) as a quotation from the public-relations officer of Glenn Martin Aircraft (*ibid.*, February 13, 1942). Occasional items on other racial minorities typically followed the same line. According to one headline (which I regarded as a partial recompense for eyestrain and boredom), "American Indians Hail Stalin as 'Warrior of 1941'; Conclave Presents Him with Feathered War Bonnet" (*ibid.*, February 22, 1942).

9 *Ibid.*, January 27, 1942; February 7, 1942; February 15, 1942; March 13, 1942.

10 This was true even of stories that pertained directly or peripherally to the evacuation—on the California election of 1942 (William Schneiderman, "The California Elections," *The Communist*, August 1942), for instance, or on the housing shortages in the state (Tom Cullen, "California's Headache: Too Many Miles," *New Masses*, June 2, 1942). "Mr. Biddle's Bombshell" was the order to

deport Harry Bridges (Abraham Unger, "Mr. Biddle's Bombshell," *ibid.*, June 9, 1942). A statement by Carey McWilliams was another demand to open up the second front (*ibid.*, August 4, 1942). A story on "The Tolan Report" was on "changes needed for effective mobilization of labor"; the committee's recommendations, we learn, were in "essential agreement" with those made earlier by Earl Browder (*ibid.*, November 3, 1942).

[11] Personal interviews. When I spoke to her in the late 1960s, Mrs. Howden was the wife of the chief of California's Division of Fair Employment Practices.

[12] Shortly before his death, Thomas wrote me about his experiences: "I can assure you that it is quite true that the Communists volubly supported the deportation of West Coast Japanese and Japanese Americans into concentration camps. They sent two men (one being a Japanese American Communist, by the way) to try to break up a pitifully small protest meeting I organized."

[13] He is so listed in the organization's *News Letter,* but the committee does not appear in the index of *Prejudice,* his major work on Japanese Americans. The *News Letter* affords a fascinating glimpse into one exotic corner of recent American history. Sponsors of its activities included such standard Party-liners as William Gropper and Max Yergan, a no less familiar contingent of captive liberals, and a number of Japanese Americans who I would suppose are not familiar to any non-Party white. Activities specific to the subnation were interspersed with such general Party affairs as a victory rally at its Jefferson Book Shop. In later issues, the "MacArthur-endorsed anti-Red campaign" in occupied Japan was contrasted with the antiwar and antifascist "Japanese People's Emancipation League," then resident in the Yenan caves of mainland China.

[14] Mr. McWilliams has deposited his papers with the Hoover Library in Stanford, California, where they are available to any interested person. This letter and the other papers mentioned in the following passage are on file there.

[15] The substance of this statement was included in his testimony before the Tolan Committee. "I appointed a committee some time ago," he said, "for the purpose of working on details of a plan which might be submitted to this [House] committee." At that time, on March 7, 1942, he still advocated individual screening of Japanese Americans, for an "indiscriminate evacuation may seriously and needlessly affect our food supply." See U.S. House of Representatives, 1942: Part 31, pp. 11788–93. The justification of the evacuation as a measure to *protect* the Japanese Americans

provided a convenient face-saving for those who supported the measure from the Left, and the alibi became part of its unofficial rationale. Later, after the whole episode was part of history, Mc-Williams commented as follows (1945: 113): "I know of only two reported instances of violence in California: on December 27, 1941, a fight occurred between Filipinos and local Japanese in Stockton; and on January 1, 1942, unknown persons fired at the home of a resident Japanese in Gilroy, California. If there was a danger, the facts do not show [it]."

16 Copyright © 1942, by Harper's Magazine Co. Reprinted from the September 1942 issue of Harper's Magazine by permission of the author.

17 Personal communication from Roger N. Baldwin, American Civil Liberties Union, New York, October 15, 1965. At one point in my consultation with Ernest Besig of the San Francisco office, he started to open up his file on the whole intra-agency dispute, but then decided against it. Without specifics, he appraised quite negatively the reaction to the evacuation of the national ACLU office and of Roger Baldwin.

18 American Civil Liberties Union, *Annual Report, 1942* (New York, 1942), p. 26.

19 See John D. Weaver, *Warren: The Man, the Court, the Era* (Boston: Little, Brown, 1967), pp. 62–63.

20 In 1936, as district attorney of Alameda County, Warren had prosecuted several members of a Communist-dominated union for the murder of one of its members; thereafter, the Communist press pictured him as a ruthless tool of the shipping interests (*ibid.*, chap. 7).

21 U.S. House of Representatives, 1942: Part 29, February 21, pp. 11011–12. Much of Warren's testimony constituted, as it were, a first draft of the *Final Report* of the Western Defense Command (U.S. Army, 1943). In his *post factum* arguments defending the evacuation, Colonel Karl R. Bendetsen borrowed whole paragraphs from the pre-evacuation testimony of the Attorney-General (see the two in parallel columns, Grodzins, 1949: 287–88).

22 In 1966, Tom Clark (who played a minor role in the affair compared with Earl Warren) stated: "I have made a lot of mistakes in my life, but there are two that I acknowledge publicly. One is my part in the evacuation of the Japanese from California in 1942 and the other is the Nuremberg trials" (Weaver, *op. cit.*, p. 113). To my knowledge, Warren has never said as much. When Bosworth was finishing his book, he wrote a courteous letter to the

Chief Justice, paying tribute to his record on civil rights and requesting a statement concerning Warren's participation in the
evacuation. Three weeks later, "an assistant to the Chief Justice
wrote that because of the pressure of his official duties, Mr. Warren would not be able to comply with the request" (Bosworth,
1967: 248).

23 In the majority decision that Justice Black wrote in the Korematsu
case, he objected that in its brief the ACLU had referred to relocation centers as "concentration camps." In an appeal for a rehearing, the ACLU lawyer rebutted the point: "A concentration camp
is one in which innocent citizens are imprisoned without charge
of crime being lodged against them and held without hearing of
any sort before a competent tribunal."

24 For example, except for Ralph Carr of Colorado, every governor of
the intermountain states protested against the West Coast's attempt, as they put it, to dump upon them its "undesirable enemy
aliens" and "potential saboteurs." Such epithets were less independent expressions of official antipathy than echoes of the well
publicized proceedings used to justify the evacuation.

25 See Tamotsu Shibutani, *Improvised News: A Sociological Study of
Rumor* (New York: Bobbs-Merrill, 1966), pp. 150–53 and *passim;*
also Leighton, 1945.

26 Daisuke Kitagawa, who was at Tule Lake, does not mention this
second version. It may be that it slipped his mind, but one wonders—given the sloppiness of the whole processing, especially at
that camp—whether the question in an amended wording was
ever distributed. Kitagawa's dignified comment was as follows: "I
publicly stated that, as an Issei, I would answer Yes to the first
question and No to the second. . . . As long as I was in the United
States and was receiving benefits of law and order from the U.S.
government [!], I would conscientiously pledge my loyalty to the
government. But as long as the law of the United States prohibited
me, as an Asian, from applying to be naturalized as a U.S. citizen, I would unequivocally answer No to forswearing allegiance
to my own country" (D. Kitagawa, 1967: 117).

27 John Okada, a veteran of the Pacific war, wrote an interesting
novel entitled *No-No Boy.* Back in Seattle from the prison where
he had served his time, the hero struggles to find his way to the
America that had rejected him and that he had rejected. The
hero's mother, who had trained him to be a Japanese nationalist,
turns out to be paranoid. A Nisei friend, just returned from the
war with a wound of which he eventually dies, is pictured as
relatively well off.

28 *Hirabayashi* v. *United States* 320 U.S. 81 (1943); *Korematsu* v. *United States* 323 U.S. 214 (1944); *Ex parte Endo* 323 U.S. 283 (1944).

29 Gordon Hirabayashi told me that several of those who have written about Japanese Americans tried, as I did, to get in touch with Fred Korematsu after the war, but all without success. Perhaps he has found the anonymity he was seeking then.

30 Edward S. Corwin, *Total War and the Constitution* (New York: Knopf, 1947), p. 91.

31 Some of the renunciants who went to Japan regretted their confused decision and hoped for a decision by the U.S. Supreme Court declaring the circumstances to be coercive. Shortly after the war, the JACL commissioned the national director of the ACLU to assist the more than 10,000 Nisei students, tourists, and visitors who had been trapped in Japan by the war. About half of these 10,000, according to the estimate of the U.S. Consul, had lost their citizenship through service in the Japanese Army, voting in a Japanese election, taking a job open only to Japanese nationals, or becoming naturalized Japanese. Under Japanese law a Nisei could be naturalized without his knowledge. Many who accepted a job were ignorant of its broader consequences; for example, a teacher in a public school, but not in a private one, lost his American citizenship (Baldwin, 1948).

32 The cases were led through the courts mainly by Wayne Collins, the ACLU lawyer in San Francisco already mentioned. I telephoned for a half-hour appointment with Mr. Collins and stayed for five hours, a fascinated listener to a flood of recollections, some of them printable, of his experiences as one of the major attorneys in "the Japanese cases." His principal adversaries were not private organizations or pressure groups of any political coloration, but a series of liberal officials in Washington and their local subordinates. In an early draft I wrote that Mr. Collins obviously enjoyed being a recurrent and increasingly painful pin in the side of Francis Biddle, whom I used, *pars pro toto,* to denote the federal legal officialdom. Collins reminded me that by the time he got involved with the Japanese cases, Biddle had been replaced as Attorney-General by Tom Clark, appointed by President Truman after his tenure of duty as a civilian liaison to the Western Defense Command. "My pleadings," Collins wrote me, "were amended from time to time to substitute various persons who held that office following Tom Clark, namely, J. Howard McGrath, James F. McGranery, Herbert Brownell, Jr., William F. Rogers, Robert F. Kennedy, and Nicholas deB. Katzenbach. I did not enjoy sticking pins into any of them. . . . [But] because of their official inhumanity

to these victims of the war and because of their generalized hostility to these innocent persons and their persistent indifference to the sufferings of the government victims, I can assure you that I would not have shed any tears for any of the officials if the pins you referred to had been swords" (personal communication from Wayne M. Collins, December 22, 1965).

Chapter 5 ◉ Six Times Down, Seven Times Up

"Military necessity" as the justification for the camps linked the Japanese subnation with America's enemy, and by the end of the war people throughout the country not only deprecated a group of whom most had had no personal knowledge, but based their hostility on gross misinformation. Only 32 percent of a national sample believed that Japanese Americans had not "destroyed any American war materials"; only 13 percent that they had not done "any spying for the Japanese government." Asked about "the *average* Japanese person who lives in this country," 50 percent characterized him as "loyal" and 25 percent as "disloyal," with the remaining 25 percent admitting that they did not know (National Opinion Research Center, 1946).

To most of these questions, the responses from the West Coast were close to the national average. In California, opposition to anti-Japanese policies remained as anomalous as before the war. The same small groups that had tried to secure the release of college students from the camps, or to mitigate the life there for the others, now undertook to facilitate the evacuees' return. Most of these activists were thoroughly respectable citizens, with hardly a political radical among them. Pasadena, the patrician suburb of Los Angeles, continued to stand out as a center of moral concern about the Japanese. In that city and similar enclaves along the Pacific, men who described themselves as "hard-headed believers in the virtues of the American form of government" organized Fair Play Committees to spread this sentiment among the general public (Modell, 1969a: chap. 11).

It was uphill work. Competitors of prewar Japanese produce wholesalers had founded an American League of California, which "sincerely" urged Japanese Americans to demonstrate their patriotism by "remaining away from the Pacific Coast." A newly organized California Citizens Council agitated for a law excluding Japanese. A post of the Veterans of Foreign Wars distributed bumper stickers proclaiming, NO JAPS WANTED IN CALIFORNIA. John Lechner, who had become one of the most active of anti-Japanese spokesmen, became obsessed during the war years, when internment whetted his appetite for more decisive measures. Fletcher Bowron, the liberal mayor of Los Angeles, warned that "the people here are thoroughly aroused, and it would be very unsafe for the Japanese themselves" if they tried to return. Three times in 1943 and 1944 a polling organization surveyed public opinion in Los Angeles County, and on each occasion about two-thirds of the respondents advocated a constitutional amendment to deport all Japanese from the United States (Modell, 1969a).

The crucial difference from 1942 was the official position of the government. Once the Supreme Court had declared detention in camps to be unconstitutional, the WRA started to issue propaganda pamphlets denouncing the whole of the policy it had been administering. Statements by U.S. servicemen on "what we're fighting for" began with a quotation from a veteran of Guadalcanal: "Our American citizens of Japanese ancestry are being persecuted as though Adolf Hitler himself were in charge" (U.S. Dept. of the Interior, 1945b). Another pamphlet, designed to dispel "common misconceptions" about Japanese Americans, refuted point by point the official rationalization of the evacuation—dual citizenship, Shinto, Japanese-language schools, concentration in strategic areas, not to mention the "honesty of the Japanese as a race" and their "soil-conservation practices" (U.S. Dept. of the Interior, 1945a). The War Relocation Authority, with its name changed to the War Agency Liquidation Unit, tried in various ways to hasten the evacuees' readaptation to a civilian environment (U.S. Dept. of the Interior, 1947).

> [During the] battle of words, ideas, and efforts to manipulate the thinking of those who differed, the social climate was . . . emotional and threatening to state and community solidarity. The extremists on both sides, for or against the

return, lined up in bitter verbal attacks in forums, sermons, discussions, letters to the editor, and mimeographed resolutions. . . . [But those favoring the return of the Japanese] happened also to be on the side of the Army, the Supreme Court, the Constitution, and the governor (Luomala, 1946).[1]

Some of the hatred of "Japs" was deflected to the "Jap-lovers." In particular, the WRA became a target of abuse, for it had allegedly "engineered" the rescission of the evacuation order (Luomala, 1946).

The long-feared homecoming began in Los Angeles late in 1944 and proceeded slowly, gradually, over the following months. The carefully prepared hostility caused only a few incidents. Until the end of 1945, the Teamsters Union boycotted Japanese produce. The California Board of Equalization issued no commercial licenses to Japanese until the WRA threatened to bring suit. Early in 1946, California's Attorney-General Robert W. Kenny charged one sheriff with malfeasance for his acts against evacuees. And this firm stand by a few official agencies helped bring about a general change of attitude. In the 1946 election, when the California ballot included a proposition to make the Alien Land Law part of the state constitution, it was defeated by 56 to 44 percent.

This does not mean, of course, that the Japanese were generally welcomed back into their old neighborhoods. According to a WRA report:

The whole occupational picture is characterized by a degrading of skilled personnel, loss of seniority and civil service status, the exploitation [as] domestic help of the families of hired agricultural workers, and the great difficulty of finding leases for farm land (quoted in Modell, 1969a: chap. 11).

The elderly in particular were beaten down and afraid. Lacking the strength to start a new fight, they settled down in trailer camps that the WRA established in out-of-the-way spots and recalled with pitiful nostalgia the relative comfort and certitude of the recent past.

The whole West Coast had been swollen by the wartime influx

of workers to new industries, and in most cities a residence was all but unobtainable. Evacuees who had laboriously constructed furniture out of scrap lumber were forced to leave the camps as they had entered them, with no more than the baggage they could carry. For more than a decade, Japanese Americans found housing to be "the single most important area of discrimination," worse in the Los Angeles area than around San Francisco, but serious everywhere (Kitano, 1960).

GOVERNMENT ASSISTANCE

The fact that, somewhat belatedly, a few official agencies declared themselves in support of the Constitution has been extrapolated into the pleasant myth that most public authorities, having recognized the grave inequity suffered by Japanese Americans, did their best to make amends. According to the *Washington Post* of October 9, 1965:

> The injustice done to the Japanese Americans will remain forever a stain on American history. There is some comfort, however, in the general acknowledgement of this injustice and in the conscientious effort that has been made to provide restitution for the property losses suffered by the evacuated citizens (quoted in Bosworth, 1967: 235).

Whether "conscientious effort" is the appropriate phrase to describe any element of the government's postwar aid program can be doubted. It is certainly not an apt designation of the decades-long litigation briefly described in the last chapter. Nor does it truly characterize the sometimes helpful activities of the WRA and its successor, whose employees "wished desperately to be rid of this bothersome group" (Modell, 1969a: chap. 11). What then of the restitution of property losses?

Immediately after the war, the JACL memorialized Congress to authorize adequate compensation for the losses incurred because of the forced evacuation. A draft of a bill was written by the WRA staff, and Dillon Myer, its director, guessed that the total payments would "probably not exceed $10,000,000," or about $91 per capita.[2] This modest estimate was based not on an approximation of the losses, but on the amount that would have to be reimbursed to evacuees who "thought they had sufficient proof to support their claims" (Bloom and Riemer, 1949: 200). The losses actually incurred can be suggested by a few examples. Robert Asazawa, who had left his 18-acre fruit farm in charge of a tenant, came home to find the tenant gone and most of the trees dead. Yoshimi Shibata found his home and his 125,000 square feet of nurseries in ruins. The Nichiren Temple in Los Angeles, where 600 families had stored their household goods, had been ransacked. George Yanagimachi found that his oyster beds had been systematically pirated, with a loss of nearly $100,000 (Hosokawa, 1969: 437).

The law as passed on July 2, 1948 (that is, some three and a half years after the dissolution of the camps started) followed Myer's logic. No payments were authorized for "death or personal injury, personal inconvenience, physical hardship, or mental suffering"; nor was any compensation made for losses in earned income and earning power, which for most families were greater than the only type of claim that could be filed, real and personal property lost as "a reasonable and natural consequence of the evacuation." Almost 24,000 claims were filed within the 18-month period stipulated in the law; 60 percent were for less than $2,500, 73 percent for less than $5,000. During all of 1950 the Department of Justice heard 211 claims and agreed to pay 137 of them. The average payment to the claimant was $450; the average cost of adjudicating the case was $1,400 (Hosokawa, 1969: 445–46).

After some undignified haggling, the government permitted two extensions of the deadline and reduced the red tape involved in settlements. The cases adjudicated from January 3, 1950, to June 30, 1956, have been collected in a book (Banse, 1956), whose dry legalese highlights the cold, official pettiness in reaction to one instance after another of guiltless suffering.

> Shigeru Henry Nakagawa sold some of his household goods for $300; he was allowed $460 to make up the difference between that amount and their "fair and reasonable value." Some Japanese books, valued at $10, for which he received no allowance, "he destroyed . . . voluntarily, and his alleged motive for doing so, the fear that he might

be punished, has no relation to the evacuation but springs from the general hysteria." He withdrew his claim for stored goods that had been stolen, since an investigation might reveal the thief and he did not want "to cause embarrassment to any person" (Banse, 1956: 93–95).

Yasuhei Nagashima received $308.75 for goods stored with the WRA and erroneously sold at public auction. However, a claim for a loss of $499 incurred in the sale of his truck was not allowed; the claimant, in ignorance of the law, had not originally included this item, and an amendment to his claim that introduced new subject matter constituted "an insurmountable bar" to settlement (Banse, 1956: 135–39).

Kihei Hashioka claimed $220 as the loss incurred in the sale of various goods, including, however, a short-wave radio that he should have deposited with the local police. Since the $80 he received included an unknown proportion for the radio; it was deemed necessary to adjust his claim downward. "A fair method of computing such price would be to allocate this unknown [amount] to $65, which represents the true value of the radio, in the same proportion as the $80 received for all the property bears to the $166 which has been found to be its true value. Thus: $(80/166) = (x/65)$, or $31.33. This $31.33, the sale price of the radio, deducted from the $80, total sales price, leaves $48.67, the sale price of the remaining property, . . . leaving claimant with a compensable loss of $52.33" (Banse, 1956: 176–77).

The last settlement was made in late 1965 to the Koda family for 5,000 acres of fertile rice land 50 miles northwest of Fresno and a large rice mill, valued at $1,210,000. When he was sent off to camp, Keisaburo Koda had left his property in charge of a white attorney and others, who proceeded to swindle him of virtually everything. During the fifteen years it took to settle the case, the original claimant died, as well as one of his two sons, two lawyers and an accountant who worked on the case, and the men most involved in the fraud (who thus avoided criminal prosecution). The settlement was for $362,500, or slightly more than the cost of the litigation.

From the first payment made—$303.36 to Tokuji Tokimasa on December 16, 1949, for books and office equipment he was forced to abandon when he evacuated his Los Angeles real-estate office—to the settlement with the Koda family, a total of about $38 million was paid out to approximately 26,500 claimants. At the time of the evacuation, the Federal Reserve Bank estimated the property losses incurred by Japanese Americans at $400 million, or slightly more than the total requested—but not paid. The payments averaged 10 cents per dollar claimed, less 10 percent in attorney's fees. The claims were at 1942 dollar values, with no allowance for the considerable postwar inflation, and no interest was paid. A year and a half after the last property settlement, in the spring of 1967, the Supreme Court released to the last individual depositors about $4 million that had been confiscated from American branches of Japanese banks. Presiding over the Court was Chief Justice Earl Warren (Justice Tom Clark abstained). Once again, grudging justice was so long delayed that many of the claimants were dead.

One of the complicating facts in the Koda case was that during the war California had filed an escheat action to seize the property because the "real owner," Keisaburo Koda, was an alien. Early in February 1942, Attorney-General Warren had recommended a tightening up of the lax enforcement of the Alien Land Law as one step in the displacement of Japanese Americans (Grodzins, 1949: 277). Of the 79 escheat proceedings taken under the law, 59 were started under Warren's prodding. One of these involved the 8 acres of farmland that Kajiro Oyama, an Issei, had bought for his Nisei son, Fred. According to a unanimous decision of the California Supreme Court, the statute prohibiting an alien ineligible for citizenship from acquiring land was improperly evaded when that alien purchased land for a citizen. It seemed, thus, that the property losses suffered in the forced evacuation would be compounded after the internees' return by the confiscation of land owned by Nisei. On appeal, the JACL took the case to the U.S. Supreme Court, which in a majority opinion reversed the decision concerning escheatage without commenting on the prohibition itself. In *Takahashi* v. *Fish and Game Commission,* similarly, the Court found unconstitutional a California wartime statute that excluded aliens ineligible for citizenship from commercial fishing in coastal waters. In these two cases, "the Supreme Court, as if in penance, struck down a racial classification involving the Japanese on what was virtually a presumption of its unconstitutionality, without applying the normal and less stringent rules of equal protection of the laws" (tenBroek, 1968: 304–10).

The most important victory of the JACL was to get a revision of the Immigration and Naturalization Act. A bill to relax the restrictions that Congressman Walter H. Judd introduced in 1950 almost passed, but was defeated for reasons irrelevant to the JACL's campaign. Two years later, as part of a general revision of American immigration law sponsored by Congressman Francis E. Walter and Senator Pat McCarran, Japan was given a token quota and race was eliminated as a bar to naturalization.[3]

> Issei . . . by the hundreds enrolled in citizenship courses sponsored by churches, JACL chapters, and other organizations. . . . In time, . . . men and women in their sixties and seventies and eighties . . . stood before federal judges and took the oath of allegiance as America's newest citizens. It was a privilege and an honor that had been a long time coming (Hosokawa, 1969: 455).

THE JAPANESE IN POSTWAR HAWAII

Though there was no general evacuation of Japanese Americans from Hawaii, their status was challenged during the war years, and they also had to take a road back after 1945. It was a different road from that traveled by the mainland internees, however, and a comparison of the same subnation in the two settings offers many insights that one could not derive from an analysis of either one alone.

The Japanese planes had hardly left the skies over Pearl Harbor on December 7, 1941, when Hawaii's governor (with President Roosevelt's approval, given two days later) proclaimed "martial law" and transferred to the local commanding general all his own authority and "all of the powers normally exercised by the judicial officers . . . of this territory . . . during the present emergency and until the danger of invasion is removed." Thus, not only did General Walter D. Short have as free a hand in Hawaii as General DeWitt in the Western Defense Command, but any rationalization for evacuation had far more plausibility than on the West Coast. Instead of less than 1 percent, the Japanese in Hawaii constituted more than 37 percent of the population; instead of merely living (like the less affluent of any race) along railroads and next to airports, they made up sizable portions of the labor force in naval yards and military depots. And Hawaii had suffered not a series of rumors but the attack on Pearl Harbor. It is true that the Japanese in Hawaii had committed no sabotage, but if Attorney-General Warren had had a counterpart in Honolulu, that would have been the most important reason for evacuating them all to mainland camps.

There were many, and not merely fanatics, who tried to accelerate the growth of hysteria. William C. Hill, a self-made businessman who had built a powerful political machine on Hawaii Island, offered the opinion that "a Jap is a Jap even after a thousand years and can't become Americanized"—a sentiment shared not only by many whites but by Filipinos, Koreans, and others in Hawaii's multi-ethnic population (Fuchs, 1961: 303). There were others, notably John A. Burns, a police captain in Honolulu, who had the courage to buck the tide and announce publicly, "I have complete confidence in Hawaii's Japanese Americans" (Inouye, 1967: 61). The abuses of civil rights that resulted from such cross pressures were relatively mild compared with total evacuation. About 1 percent of the adult Japanese population, alien and citizen, were interned and sent to mainland camps (Lind, 1946: 73; cf. tenBroek, 1968: 135–36). After the immediate threat of invasion had passed, an effort was made in the courts to restore the right of *habeas corpus;* and on December 7, 1945—four years to the day after the attack—the U.S. Supreme Court found that the martial law had been unconstitutional.[4]

Although the worst excesses were avoided, the Japanese were objects of suspicion, humiliation, and discrimination:

Before systematic curtailment of Japanese community life was imposed by outsiders, the Japanese themselves strenuously repressed manifestations of their own culture. The youngsters from college and high school told their mothers to put away their kimonos, stop eating Japanese food, throw away the small shrines and family swords, preserved for generations; and the old folks had to listen (Fuchs, 1961: 304).

As one important expression of this self-abnegation, Japanese candidates voluntarily withdrew from politics during the war, so that the 1943 state legislature was the first in many years without a single person of Japanese ancestry in either house.

Once it became possible for Japanese Americans to demonstrate their patriotism, they did it with the same fervor as on the mainland. The Nisei bought more war bonds than any other group in the islands. In the first weeks of the war the Nisei in the National Guard units had been summarily discharged, and those in the ROTC and the Territorial Guard stripped of their weapons. But when the Army reversed its stand, approximately 80 percent of the male Japanese Americans of military age showed up to volunteer (Inouye, 1967: 61–68). And as soldiers they established a record for heroism matched only by their counterparts from the West Coast (Murphy, 1954). In the Army, they also lost much of their provincialism, the easy-going acceptance of their second-class place in Hawaiian society.

This awakening to new opportunities coincided with the coming of age of a whole generation of native-born citizens. From 1924, the year that Daniel Inouye was born, to 1947, when he was discharged from the Army, the Nisei increased from 5 to 30 percent of Hawaii's electorate. "In the summer of 1947," he recalls, "I was signed up as a member of the Democratic Party by that one-time police captain, John Burns" (Inouye, 1967: 201, 207). As police representative to an unofficial organization called the Morale Contact Group, Burns had worked behind the scenes to distribute small favors to the demoralized Japanese. Sometimes he was able to render important assistance to the whole subnation, as when he helped block a bill that would have denied to Japanese Americans all types of employment in the territorial government. The faction in the postwar Democratic party that he built had as its nucleus Nisei and Sansei who remembered his help.

Its political prospects seemed good. According to opinion polls, by 1948 the routine Republican dominance of the islands was resting on a minority of the electorate. The two largest nonwhite sectors, Japanese and part-Hawaiian, professed a Democratic preference in the largest proportion; and even the Chinese, by that date thoroughly middle-class, were Democrats by a sizable majority. To convert this sentiment into votes took time, however, for it was a new idea to many among the ethnic minorities that they could realize social and economic goals through politics. In any case, the Democratic party was too much involved in an internal struggle to be able to win any elections. The Communist Party, acting through its members in the leadership of the International Longshoremen's and Warehousemen's Union, "decided in late 1947 to use every re-source to capture the machinery, personnel, and policies of the weakened Democratic Party" (Fuchs, 1961: 311).[5] In a fight that lasted several years, the Communist-ILWU faction was thoroughly defeated by a group made up of such rising party leaders as Burns (later the governor) and Inouye (later a U.S. Senator), who built a strong state organization linked to the Johnson-Humphrey wing of the national Democratic party.[6] In the Democratic landslide of 1954, Nelson K. Doi, a Nisei Demo-cratic newcomer, won a seat in the state Senate over William C. Hill (who had long since regretted his wartime diatribes). Nearly half the seats in the state legislature were captured by Japanese Americans, and in every local government except on Hawaii Island, control was taken by Democrats, with a large proportion of Nisei among them (Fuchs, 1961: chap. 13).

Ever since the establishment of the Hawaiian Republic, the dominant whites had been seriously concerned about the po-tential power of the several Oriental minorities (cf. pp. 45–48). To the frequently repeated charge that Orientals practiced bloc voting, liberal social scientists have usually replied, "It is so slight as to be inconsequential" (Lind, 1957).[7] And this cer-tainly was true at least of the Japanese in the early years of this century (Table 5-1). Up to 1920, while most Nisei were still under 21, the Japanese had few votes and no government

Table 5-1. *Percentage Japanese among the Electorate and Government Officials, Hawaii, 1910–1955*

YEAR	ADULT CITIZENS	ELECTED OFFICIALS	APPOINTED OFFICIALS
1910	0.3	0	0
1920	5.5	0	0
1930	15.3	2.2	1.6
1940	26.6	14.3	2.9
1950	34.7	25.3	10.0
1955	41.0 (est.)	43.0	19.1

SOURCE: George K. Yamamoto, "Political Participation among Orientals in Hawaii," *Sociology and Social Research*, 43 (1959), 359–364.

posts, either elected or appointed. Thereafter, their proportion of the electorate increased rapidly, but there was a decided lag in the percentage of elected and, especially, appointed officials of Japanese ancestry. The breakthrough came, as we have noted, in 1954, when for the first time in the Territory's history Democrats controlled the legislature. From an analysis of that election, one writer concluded, "Ethnic considerations do enter into the vote in Hawaii . . . and, in a close election, could be decisive" (Digman, 1957). The political salience of subnations, already strong by the early 1950s, was reinforced by the effort to join the Union as the 49th state. Until Hawaii was admitted in 1959, the principal argument voiced (or often only intimated) by opponents in Congress was that "the various groups of recent arrivals with Oriental traditions predominate and set the tone of the entire culture."[8]

During the past fifteen years or so, "the ethnic composition of [Hawaii's] legislature has tended to reflect that of Hawaii's adult citizen population, with the Japanese component currently a little exaggerated" (Meller and Tuttle, 1969). In 1968 one U.S. Senator was of Japanese ancestry, the other of Chinese; and both of the two members of the House were Japanese. The governor was John A. Burns. Of the 17 departments of the state government, 5 were headed by Japanese. The 25 members of the state Senate included 11 Japanese (9 Democrats and 2 Republicans), plus the clerk and the sergeant-at-arms. In the state House of Representatives, 31 of the 51 members were Japanese (27 Democrats and 4 Republicans), plus the clerk.[9]

These statistics are not cited to suggest that the high proportions are unfortunate in any way. As a group, Japanese have all the civic virtues—education, diligence, honesty, competence; and if they apply these admirable qualities to public problems, the whole community gains thereby. On the other hand, it would be naive to suppose that Hawaiian Japanese, so recently under unjust attack as potential saboteurs, could fail to identify with those of their subnation who have now been elected to high office. This route up, virtually closed to the small proportion on the mainland (though in 1971 a Nisei was elected mayor of San Jose), is in some measure a realization of the American promise for every Japanese in the islands.

UPWARD MOBILITY

The main key to material success in the United States for anyone is education. Since 1940, Japanese have had more schooling than any other race in the American population, including whites. In Figure 5-1, note the position of "nonwhites"—virtually the same as that of Negroes, but a gross distortion of the level of other subnations included in that artificial category. Note also that among other racial minorities (Filipinos, Chinese, and to a lesser degree Negroes) females acquired more education than males, but that Japanese of both sexes ranked highest. By 1960, almost 7 out of every 10 Japanese of either sex had at least a high school diploma (Schmid and Nobbe, 1965), and a high proportion of these went on to college.

Adding to these census data is difficult, for most other statistical series are not broken down by race. Detailed knowledge can be based on only a few scattered studies, but in general their findings reinforce one another.

In the 1930s, many Nisei children had a poor command of English, as a consequence of both their home environment (see pp. 203–204) and, sometimes, the more or less segregated schools they attended (Hormann, 1957; R. Bell, 1935: 7–8). In any scholastic or "intelligence" test based on language ability,

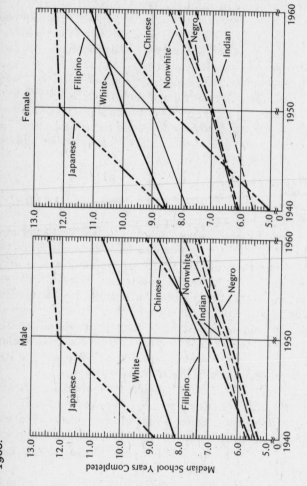

SOURCE: Census data as compiled in Calvin F. Schmid and Charles E. Nobbe, "Socio-economic Differentials among Non-white Races," *American Sociological Review,* 30 (1965), 909–22. Reprinted by permission of the authors.

therefore, their performance was often mediocre, but they did so well in such other elementary subjects as arithmetic and spelling that they typically placed at the top of their class (Strong and Bell, 1933: chap. 3). In later grades, however, as less qualified whites dropped out of school while a much higher proportion of Nisei remained, the competition became keener, so that in high school whites and Nisei ranked about equal (R. Bell, 1935: 61).

According to a number of postwar studies in Hawaii, the "cultural traditions of national-ethnic groups" are important in determining both whether students go on to college and, if so, what they study there (Dole, 1961; Dole and Sherman, 1962). In 1959, when entering freshmen at the University of Hawaii were surveyed, 57.5 percent were Japanese and 16.9 percent Caucasian, with the remaining 25.6 percent scattered among six other racial categories. In a survey of seniors the following year, the percentages were, respectively, 64.6, 13.8, and 21.6 (Dole and Iwakami, 1960a; 1960b). Since no other table in these two studies is classified by race, they tell us nothing about Japanese students except that proportionately many start and even more finish.[10] According to the indications from two minor studies, the scholastic performance of Sansei has remained high in Hawaii (Arkoff and Leton, 1966), but may have fallen somewhat on the mainland (Kitano, 1962).

From the files of the University of California placement bureau, I was able to derive a composite impression of the Japanese who had attended the Berkeley campus during the late 1950s and early 1960s. Their marks were good to excellent, but apart from a few outstanding individuals, this was not a group that would succeed solely because of extraordinary academic achievement. The extracurricular activities they listed were prosaic—the Nisei Student Club,[11] various fraternities, field sports. Their education had been conducted like a military campaign against a hostile world, with intelligent planning and tenacity. Their heavy dependence on the broader Japanese community was suggested in a number of ways. The personal references students listed were often from Japanese professors in totally unrelated fields, and the part-time jobs they held (almost all had had to work their way through college) were typically in plant nurseries or other Japanese business establishments. Their degrees, almost never in liberal arts, were in business administration, optometry, engineering, or some other middle-level profession. For them, education was obviously a means of acquiring a salable skill that could be used either in the general commercial world or, if that remained closed, in a small personal enterprise. Asked to designate the beginning salary they wanted, the applicants' guesses ranged between precisely the one they got in their first professional job and something under that.

In a word, these young men and women were squares. Any doubts they may have had about the transcendental values of the American middle-class life did not reduce their determination to achieve at least that level of security and comfort.

For years after World War II, no firm in San Francisco's financial district would hire a Japanese American, and nothing the Berkeley placement bureau did could break this ban. Finally, the director herself went to the president of one of the largest and most prestigious companies, offered to pay out of her own pocket a Nisei applicant's salary during a trial period, and thus shamed the corporation into hiring the young man. The personnel officer soon became enthusiastic about not only him but any of his race. Some months later, when the same company called the placement bureau specifically requesting more Nisei, the director gently reminded her client that it was against state law to discriminate on the basis of race.

It is difficult to find data on discrimination more broadly based than such personal anecdotes. In a 1947 survey in Seattle, Frank Miyamoto and Robert O'Brien asked their Japanese respondents to compare job discrimination then with that just before the war. The distribution of the answers was:

	NISEI	ISSEI
Less	28%	20%
Same	56	68
More	16	12

What these replies signify is hard to tell, for before the war many Issei had been so thoroughly embedded in the Japanese community that they never in fact tested the tolerance of the whole city. "There was generally a tendency to regard conditions as better than expected" (U.S. Dept. of the Interior, 1947: 132). In the early 1950s Alan Jacobson and Lee Rainwater conducted a study of how 79 firms evaluated their Japanese employees. In spite of the probable race prejudice of some respondents, undoubtedly reinforced in some cases by surviving wartime hostility, an extraordinarily high proportion of the white employers expressed satisfaction.[12] More than two-thirds were "very positive," and the occasional negative remark was typically that Japanese are "too ambitious and want to move on to a better job too quickly" (Caudill and DeVos, 1956).

In Hawaii, there was a long tradition that Japanese were most suitably employed at a menial level. For males, as we have seen, the route out of field work was usually into either small business or a skilled craft; for females, it was generally into domestic service. From the beginning of the century to after World War II, well over half the servants in Hawaii's private households were Japanese (Lind, 1951). In the mid-1930s, according to the employment secretary of the Honolulu YWCA, persons seeking employees "generally express[ed] a racial preference," and for household work the principal demand was for Japanese women, especially Issei. A Japanese girl who worked as a waitress or salesgirl was routinely paid less than a Caucasian or Portuguese (Dranga, 1936). Some worked as barbers, getting an average weekly wage of $12, compared with $15 for a Japanese male performing the same service (Kimura, 1939).

Whether any anti-Japanese discrimination exists in postwar Hawaii is hard to determine. In 1964, a fair-employment practices law went into effect, but its enforcement has not been very stringent. During the first four and a half years, only 40 complaints were investigated, of which 11 were found to be well based. Only 2 complaints involved a Japanese, both filed by the same woman, who charged discrimination on the basis of her age.[13] The Fair Practices Training Council, a private firm operating under a federal grant to train unemployed persons, put a total of about 1,100 persons through its program. Though no statistics on race were kept, the director estimated that 90 percent were "non-Caucasians," including a small number of Japanese.

Whatever discrimination remained after the war, both in Hawaii and on the mainland large numbers of Japanese succeeded in moving up to middle-class positions. As with every nationality, the first data available were about outstanding individuals who were the first to achieve some post or honor. Takeshi Yoshida was the first Nisei admitted to Annapolis; Minoru Yamazaki became a world-famous architect; Stephen C. Tamura became superior judge of Orange County, California (Morita, 1967: chap. 6). The Nisei honored by the JACL at one of its postwar conventions included—in addition to those distinguished for their services specifically to the civil rights of Japanese Americans—Tomi Kanazawa, the first Nisei given a leading role with the Metropolitan Opera Company; Ford Hiroshi Konno, "America's greatest swimmer"; John F. Aiso, a justice of the California Court of Appeals; Jack Murata, an agricultural chemist with the U.S. Department of the Interior; and Kijo Tomiyasu, technical director of General Electric's laser laboratory (Hosokawa, 1969: chap. 27). According to the Japanese American Research Project currently under way at UCLA, Naoki Kikuchi, a watch repairman in Seattle, had ten children, of whom two died. One daughter is married to a pharmacist; the other is president of a women's college. His sons are a professor of physics, a printing technician, an artist, a research physicist, an architect, and an electrical engineer.

Such individual cases, once a sufficient number accumulates, are significant in themselves, but they merely suggest the social mobility of the subnation as a whole. Another kind of data is needed to give a broader indication of the movement of Japanese into the upper middle class—for example, the membership lists of various professional associations in Hawaii. Japanese were identified as such by their names, which for this nationality are an excellent index. At the specified dates, the numbers in the more important professions were as follows:

Civil Engineers: In 1951, 18 of the professional association's total membership of 124 (14.5 percent) were Japanese Americans; in 1968, 167 of 350 (48 percent). At the latter date, four of the six officers plus six of the seventeen committee chairmen were Japanese.[14]

Professional Engineers: Of the 92 resident engineers registered in Hawaii in 1928, only 6 (or 6 percent) were Japanese. In 1967 the comparable figures were 331 of a total of 795 (42 percent).

Architects: None of the resident architects registered in Hawaii in 1928 was Japanese. In 1967 there were 50 of a total of 196 (25 percent).

Surveyors: Of the 61 resident surveyors registered in 1928, only 7 (11 percent) had Japanese names. Of the 151 registered in 1967, 69 (46 percent) were Japanese.[15]

Physicians: The Japanese among residents licensed to practice medicine constituted 95 out of 346 (27 percent) in 1940, 176 out of 600 (29 percent) in 1959, and 223 out of 978 (only 23 percent) in 1968.[16] Why in this case there was a relative decline is not known.

Lawyers: In 1959, 119 out of the total of 416 who had been admitted to the bar (28 percent) were Japanese, compared with 168 out of 603 (again, 28 percent) in 1968. Though there was no change over this period in the proportion among all lawyers, a far larger number moved up within the profession. Of the 48 members of legal firms in 1959, only 2 (Shiro and Genro Kashiwara, members of their own firm) were of Japanese origin. In 1968, 32 out of 150 (thus, 21 as compared with 4 percent) were Japanese; and of these, 12 were in firms that included non-Orientals as members.[17]

The information on lawyers can be supplemented by a survey of 75 Japanese practicing in Honolulu in 1959 (Yamamoto, 1968). Almost all had moved up from their fathers' occupations, which in the main were either blue-collar (26 percent) or small retail proprietor or farmer (27 percent). Three-fifths had been able to attend law school only with veterans' benefits. After they were admitted to the bar, more than one in four worked for a government agency. Though all had received their degrees from distinguished law schools, as of that date none had become a partner in any of the large firms, in part because the Japanese lawyers preferred the greater independence of a small establishment. There was then a marked division of labor between the two types of firms, with the first concentrating on the commercial counseling of large corporations, the second on general practice.

On a national scale, the great shift in occupational status took place during the 1950s (Figure 5-2). From findings of this type, one analyst (Varon, 1967) concluded that Japanese Americans no longer constitute a "minority," since (by Louis Wirth's definition) "minority status carries with it the exclusion from full participation in the life of the society." If the Japanese have moved to or beyond parity with the whites in their education and occupational status, Varon hypothesized, then by other criteria their social status must also be rising almost as fast. Even if we do not quite accept this prognosis, it is significant that anyone could make it from a conscientious study of a colored minority in the United States.

In spite of their advances in education and occupational status, mainland Japanese had not achieved parity with the income of whites by 1959 (Table 5-2). Japanese males earned

Table 5-2. *Median Personal Income, White and Japanese Males Aged 14 and Over, Mainland United States and California, 1959*

| | WHITE | JAPANESE | | | |
		Census	I.D.*	Stand- ardized†	I.D.*
Mainland					
United States	$4,339	$4,305	2	$4,064	3
California	5,109	4,385	10	4,149	13

* The "index of dissimilarity"—that is, the percentage of Japanese which would have to change to another income category in order to make the two distributions identical.
† Standardized to the age distribution of the white population.

SOURCE: Census data as reported in Monica Boyd, "The Japanese Americans: A Study in Socio-Economic Integration," paper presented at the meeting of the Southern Sociological Society, Atlanta, Georgia, 1968.

more in California than elsewhere, but the discrepancy was also greater there. If the age structures of the two races had been the same, the differences in the median incomes would be still larger. At least as of that date, a considerable discrimination

FIGURE 5-2. *Relative Occupational Level of Males in the Labor Force, by Race, United States, 1940–1960.*

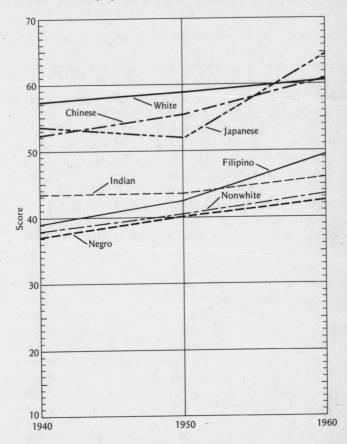

* The scores were computed essentially by the method described in Charles B. Nam, *Methodology and Scores of Socio-economic Status,* Working Paper No. 15 (Washington, D.C.: U.S. Bureau of the Census, 1963). The scores represent weighted averages, which in the Schmid-Nobbe paper are combined with education and income scores to derive a graphic profile for each race.

SOURCE: Calvin F. Schmid and Charles E. Nobbe, "Socio-economic Differentials among Nonwhite Races," *American Sociological Review,* 30 (1965), 909–922. Reprinted by permission of the authors.

persisted, since a group with qualifications that should have commanded larger salaries in fact earned less on the average.

MAINLAND-HAWAII CONTRASTS

The postwar rise of all Japanese Americans, however remarkable in itself, does not fully demonstrate the thesis of this chapter—that in spite of discrimination as degrading as the incarceration in prison camps, the former inmates have progressed remarkably in the subsequent period. In order to analyze this relation, one should separate those who were in camps from those who were not, but such a division cannot be made precisely with census data. However, a comparison of Hawaii and California (where about 60 percent of the mainland Japanese reside) with the national totals would be indicative. Data on internal migration support the implied assumption that the Hawaii-mainland movement of Japanese has been too small to affect such a contrast significantly.[18]

A comparison of educational attainment (Table 5-3) shows several things. The suggestion from other data that immigrants to the mainland were superior to those to Hawaii (cf. pp. 27–29) is confirmed by a comparison of persons aged 45 and over. By both measures and for both sexes, the elderly in California consistently ranked higher than those in Hawaii. For the youngest group, aged 14 to 24, the differences were generally slight; the one interesting datum for these ages is that the national percentage of college graduates was higher than in either of the two states, so that the relatively small Japanese populations living elsewhere must have had a very high proportion of college-trained persons. The most interesting group is the middle one, aged 25 to 44 in 1960, or 10 to 29 when the war ended in 1945. These included the Nisei who left the camps to go to college, and also most of those who acquired their secondary and higher education during the postwar years. A slightly higher proportion of Hawaiian females, but a decidedly higher percentage of Californian males, had received college degrees.

The plausible conclusions from these data on education seem

to be reinforced by a comparison of the occupational structures (Table 5–4). More than 20 percent of the occupied males in California (compared with only 3 percent in Hawaii) were classified as farmers and farm managers. In Hawaii 30 percent (compared with 10 percent in California) were craftsmen or foremen. These are the grossest divergencies between the two sectors of the Japanese population, but they suggest differences in the two economies rather than in rates of social mobility. More directly comparable are the percentages of professionals (15 in California versus 10 in Hawaii) and of nonfarm laborers (6 in California versus almost 7 in Hawaii). The proportion of

Table 5-3. *Indices of Educational Level, Japanese Population 14 Years and Over by Age Group and Sex, United States, California, and Hawaii, 1960*

AGE GROUP AND SEX	MEDIAN SCHOOL YEARS COMPLETED			PERCENT WITH FOUR OR MORE YEARS OF COLLEGE		
	U.S.	Cali-fornia	Hawaii	U.S.	Cali-fornia	Hawaii
14–19						
Male	10.3	10.6	10.2	0.1	0.05	>0.05
Female	10.4	10.6	10.2	—	—	—
20–24						
Male	12.9	13.2	12.7	10.5	9.0	7.8
Female	12.8	13.0	12.7	10.2	9.3	9.9
25–34						
Male	12.8	12.9	12.5	22.8	20.5	14.5
Female	12.5	12.6	12.5	9.4	9.0	10.3
35–44						
Male	12.4	12.6	12.1	14.3	14.6	7.5
Female	12.3	12.5	11.2	5.8	5.1	4.1
45–64						
Male	9.6	11.3	8.6	8.6	8.9	5.9
Female	8.6	10.3	7.7	3.6	3.5	3.0
65+						
Male	8.1	8.6	5.0	3.0	3.6	0.7
Female	4.5	8.0	2.1	1.1	1.5	0.3

SOURCE: *U.S. Census of Population, 1960: Subject Reports,* "Nonwhite Population by Race," Final Report PC (2)-1C (Washington, D.C.: U.S. Government Printing Office, 1963), calculated from Table 21.

Table 5-4. Percentage Distribution by Major Occupational Categories, Employed Japanese by Sex, United States, California, and Hawaii, 1960

MAJOR OCCUPATIONAL CATEGORY	MALE			FEMALE		
	U.S.	California	Hawaii	U.S.	California	Hawaii
Professional, technical, and kindred workers	14.8	15.0	10.1	11.8	10.1	11.7
Farmers and farm managers	11.0	21.3	3.2	2.2	3.2	1.8
Managers, officials, and proprietors (except farm)	9.8	7.9	10.5	3.7	2.8	4.3
Clerical and kindred workers	7.7	6.8	8.6	29.2	32.4	28.3
Sales workers	5.6	5.9	6.2	6.4	4.4	8.9
Craftsmen, foremen, and kindred workers	19.3	10.4	30.2	1.3	0.9	1.4
Operatives and kindred workers	10.9	9.1	13.0	16.2	16.4	14.5
Private household workers	0.7	1.1	0.2	7.8	11.6	6.3
Service workers (except private household)	4.9	3.5	5.1	12.3	6.8	16.1
Farm laborers and foremen	5.6	9.2	3.3	4.2	6.9	2.7
Laborers (except farm and mine)	5.8	5.9	6.6	0.7	0.9	0.7
Occupation not reported	3.9	3.9	3.0	4.2	3.6	3.3
Total	100.0	100.0	100.0	100.0	100.0	100.0
	(118,144)	(44,019)	(52,154)	(74,393)	(25,665)	(35,339)

SOURCE: U.S. Census of Population, 1960: Subject Reports, "Nonwhite Population by Race," Final Report PC(2)-1C (Washington, D.C.: U.S. Government Printing Office, 1963), calculated from Table 34.

males at the lowest occupational level was small in both states, and at what is usually taken to be the highest, it was significantly greater in California. Note that the percentage of California females engaged in private household work was almost double that in Hawaii, but that among service workers outside private households the ratio was reversed. Once again, these figures probably reflect a difference in low-income opportunities in the two states rather than different propensities to rise from that level.

Perhaps the clearest single index of overall social-economic level is the median income (Table 5-5). In Hawaii this was

Table 5-5. *Median Income of the Japanese by Sex,*
United States, California, and Hawaii, 1959

GROUP	UNITED STATES	CALIFORNIA	HAWAII
All persons with income	$3,205	$3,401	$3,188
Male	4,304	4,388	4,302
Female	1,967	2,144	1,979

SOURCE: *U.S. Census of Population, 1960: Subject Reports,* "Nonwhite Population by Race," Final Report PC(2)-1C (Washington, D.C.: U.S. Government Printing Office, 1963), Table 34.

about on a par with the national figure for Japanese, but in California it was somewhat higher, especially for females. The cost of living, though high in California by national standards, was still higher in Hawaii.[19] In real terms, thus, the differences would be somewhat greater.

Everywhere in the country, the postwar rise of Japanese Americans has been amazingly rapid. From the membership lists of Hawaii's professional societies, one can see how many in that state moved up into this highest occupational category. From the three comparisons between Hawaii and California, however, the general conclusion is that the upward mobility on the mainland was at least as fast or, by some indices, even faster. In other words, the national data do not represent mainly the postwar experience of that considerable sector of the Japanese population that had not been interned.

A truly prodigious effort was needed to overcome the economic and psychological consequences of the camp experience, and by all reasonable standards one should have anticipated a subnation pushed into more or less permanent degradation. But the Japanese Americans lived up to the proverb of their forebears used as the title of this chapter. Since the former camp inmates made that prodigious effort, the very shattering of the community's structure brought some eventual advantages. The occupational traps of the young Nisei tending vegetable stands in Los Angeles, the seemingly unreasonable control that Issei exerted in their families, the restrictive life in a Little Tokyo— these elements of prewar existence were reduced in importance or eliminated, together with the agricultural economy, the Japanese Associations, consular authority, and much of the informal community solidarity. This is what is meant by the preposterous statement that, in one version or another, is found in several accounts of the internment—that today many Japanese "are grateful for the evacuation experience" (Arrington, 1962: 42). In Hawaii, on the contrary, the impetus to rise was to some degree countered by the pressure to take over one's father's retail store, to follow one's father in his skilled trade. And if, as has been hypothesized, the electoral gains in the islands were accompanied by similar increases in the proportion of Japanese in the lower and middle ranks of the state's civil service, this was another relatively easy route to modest financial security. On the mainland, the postwar rule had to be the famous slogan of the 442nd, "Go for broke"—all or nothing; for there were no easy routes to a middle-level status.

Notes

[1] Governor Warren announced that he favored maintaining the evacuation until after the war's end, but that since the Army (in fact, the Supreme Court) had decided otherwise, it was everyone's duty to comply loyally and cheerfully (Luomala, 1946). This statement supports the earlier interpretation of Warren as a politician mainly responding to pressures rather than following his own principles.

[2] With a probable schedule of average claims ranging from $250 to a

maximum of $2,500, the total to be paid out, allowing one claim per family, would have been not $10 million, but $52.6 million. If two claims per family had been allowed under a community-property rule, the estimated total would have been $79.3 million; if each person aged 18 or over in 1942 had been permitted to file, it would have been $90.1 million (Bloom and Riemer, 1949: 202–3). The direct cost of the evacuation and detention has been roughly estimated at $350 million, including $70 million for the construction of the assembly and relocation centers and $150 million for maintenance of the inmates (Arrington, 1962: 6; cf. Girdner and Loftis, 1969: 480–81). Given a total expenditure of this order, Mr. Myer proposed an addendum of less than 3 percent to make up the losses to the evacuees.

3 These three members of Congress, each of whom was deeply involved in the effort to permit again the immigration and naturalization of Asians, most liberals would classify as thorough reactionaries. As in other instances, justice for Japanese Americans was never incorporated as part of the liberal program. When the McCarran-Walter Act passed Congress the first time, President Truman vetoed it—mainly because it continued the national-quota system. And when Congress passed it over his veto, he appointed a President's Commission on Immigration and Naturalization, which submitted a report analyzing all the new law's faults and limitations (*Whom We Shall Welcome*, Washington, D.C.: U.S. Government Printing Office, 1953). The section on Japanese immigration reads: "That racial and national discrimination is the essence of the Immigration and Nationality Act of 1952 is shown . . . [for example, by] the fact that although the law repeals the Japanese Exclusion Act and sets up a minimum quota for Japanese, it establishes a racial quota under which Orientals are to be charged to the 'Asia-Pacific Triangle' on the basis not of place of birth—as is true in all other cases—but of their own racial background" (p. 90). The discussion of citizenship (chap. 16) does not mention the fact that under the new law foreign-born Asians became eligible for naturalization.

4 Edward S. Corwin, *Total War and the Constitution* (New York: Knopf, 1947), pp. 100–5. Mr. Corwin comments, "Enough has come to light . . . to create a strong suspicion that the military authorities were guilty at times of acts of injustice. . . . Fulton Lewis, Jr. [of all people] has produced some pretty convincing evidence of gratuitous harshness on the part of Hawaii's military rulers in certain individual cases, and even of a labor draft suggestive of peonage in some parts of the Islands" (*ibid.*).

5 A liberal professor of political science, Fuchs did not make such

statements lightly or without evidence. In Hawaii, on the contrary, his book was often criticized for understating Communist influence. For example, the magazine *Paradise of the Pacific* published four reviews, of which two, both in the October 1962 issue, stressed this fault. The fairest appraisal in the opinion of the magazine's editor was by Don Woodrum, an advertising executive and an active member of the Republican party (October 1962), who found the worst flaw of *Hawaii Pono* to be its analysis of Communism. Fuchs, he wrote, "has discussed the Communist influences in Hawaii in some detail but has shied away from the main point of this influence, i.e., that persons with Marxist-Leninist backgrounds hold many of the important leadership positions in the union that dominates Hawaii's waterfront and its basic sugar and pineapple industries. These men wield enormous economic power, . . . [which] has been extended to the political and social fields."

6 When I was on the campus of the University of Hawaii during the summer of 1968, I noticed that the McCarthy table, unlike virtually every other activity at that heterogeneous institution, was inevitably manned by whites. One day I stopped and spoke to two of them, a man and wife, both graduate students from the mainland; and they confirmed my impression. The McCarthy group had attempted to recruit six Orientals to tour the outer islands, but were unable to find that many Japanese or Chinese students who would support their candidate! One reason, they thought, was that Inouye was closely linked to Humphrey. But more important was the fact that Japanese students viewed college as a place to acquire training for a life's profession, a "middle-class orientation" that my informants found thoroughly reprehensible. The very few Japanese rebels on campus supported not McCarthy, but the Peace and Freedom party or a local extremist sect of similar views.

7 For a similar equivocation from a more recent publication, see Meller and Tuttle, 1969: "Pending further research results, it may be tentatively hypothesized that generalized ethnic cohesion rather than unmitigated ethnic bloc voting characterizes the Island voting public."

8 Senator Hugh Butler of Nebraska, quoted in Cheng, 1951. In case there were any who missed his point, Senator Butler continued: "If Hawaii had been settled and primarily populated by Americans from the mainland, there might be no great problem about admitting it as a state. Unfortunately, that was not the case."

9 I was able to find no statistics on the ethnic composition of the entire state civil service, and I doubt whether they exist. It was my impression, going from one state office to another seeking in-

formation for this study, that Japanese are no less strongly represented at lower levels than at the top. However, according to a health survey made in 1964–1966 on Oahu Island, only 15.5 percent of Japanese in the civilian labor force, as compared with 18.0 percent of all other races combined, were employed in "public administration"—which includes, of course, federal and local as well as state employment (Schmitt, 1967a).

10 Although the question on race was specified as optional in both these surveys, less than 0.5 percent of the respondents chose not to answer it. Even so, the administration of the university has become absurdly touchy on this matter. Not only are no data compiled by race (or so I was told), but several administrators refused point-blank to permit me to use lists of students in order to compare Japanese (identifiable by their names) and non-Japanese as groups. This resistance was in contrast to the cordial cooperation given me in every other facet of my research.

11 The University of Hawaii has no counterpart to the Nisei Student Club typical on West Coast campuses. In the 1967/68 academic year, the Honolulu campus had a total of 96 officially recognized student organizations, variously based on professional interest, residence hall, social or cultural activities, and religion. Two presumably were predominantly Japanese—a Young Buddhist Association and a society to enhance members' knowledge of Japanese culture. Among the others, 38 had presidents with Japanese names.

12 But the reason—according to this interpretation—did not suggest that the Nisei deserved any commendation. "Because of the compatibility between Japanese and American middle-class cultures, individual Nisei probably have a better chance of succeeding than individuals from other ethnic groups where the underlying cultural patterns are less in harmony with those of the American middle class" (Caudill and DeVos, 1956). In other words, it was pure coincidence that American employers preferred promptness, accuracy, diligence, cleanliness, neatness, and so on; and these traits, of no particular relevance to the conduct of their business, just happened to be characteristic of their Nisei employees.

13 Interview with K. Tanimoto, a specialist in fair employment, State Employment Relations Board, Honolulu, August 1968. Of the 15 complaints during the first three and a half years based on alleged discrimination by race, religion, color, or ancestry, 8 were filed by Caucasians, 5 by Negroes, 1 by a Cambodian, and 1 by a Hawaiian-Portuguese.

14 *Directory of the American Society of Civil Engineers, Hawaii Sec-*

tion, various dates, supplemented by an interview with Mr. Ben Taguchi, secretary of the section in 1968.

[15] *Roster of the State Board of Registration of Professional Engineers, Architects and Land Surveyors, State of Hawaii,* various dates.

[16] *Roster of Physicians Licensed in the State* (or *Territory*) *of Hawaii,* various dates.

[17] *Martindale-Hubbell Law Directory, Hawaii,* various dates.

[18] Robert C. Schmitt, "Recent Migration Trends in Hawaii," *Social Process,* 25 (1961–62), 15–22.

[19] Honolulu Redevelopment Agency, "Recent Research on the Cost of Living on Oahu," September 1968.

Chapter 6 ◉ Social Pathologies

Extraordinary as has been the positive record analyzed in the previous chapter, the lack of a countervailing negative one is in a sense even more surprising. Indeed, the statistics on various types of social pathology are notoriously poor, and many of the series, moreover, do not distinguish Japanese from other "nonwhites."[1] Even so, the data suffice to make the point. Of all types of crime, delinquency, dependency, or social disorganization about which we have usable statistics, the incidence is lower for Japanese than for any other ethnic group in the American population, including native whites of native parents.

SOCIAL WELFARE

In the prewar years it was axiomatic that the Japanese community took care of its own, and few applied for welfare benefits of any kind, even during the depression of the 1930s.[2] At the time of the first evacuation, the Federal Security Agency borrowed about a dozen social workers from other bureaus to carry out a direct relief program for the families forcefully evicted from their homes.

> Few Japanese in Los Angeles County ever [had] been on relief, [for] . . . accepting relief—being a pauper—carried a stigma. . . . During the first days after the FSA offices opened there were almost no applications for assistance. . . . When finally Japanese families began using the facilities provided for assistance or information, they generally came not on their own initiative but . . . referred by their minister or a representative of [a private agency]. . . . A humorous touch [!] was added to [such] situations when the social worker groped for elementary synonyms for "social security benefits," "eligibility," "regulations," "re-

sources," and other stock-in-trade terms. . . . The assistance
rendered only partially met the need (Nickel, 1942).

This initial humiliation was one of a long series. In the camps,
the inmates became public charges; professionals who worked
there could earn about 10 cents an hour, others somewhat less.
Dependence might have become habitual, but it did not. In
1960, only 2.8 percent of the Japanese labor force in the whole
of the country was unemployed—the lowest proportion for any
subnation classified in the statistics. From a detailed breakdown
for California, one can see how wide the range was (Table 6-1).

Table 6-1.   Rate of Unemployment by Sex and
Ethnic Group, California, 1960*

GROUP	MALE	FEMALE
Japanese	2.6	3.1
Chinese	4.9	4.1
White (inc. Spanish-surname)	5.5	6.3
Spanish-surname	7.7	11.2
Filipino	7.8	13.6
Negro	12.7	11.4
American Indian	15.1	11.4

* Percentage of each group in the labor force who on a specific
day were not employed and were actively seeking work.

SOURCE: Bureau of Labor Statistics data, collated in "American
Indians in California," published by the California Fair Employment Commission, San Francisco. Reprinted by permission.

The code of family responsibility lost a bit of its traditional
rigidity in the post-1945 period. That this slight relaxation was
independent of the camp experience can be seen from the trend
in Hawaii. A small sample of Honolulu Nisei, comprising white-
collar workers who were also oldest sons, were interviewed in
1954 concerning their attitude toward dependent parents. The
duty of filial piety was still almost inviolate; to send one's father
or mother to a home for the aged would be shameful, and to
ignore their need was not even mentioned as a possibility.
Though the obligation was recognized, some of the younger
Nisei also expressed doubt and conflict. Rather than to take

parents into their own home, the respondents now saw the ideal solution to be a separate residence paid for by the oldest son or all the children jointly. A few went further and admitted that, if a choice had to be made, they would put the welfare of their wives and children over that of their parents (Glick, 1958; cf. Kanagawa, 1955).

The beginning change in attitudes reflected in this Hawaii survey developed slowly over the next decade. At one end of a social-political spectrum was a conservative organization, Hojukai, which tried to reestablish traditional family norms to the full. Its head, Rev. K. C. Kondo, testified against a bill in the Hawaii legislature that would have eliminated the legal duty to assist any relatives except one's own minor children. However little they followed his precepts, Kondo spoke for the consciences of many Japanese, who were still ashamed if their parents depended on public support. Even so, the proportion requesting old-age benefits rose during the 1960s, in part because of the large number of Issei reaching retirement age. Another reason was that Hawaii, though far from a wealthy state by national standards, provided welfare benefits that compared favorably with those of almost any other. The cost of living was high (a simple wooden frame house on a small plot in a middle-class neighborhood of Honolulu cost about $35,000 in the late 1960s), and that of special care for the aged even higher (a private nursing home charged $400 to $600 a month, or far more than most families could manage). By a frequent compromise, both parents worked outside the home and the grandparents were baby-sitters.[3] In spite of this partial adaptation to the general norms, Hawaiian Japanese still applied for only a portion of the welfare payments to which they were entitled. Among aged residents receiving aid of all types during June 1965, only 17 percent were Japanese,[4] though according to the 1960 census the Japanese made up 32.3 percent of the state's total population and, because of their age structure and longevity, a still higher proportion of those eligible for old-age benefits.

In sum, despite the slight relaxation both in Hawaii and on the mainland in the obligation to one's family, many Japanese still do not apply for the public benefits legally due them because of age or other disabilities. In spite of all the pressures, including the strong will to accommodate to general American standards, community pride has remained a symbol to which some sacrifice must be made.

CRIME AND DELINQUENCY

Harry Kitano, a Nisei professor of social welfare at the University of California who has written about crime and delinquency among Japanese Americans, has had some difficulty in finding enough to discuss. According to his analysis of probation records in Los Angeles County, the crime rates of adult Japanese rose from 1920 to a peak in 1940 and then declined sharply to 1960; but throughout those forty years the rate was consistently under that for non-Japanese. In Los Angeles in the 1960s, while the general crime rate rose, that of Japanese adults continued to fall (Kitano, 1969: 159). His more general conclusion, based on an analysis of national statistics of arrests of both adults and adolescents, is that the Japanese rate has been markedly lower than that of any other identifiable group (Kitano, 1969: 118).

Not only is the number of offenses small, but they are typically not very serious. Of all convictions in California over a 28-year period, only 6 percent of the crimes by Japanese were against persons or property (Table 6-2). The two causes of arrest with the highest incidence were drunkenness and gambling, which are perceived much more tolerantly in the traditional Japanese culture than by American norms. As for such

Table 6-2.   *Distribution of Crimes by Japanese,*
California, 1900–1927

TYPE OF CRIME	NUMBER	PERCENT
Offenses against persons	393	2.3
Offenses against property	632	3.7
Offenses against public policy and morals	7,275	42.5
Offenses against public health and safety	8,803	51.5
Total	17,103	100.0

SOURCE: Walter G. Beach, *Oriental Crime in California: A Study of the Offenses Committed by Orientals in That State, 1900–1927* (Stanford, Calif.: Stanford University Press, 1932), Table 44.

others as the violation of traffic regulations, garbage ordinances, and similar relatively minor breaches of the law, "it is fair to assume that a considerable percentage . . . express the difficulties of understanding which always characterize immigrant life in process of adjustment" (Beach, 1932: 64).

So far as one can tell from the sparse data and small number of studies, the Japanese have been exceptionally law-abiding since their first arrival in either Hawaii or mainland United States. It would serve no purpose to give an array of statistics, but one set—the earliest I was able to find—may be of interest. During the first ten months of 1902, the rates per 1,000 population of commitments to the Oahu Prison in Honolulu were as follows:[5]

Japanese	1.1
Chinese	3.0
Whites	5.3
Hawaiians	6.1
Puerto Ricans	33.2

Most of the theories criminologists have developed to explain crime and delinquency do not fit the Japanese Americans. To attempt a full reconciliation of these theories with this deviant case would go beyond the scope of this chapter, and what follows is only a brief comment on the most important discrepancies.

DELINQUENCY AREAS. From the ecological analysis of Chicago and some other cities, a number of sociologists concluded that certain neighborhoods have a consistently high incidence of all types of delinquency, irrespective of the nationalities residing in such "delinquency areas."

Diverse racial, nativity, and national groups possess relatively similar rates of delinquents in similar social areas. . . . [Therefore,] it is difficult to sustain the contention that, by themselves, the factors of race, nativity, and nationality are vitally related to the problem of juvenile delinquency. It seems necessary to conclude, rather, that the significantly higher rates of delinquents found among

the children of Negroes, the foreign born, and more recent immigrants are closely related to existing differences
in their respective patterns of geographic distribution
within the city.[6]

Perhaps the best refutation of this generalization was a study
of Japanese in Seattle. One sector within a high-delinquency
area, the Bailey Gatzert school district, showed all the earmarks
of a slum in an advanced stage of deterioration. In addition to
the poor physical facilities, it had "the highest concentration of
homicides, houses of prostitution, unidentified suicides, and
cheap lodging-houses in Seattle." According to the president of
the district's PTA, "Our children cannot sleep at night because
of drunken noise-makers. . . . We have a list of twenty places
where there is much night life, as you call it." However, 90
percent of the boys attending the school were Japanese; and this
fact canceled out all the other "causes" of delinquency. Of the
710 Seattle boys sent to a special school for delinquents during
the period 1919–1930, only 3 were Japanese; and those 3 lived
in mixed neighborhoods where they had few contacts with other
Nisei (Hayner, 1934).

In a subsequent paper, Hayner (1938) concluded that "the
extent of criminality among Orientals in America seems to vary
inversely with the extent to which they are incorporated in
closely integrated family and community groups." The decisive
fact about the three Nisei delinquents was not that they lived in
a slum but that they did not live in a Japanese ghetto, where
their behavior would have been subject to such informal but
powerful controls as face-to-face contacts and gossip. Lind
(1930b) studied two adjoining areas of Honolulu, both with
about the same poor housing, inadequate recreational facilities,
and other slum characteristics. The first, with a very high concentration of Japanese population, had no juvenile delinquency.
In the second, where a few Japanese lived among Hawaiians,
part-Hawaiians, Portuguese, Puerto Ricans, Koreans, Chinese,
Filipinos, and others, 3 out of the 15 Nisei school children had
been before the juvenile court (cf. also Lind, 1930a).

BIAS IN LAW ENFORCEMENT. That the crime rates of various
races differ, it is sometimes alleged, is due partly or mainly to

the attitudes of enforcement personnel. One criticism of Shaw and McKay's study of "delinquency areas," thus, was that they ignored the facts that police vary in their policy concerning arrest and courts in that concerning conviction, so that any set of statistics reflects differences in both behavior and liability.[7] The point is usually made more specifically—that "all of the procedures in criminal justice are frequently biased against minority groups," especially Negroes.[8] It is true that when blacks commit crimes *against whites*, both police and courts may react more harshly than against comparable white offenders. But the principal expression of white bias is an official indifference to whatever black criminals do to other Negroes, and this attitude has precisely the opposite effect on racial differences in crime statistics.[9]

In any case, the explanation has little to do with Japanese Americans. From the school crisis in San Francisco to the California sheriff disciplined for malfeasance, it was sometimes the law-enforcement agents who helped persecute the Japanese, either directly or by refusing to give them protection from militant whites. One can reasonably assume that if the West Coast's palpable official prejudice found expression in the administration of justice, the consequence would have been a greater liability of Japanese to arrest and conviction. If we accept Sutherland and Cressey's extrapolation from Negroes to "minority groups," the anomaly of the low incidence of Japanese crime is only heightened.

FRUSTRATION-AGGRESSION. The theory that frustration leads to aggression is often couched in a psychological, or even a psychiatric, frame of reference.[10] In a social-political context, it expresses one of the important dilemmas of a democratic, open society.

> When a system of social values extols . . . *common* success-goals for the population at large while the social structure rigorously restricts or completely closes access to approved modes of reaching these goals *for a considerable part of the population,* deviant behavior ensues on a large scale.[11]

This proposition has been accepted as almost axiomatic by most sociologists. It was an early statement of the thesis, since become popular, that high crime rates among ethnic minorities cannot be ascribed to irresponsible individuals or even to local social environments, but must be charged to the "white racism" of the whole country. But obviously the proposition is grossly overstated. Not all frustration leads to crime: some whose ways are blocked exert still greater effort, and others become apathetic. According to impressionistic studies, the reaction depends in part on the person's reference group. If he associates mainly with his own social class, he is likely to be more comfortable; but if he strives to move up, comparing his attainments with those of persons who already have more, he will suffer greater tension.[12]

No group has desired upward mobility more avidly than Japanese Americans. Their hungry absorption of as much education as they could acquire, their behavior on the job as reported by a variety of employers, have marked them as the eagerest of beavers. In part because the bars to their rise were institutionalized, made part of the formal law of the country, blocks to their social mobility were more restrictive than those faced by any non-Asian minority during the past generation. And so long as most Japanese lived in slums or near-slums— say, until World War II—the opportunities to learn and practice deviancy invited them no less than any others residing in the same environment. From Merton's theory, even as refined by data from criminologists, the Japanese should have had not the lowest but the highest rates of delinquency and crime.

In a recent test of Merton's proposition, an analyst compared an entire junior class of one Seattle high school, comprising 159 whites, 111 Negroes, and 76 Orientals. The main purpose was to compare the students' social class and race with the delinquent acts that they reported.

> There is no significant difference in the incidence of delinquent behavior between the most disadvantaged group economically (Negroes) and the most favored group (whites). Orientals were significantly less delinquent than either whites or Negroes but were intermediate in socioeconomic status (Epps, 1967).

GENERATIONAL CONFLICT. One important cause of crime is what is sometimes termed "culture conflict": a person marginal to several subcultures is trained in more than one moral code. "A conflict of norms is said to exist when more or less divergent rules of conduct govern the specific life situation in which a person may find himself."[13] One frequent type of culture conflict is antagonism between parents and their adolescent children, in part a universal consequence of the shift from dependent childhood to independent adulthood, but sharper in a society like the United States. Generational conflict is likely to divide immigrant parents from their native-born children, especially in "nationalities whose values have been most in contrast with the prevailing mode in the United States."[14] The open structure of American society permits the second generation to rise above their parents' social class, and in anticipation of this possibility the teenager already feels superior to those in authority over him. He speaks better English than his father, and in other respects has a fuller, more natural acquaintance with American culture. Thus, the thesis goes, as the young man comes to view his father with contempt or shame, he generalizes this perception into a rejection of all authority.

> The second generation found itself living in two different worlds. . . . The second-generation child, especially the boy who was never insulated from the nasty world by the sanctuary of the home, could hardly conform to one moral code without being delinquent with respect to the other. A combination of moral confusion and ethnic self-hatred frequently resulted in legally "delinquent" behavior.[15]

Not only would the theory seem to hold for Nisei youth, but their particular circumstances aggravated the usual tensions (see pp. 201–207). If deviance is explained by the generational conflict in immigrant families, then there should have been not only a high delinquency rate among Nisei but the highest.

DIFFERENTIAL ASSOCIATION. According to a theory developed mainly by Edwin Sutherland, criminal behavior is learned, and it is learned primarily in intimate personal groups rather than through mass media. A young person consorts with those who define legal codes either favorably or unfavorably, and such associations vary in frequency, duration, and intensity. "A person becomes delinquent because of an excess of definitions favorable to violation of law over definitions unfavorable to violation of law. This is the principle of differential association."[16] How difficult it is to test this theory empirically is suggested by a study comparing Hawaii's subnations with the highest and lowest rates of delinquency—respectively, Hawaiians and Japanese. Data were gathered from an anonymous questionnaire administered to 15 percent of the seventh-grade pupils in Honolulu's schools, plus a sample from the school for delinquents. The author's hypothesis was that a positive picture of the self insulates a child from delinquency; he tested it by comparing the more and less delinquent for their reported self-conceptions. Nothing was introduced into the study to permit him to escape from the argument's perfect circularity (Voss, 1961).

If children or adolescents have *accidental* associations with delinquents, then an alternative statement of etiology would seem to be that the main reason is the lack of supervision by parents or other persons of authority. The proximate reason for the low rate of crime and delinquency among Japanese Americans is that the whole community cooperates to prevent it.

> Part of good Americanism was staying out of trouble, and in this the Japanese community of Los Angeles was undeniably successful. The gamut of group sanctions [ran] from gossip (made more potent by residential segregation) to the publication of disgraced names to ostracism. . . . The Japanese Association, church, and lay groups worked to reduce crime and discourage undesirable elements, in the emulation of an idealized crimeless Japan (Modell, 1969a).

The English section of the vernacular newspaper published a "police blotter" listing offenders. Two among those in Los Angeles subjected to ostracism were a licentious minister and an abortionist. Moral offenders who did not respond to other sanctions were sometimes helped to return to Japan.

The community reacted vehemently also to the more recent

slight rise in the rate of delinquency among California Sansei. For these third-generation Japanese, the camp experience is either a half-forgotten childhood memory or something not quite believable that happened to their parents and grandparents. They have grown up, most of them, in relatively comfortable circumstances, with the American element of their composite subculture becoming more and more dominant. Part of their full acculturation to the general pattern is that they are beginning to show some of the faults of American society that were almost totally lacking in their parents' generation. The rate of delinquency among Sansei is still lower than that of any other group in California's population, but it has become visible. During the late 1960s, Frank Chuman, a Los Angeles lawyer, was counsel for almost two hundred young Japanese offenders charged with everything from petty theft to murder. Some were organized into gangs of ten to fifteen members, of whom a few were sometimes blacks or Mexicans. Nothing obvious in their background accounted for their deviance from the group norm. Typically, they had lived at home with solid middle-class families in pleasant neighborhoods; their brothers and sisters were not in trouble. According to Yori Wada, formerly a Nisei member of the California Youth Authority, some of these young people were in revolt against both the narrow confines of their subculture and also what they saw white society to be. In one instance, a Sansei charged with assault with intent to kill was a member of the Black Muslims; lacking any other spiritual home, he sought an identity among extremist black nationalists.

Their parents were far from accepting this trend as inevitable. In several Japanese communities, San Francisco and San Jose among others, councils were formed to attack the problem of delinquency head on. The effort can be illustrated best from the action taken in Sacramento, which was something of a model for other California cities. Several Sansei teenagers had been arrested there for shoplifting—according to the police, "nothing to be alarmed at." The Nisei generation disagreed. The local JACL called a meeting, which organized a Japanese Family Guidance Council. The co-chairmen were the Nisei pastor of a Seventh-Day Adventist Church and a Nisei optometrist.

Officers included ministers or lay leaders from the Presbyterian, Buddhist, and Methodist churches; leaders of the Lions Club, the Nisei Veterans, and the JACL.

> The purpose of this council is to make available counseling service for any teenage problems; to provide advice on marital problems; to promote a public educational service by mass meetings dealing with juvenile delinquency and a better home relationship; and [to establish] a teenage committee for standards on behavior and morals.[17]

At public meetings sponsored by the council, the attendance was between 400 and 500 persons, or most of the Japanese adults in the Sacramento area. They heard talks by such experts as the chief psychiatrist of the California Youth Authority and a deputy probation officer of Sacramento County. The pressure was only partly on the teenagers; the council's principal effort was to arrange for whatever services might seem appropriate when parents were unable (or unwilling) to control their offspring. According to several of the Sacramento Nisei who discussed the campaign with me, the publicity alone was salutary, for it brought parents back to a sense of their responsibility.

The final success of such community efforts is to instil a sense of shame for wrongdoing in the minds of the young people themselves. From my slight acquaintance with the Japanese students on the Berkeley campus, it was clear to me that these young Sansei, living away from home in the midst of a revolting university, had organized an unofficial "council" of their own. A sizable proportion of the Berkeley student body was involved to one degree or another in the riots of the 1960s; on one occasion, for example, 779 were arrested. Only five Japanese were prominent in the radical movement, and they were as atypical as the Sacramento delinquents. (One, the daughter of a man who twenty years before had been an officer of a Communist front, was no more a symbol of generational revolt than the more notorious Bettina Aptheker, the daughter of the Communist Party's principal theorist.) For some of the Sansei students, these few extremists constituted a poignant moral problem. Brazenly to break the law invites retribution against the whole community, and thus is doubly wrong. But such acts, however one judged them on other grounds, also symbolized an escape from the persistent concern over "the Japanese image." Under the easygoing middle-class life, in short, there lurked both a wariness born of their parents' experience and a hope that they really will be able to acculturate in a sense not yet deemed possible. In discussions of such ethical dilemmas, every Sansei reflected both his own opinion and an almost palpable group pressure to stay out of trouble, obey the law, reflect honor on himself and the subnation.

ILLNESS AND DEATH

The Japanese have generally close to the lowest rate of mental illness among all identifiable ethnic groups (Kitano, 1969: 122–25). The patient is likely to be an elderly, lower-class male; and if adjustments were made for the differences in age structure among the various subnations, the Japanese rate would probably be still lower. The most common diagnosis is schizophrenia (Kitano, 1969; Schmitt, 1956), and one interesting study compared all Japanese and Filipino patients admitted over a six-year period to the Hawaii State Hospital and diagnosed as schizophrenics, paranoid type. Since the identical diagnoses were based on a common set of symptoms, the divergence between the two races is particularly striking.

> Such terms as "preoccupied," "confused," and "obsessed" are applied much more frequently to Japanese patients than Filipino. . . . Filipinos are often convinced that someone wishes to kill them, while the delusions of the Japanese are confined to less drastic forms of persecution. . . . Delusions that one is being influenced, hypnotized, or controlled is almost exclusively Japanese. . . . The disturbing behavior of the Filipinos tended to be more violent, wild, and uncontrollable than that of the Japanese. . . . Thus, the Japanese were [more often] described as "suspicious," "guarded," "irritable," etc., while the Filipinos more frequently threatened others, carried weapons with them, or were described as menacing or frightening to others. . . . The Japanese much more frequently exhibited apathy, loss

of interest in their surroundings, and social isolation. . . .
The withdrawing Japanese tended to stay in his room; the
withdrawing Filipino was more likely to go out and hide
in the cane fields. . . . The Filipinos believed themselves to
be God, commanded the moon and stars, and felt they
could fly around the world in a few minutes. In contrast,
the Japanese only went as far as talking to God or Jesus
and concentrated their grandiosity on achieving social
recognition and prestige. For instance, they felt they were
more intelligent than anyone else, possessed honorary
scholastic degrees, read minds, and knew famous people
(Enright and Jaeckle, 1961–62).

One reason for the low reported incidence of mental illness may
be that Japanese marginal to that vaguely defined state more
often receive care at home and thus do not get into public statistics. The low reported incidence of mental illness may *not*
be spurious, however, for by a number of other measures Japanese are now an extraordinarily healthy population.

This was not always the case. In 1889–1892 the crude death
rates in Honolulu ranged from 14.4 for Americans to 52.8 for
Japanese. The Board of Health noted that Japanese "are not in
the aggregate as healthy as other nationalities, a larger percentage being off duty from slight ailments." According to one
government physician, enteric fever was "almost entirely confined to the Japanese." Another remarked that "the Japanese
laborer seems to lack sufficient stamina to withstand even the
slightest ailment." A third observed a considerable incidence of
beri-beri among the Japanese (Schmitt, 1967b).

A contrasting picture of the health of Hawaiian Japanese is
provided by the data of a recent survey conducted on Oahu
Island (about 80 percent of the state's population). Roughly
one-third of Oahu's population was Japanese and one-third
Caucasian, with all the small subnations making up the balance. For the direct comparison with Japanese, all others were
consolidated into "non-Japanese." Several measures of health
were taken, and by each the Japanese were in general superior
both to other residents of Hawaii and to the American population as a whole. For example, in days partly or wholly lost from
work, one conventional index of health, the Japanese ranked

between only half and three-quarters of the incidence of other population sectors (Bennett, 1963). One hypothesis to explain the difference might be that the more stoic Japanese keep going when others would lose time from work.

However much validity this thesis may have, it does not help to explain differences between Japanese and others in the incidence of acute or chronic afflictions (Table 6-3). With one minor exception (the last item, with a low incidence for all three populations), the rates for Japanese were lower than those of non-Japanese in Oahu, in some instances by a considerable margin. In most cases, the Japanese rates were also under those for the mainland population; and in those instances when they were not, the differences were probably due to the special hazards of the Hawaiian environment (thus, tropical sun as a factor in skin diseases, vegetation in asthma and hay fever).

In another Hawaiian study, conducted on Kauai Island, a team of pediatricians, psychologists, and public-health workers studied more than a thousand children from birth to age ten. In various tests of health, intelligence before age two, social maturity at age two, school achievement at age ten, relative lack of problems in language, perception, or behavior, and so on, the Japanese sample ranked either first or, in one or two instances, second to Anglo-Caucasians. The explanation given was the routine one: "in the majority of the Japanese homes emphasis is placed on the value of education, on disciplined work habits, and on respect and esteem for intellectual pursuits" (Werner, 1971: chap. 10).

The available data on the health of the mainland population show differences of the same general range. For example, during 1965 the Human Population Laboratory of Alameda County, California, used a household survey of 6,928 randomly chosen adults to compare the various races' health. Each respondent was located along a "physical health spectrum" according to the number of his or her chronic conditions or symptoms. Only 1 percent of the Japanese reported a disability, compared with 15 percent of the whites and 16 percent of the Negroes. At the other end of the scale, 42 percent of the Japanese reported a complete absence of any disabilities, chronic conditions, or specified symptoms, compared with 28 percent of the whites and 30

Table 6-3. Rates of Selected Acute and Chronic Ailments per
1,000 Population, Japanese and Others, Oahu 1958–1959
and United States 1959–1960

| | OAHU | | MAIN-LAND |
| | | | UNITED |
AILMENT	Japanese*	Non-Japanese*	STATES
Acute†			
Infectious and parasitic diseases	100	150	260
Diseases of the ear	70	80	50
Upper respiratory ailments	780	1,160	830
Other respiratory ailments	340	570	430
Ailments of the digestive system	90	190	120
Diseases of the skin	50	120	30
Current injuries	270	400	290
All other	140	260	150
Chronic‡			
Heart conditions	12	19	30
High blood pressure	27	38	31
Diabetes	13	17	9
Peptic ulcer	5	9	14
Arthritis and rheumatism	14	41	64
Hernia	3	8	15
Asthma, hay fever	70	75	54
Chronic bronchitis	5	12	12
Chronic sinusitis	22	27	59
Visual impairments not corrected by glasses	8	16	18
Hearing impairments	31	26	34
Paralysis of major extremities or trunk	6	5	6

* Standardized for age to the U.S. population, 1959–1960, as estimated for the National Health Survey.
† Conditions which had their onset within the two weeks prior to the week of the interview and for which the person afflicted had seen a physician or reduced the amount of his usual activities for at least one day.
‡ Either one of a list of morbid conditions ordinarily classified as chronic or one that was noted more than three months prior to the week of the interview.

SOURCE: Charles G. Bennett, George H. Tokuyama, and Paul T. Bruyere, "Health of Japanese Americans in Hawaii," *Public Health Reports*, 78 (1963), 753–62.

percent of the Negroes. In the same county during the period 1960–1964, the age-adjusted annual rates of cancer incidence ranged from 265 per 100,000 whites down through intermediate figures for Negroes and Chinese to 189 for Japanese (Breslow and Klein, 1971).

The lower incidence of diseases of various types leads to a lower death rate (Table 6-4). As compared with the residents of Japan, Japanese Americans—like all Americans of their social class—have a low mortality from such causes as childbirth. As compared with white Americans, however, Japanese Americans have markedly lower mortality from two of the most important causes in the United States, diseases of the heart and most cancers. The differences could, of course, be spurious, based on various types of misreporting or other consistent errors. "But it is difficult to imagine an artifact that would account for all of the features of the reported mortality. Nor is there any internal evidence suggesting it is unreasonable to take the main features of the data at face value" (Gordon, 1967). We can plausibly conclude that the lower mortality of

Table 6-4. *Deaths per 1,000 Population of Japanese Americans and Comparable Populations, ca. 1950 and ca. 1960*

	MALE		FEMALE	
POPULATION	1950	1960	1950	1960
Japanese				
Mainland United States	8.99	6.46	3.53	2.51
Hawaii	6.54	6.42	3.90	4.10
Japan	10.42	8.2	9.44	6.9
White, United States	10.90	10.98	8.03	8.01

SOURCES: Tavia Gordon, "Mortality Experience among the Japanese in the United States, Hawaii, and Japan" and "Further Mortality Experience among Japanese Americans," *Public Health Reports,* 72 (1957), 543–53; 82 (1967), 973–84. United Nations, *Demographic Yearbook, 1966* (New York, 1967), Table 19.

Japanese Americans is the consequence of three factors—genetic superiority,[18] the good health care available to middle-class Americans, and certain cultural practices specific to this subpopulation.

According to California life tables for 1959–1961, Japanese in that state had life expectations of 74.5 years (males) and 81.2 years (females). This was six to seven years longer than that of California whites, a relatively favored group by national standards.[19] So far as I know, this was the first time that a longevity of more than 80 years was recorded for any population anywhere in the world.

As the reader may recall from the outline given in the introduction, this chapter completes the presentation of the anomaly to be analyzed. The Japanese were subjected to worse injustices, greater degradations, than any other ethnic group during the past generation. Internment in the camps was capped by a quarter-century of official haggling over the losses the guiltless inmates had suffered. Yet in that same generation the mainland Japanese pulled themselves up and in some respects surpassed even the postwar progress of their Hawaiian counterparts. And this phenomenal positive record was matched by an even less explicable lack of any significant social pathology.

The problem is why, in the case of *this* colored minority, discrimination did not lead to self-destructive hostility or apathy. Answers are sought in the next four chapters, respectively, on the home-country background, religion, the family, and the subnation.

Notes

1 Some of the replies to my inquiries illustrate the range of ignorance. The Family Court in Hawaii no longer accumulates data on the race of delinquents. The U.S. Bureau of Prisons compiles such statistics, but the various states differ so much in their definitions and reporting that it considers only three races—white, Negro, and Indian—to be reliably classifiable, with all others assigned to a miscellaneous category. The California Youth Authority has published a pamphlet on drug use by juveniles, but it contains no breakdowns by ethnic group. The California Department of Justice classifies convicted criminals by race, with the small number of Japanese grouped in a general category of "all other races." The Hawaii Office of Health Statistics determines the race of each child born, but the individual is not so identified in any public record. This policy was instituted in spite of the fact that "in registering

about 175,000 vital events over the course of seven years, only 2 cases have come to the attention of the Registrar General when opposition to the racial items was raised"—Hawaii Office of Health Statistics, "The Race Item in Vital Statistics Records" (Honolulu, n.d.).

2 In Los Angeles, for example, of the 7,429 persons who received relief in 1923, 7 were Japanese; of the 4,877 who were given Christmas baskets in that year, 2 were Japanese. Even at the depth of the depression, when many Japanese were underemployed, only 61 families received a dole. The Japanese Associations sometimes helped those unable to cope to return to Japan (Modell, 1969a).

3 Personal interview with Yukio Gotanda, assistant director of the research section, Hawaii Department of Social Services, Honolulu, August 1968. According to Mr. Gotanda, it is the state's policy generally to avoid classifying data by ethnic group, so that the great differences in the various races' use of social services is usually not recorded. The one recent exception that his agency made to this rule happened to be the data on old-age dependency.

4 Hawaii Department of Social Services, "Characteristics of Aged Persons Receiving Aid to the Aged, Blind and Disabled, Hawaii, June 1965" (Honolulu, 1965), p. 4.

5 U.S. Bureau of Labor Statistics, *Report of the Commissioner of Labor on Hawaii*, 1902 (Washington, D.C.: Government Printing Office, 1903), p. 29.

6 Clifford R. Shaw and Henry D. McKay, *Juvenile Delinquency and Urban Areas* (Chicago: University of Chicago Press, 1942), p. 156.

7 Christen T. Jonassen, "A Re-evaluation and Critique of the Logic and Some Methods of Shaw and McKay," *American Sociological Review*, 14 (1949), 608–17.

8 Edwin H. Sutherland and Donald R. Cressey, *Principles of Criminology*, 5th ed. (Chicago: Lippincott, 1955), p. 139. The passage continues: "It has been shown conclusively that Negroes who commit crimes against white persons have a larger percentage of arrests resulting in convictions than do white offenders, have a larger percentage of convictions resulting in imprisonment, frequently have a longer period of detention in prison for the same crimes, and less frequently secure probation, parole, and pardon." There is a footnoted reference to Thorsten Sellin, "Race Prejudice in the Administration of Justice," *American Journal of Sociology*, 41 (1935), 212–17. In fact, however, Sellin's article is on only one point—a comparison of the sentences that judges give native whites, foreign-born whites, and Negroes convicted of the same

crimes. For only three out of the ten crimes he analyzed—rape, other sexual offenses, and burglary—were Negroes given longer average sentences than *native* whites; but foreign-born whites, who consistently received longer sentences than either of the other two groups, were by this criterion the principal object of administrative bias.

9 See Kenneth B. Clark, *Dark Ghetto: Dilemmas of Social Power* (New York: Harper Torchbook, 1965), p. 87.

10 See in particular John Dollard *et al.*, *Frustration and Aggression* (New Haven, Conn.: Yale University Press, 1939). For a critical comment, see William Petersen, *The Politics of Population* (New York: Doubleday, 1964), pp. 242–44.

11 Robert K. Merton, *Social Theory and Social Structure*, rev. ed. (New York: Free Press, 1957), p. 180. For a longer exposition of the same theme, see Albert K. Cohen, "Deviant Behavior and Its Control," in Talcott Parsons (ed.), *American Sociology: Perspectives, Problems, Methods* (New York: Basic Books, 1968), pp. 237–39.

12 Richard A. Cloward, "Illegitimate Means, Anomie, and Deviant Behavior," *American Sociological Review*, 24 (1959), 164–77; Richard A. Cloward and Lloyd E. Ohlin, *Delinquency and Opportunity* (New York: Free Press, 1960).

13 Thorsten Sellin, *Culture Conflict and Crime* (New York: Social Science Research Council, 1938), p. 30.

14 Donald R. Taft and Richard Robbins, *International Migrations: The Immigrant in the Modern World* (New York: Ronald Press, 1955), p. 522.

15 Joseph Lopreato, *Italian Americans* (New York: Random House, 1970), p. 124. For other analyses of the thesis applied to second-generation Italians, see William Foote Whyte, *Street Corner Society* (Chicago: University of Chicago Press, 1943); Francis A. J. Ianni, "Minority Group Status and Adolescent Culture," in David Gottlieb and Charles Ramsey (eds.), *The American Adolescent* (Homewood, Ill.: Dorsey Press, 1964), chap. 12. For more general statements of the theory, see, for example, Louis Wirth, "Culture Conflict and Misconduct," in *On Cities and Social Life: Selected Papers* (Chicago: University of Chicago Press, 1964), chap. 16; Eleanor Glueck, "Culture Conflict and Delinquency," *Mental Hygiene*, 21 (1937), 46–66.

16 Sutherland and Cressey, *op. cit.*, pp. 77–80. No one doubts, of course, that an accidental event may occasionally set off a causal chain; the arrival of a new family in a neighborhood may have devastating consequences on its hitherto nondelinquent children.

Nor would anyone deny that associations typically reinforce already existent predispositions toward deviance. But Sutherland viewed the principle of differential association as a *universal* theory to explain the *genesis* of crime. It is virtually impossible to collect data that support this interpretation rather than one of several others; cf. Sheldon and Eleanor Glueck, *Unraveling Juvenile Delinquency* (Cambridge, Mass.: Harvard University Press, 1950), p. 164; Travis Hirschi and Hanan C. Selvin, *Delinquency Research: An Appraisal of Analytic Methods* (New York: Free Press, 1967), p. 70.

17 *Japanese Community News*, news release, June 16, 1965; cf. *Hokubei Mainichi*, June 22, 1965.

18 Japanese (and Koreans) show a relatively high frequency of only three simply inherited ailments: acatalasemia (a lack of a particular enzyme in the blood), dyschromatopsia universalis hereditaria (general color blindness), and Oguchi's disease (a form of night blindness). All three are rare, and the last two are never the cause of death. Among ailments with a complex or unproved genetic component, Japanese show a high frequency of four: gastric cancer, cerebrovascular accidents, cleft lip or palate, and trophoblastic disease (an ailment of the tissue that links the ovum to the uterine wall). They show a low incidence of six others that may have a genetic component: cancers of the breast or prostate, chronic lymphatic leukemia, congenital hip disease, otosclerosis (loss of hearing due to a change in the bones of the inner ear), and acne vulgaris. See Albert Damon, "Race, Ethnic Group, and Disease," *Social Biology*, 16 (1969), 69–80. On cancers, see also Philip Buell, "Cancer Mortality of Selected Sites, Racial Groups of California," *Chronic Disease Quarterly*, No. 6, Supplement (May 1965).

19 H. H. Hechter and N. O. Borhani, "Longevity in Racial Groups Differs," *California's Health*, 22 (February 1, 1965), 121–22.

Chapter 7 ◉ The Country of Emigration

There are several reasons for positing the probable continuing importance of the beliefs, customs, and norms that Japanese immigrants brought with them to the United States. (1) Far more than most immigrant groups, the Japanese were denied ready access to American culture, partly because of their non-European origin, partly because their native country was viewed as a potential enemy of the United States. (2) Within their enclaves, the Japanese typically endeavored through such institutions as their temples or the Japanese-language schools to retain a cultural (or even a political) link with the old country. (3) Most significantly, Japan is the one non-Western country (apart from the marginal case of the Soviet Union) that acquired a fully modern economy, and the accompanying social transformation was under way during the decades of the main emigration. It is reasonable to hypothesize that there is a common factor in the unexpected deviation from the norm in these two cases, Japan's modernization and the upward mobility of Japanese Americans.

This chapter, a general introduction to later, more specific analyses of the key Japanese institutions, briefly describes the rise of modern Japan and, more speculatively, the characteristic patterns of thought and behavior during the late nineteenth century.

THE TOKUGAWA BACKGROUND

In 1854, when Commodore Perry sailed up Suruga Bay for the second time and refused to leave until Japan ended the self-seclusion it had imposed two centuries before, his action was a last dramatic blow to the disintegrating Tokugawa regime. The bonds that held Japanese society in its supposedly rigid hierarchical mold had been weakening for more than a century and, with or without the intrusion from the West, could not have prevented a fundamental change for very much longer.

The nominal head of the Japanese state was the emperor, who for several centuries had reigned without ruling. The actual head was the *shogun,* or commander-in-chief, who was also the head of the Tokugawa clan, one of several hundred noble houses. Under this top layer of emperor, shogun, and nobility, the next social class was the *samurai,* or knights. When the long intermittent civil war had been brought to an end at the beginning of the seventeenth century, they lost their function in society, but they were generally too proud of their warrior heritage to find another role. They tried in their poverty still to follow the knightly code of *bushido,* which with artistic-literary embellishments enjoined on them an exaggerated patriotism, a scorn of danger and death, an absolute adherence to personal honor. Comprising perhaps 7 or 8 percent of the population in the middle of the nineteenth century, the samurai constituted a heady stimulus to social unrest.

The basic social class was the peasantry, who made up more than three-fourths of the nation. In a common saying, they were likened to sesame seeds, for the harder you squeezed them, the more sustenance could be pressed out. Traditionally, the yield from the land was divided four parts to the lord and six to the peasant, but in fact—with taxes, bribery, and interest to usurers—peasants kept as little as 30 percent of their produce. The two remaining classes, artisans and merchants, were small and of limited importance. Merchants sometimes prospered materially, but they were controlled by a thousand petty regulations governing their business, their clothing, their names, and every other detail of their life. A basic characteristic of Japan's subsequent industrialization, the chronic shortage of capital, was partly due to this centuries-long discrimination against trade, which prevented the growth of a class of mercantile princes comparable in size or aggregate wealth to that in several preindustrial societies of the West.

That the four main classes of Tokugawa Japan—samurai,

peasants, artisans, and merchants—were fixed in law did not prevent an actual social mobility of various types. Children were kidnapped from the cities and sold to peasants, who thus acquired field laborers without the cost of rearing them. More frequently, peasants sent their children into the cities as apprentices or maids. By a usage that gradually acquired legitimacy, any househead still lacking an heir at age fifty could adopt anyone he chose in order to prevent the extinction of the family line. From the early eighteenth century on, the purchase of samurai status became common, and "it was often the most ambitious or worthy of the commoners who, as a first step in their careers, bought positions as low-grade samurai" (Sansom, 1931: 513). On the other hand, the stability of the social structure was reinforced by the total lack of population growth. Between 1726 and 1852 the estimated number of inhabitants fluctuated slightly around 25 million, with the low and the high during this century and a quarter differing by less than one-tenth (Taeuber, 1958: 21). Fertility was kept on a level with mortality by conscious family limitation, achieved mainly through infanticide (euphemistically termed *mabiki*, literally "thinning," as of rice seedlings when some are pulled up to encourage the growth of the remainder).

The effect of internal restrictions of all types was reinforced by Japan's not quite total seclusion from the outside world. After 1640, except for certain authorized Chinese and a handful of Dutch at the port of Nagasaki,[1] no foreigner was permitted to enter Japan, and, on pain of death for himself and severe punishment for his whole family, no Japanese was allowed to leave the country. Until the mid-eighteenth century, it was forbidden to translate or even to read European books. Thereafter some of the upper classes were able to acquire what was known as "Dutch learning"—that is, a knowledge of Western astronomy, anatomy, medicine, and military science through the medium of the Dutch language. However important their new knowledge was to the students, the overall impact of Dutch learning on Tokugawa society was slight.

To its Western contemporaries, Japan was a land of mystery. The first edition of the *Encyclopedia Britannica* (1768) summed up the available knowledge about the country in a single short sentence, giving its latitude and longitude. And scholars of today, whether Japanese or Western, have achieved no consensus on how to characterize that society. Writers have played a kind of game in specifying the century of European history that best corresponds to the Japan of 1850—whether 1650 (E. O. Reischauer, 1965: 108), the sixteenth century (Orchard and Orchard, 1930: 71), late Tudor England (Jansen and Stone, 1967), or fourteenth-century England (Utley, 1937: 218). There is a considerable literature, as another instance, on whether the word *feudal* can be properly applied to any society outside medieval Europe and, if so, whether specifically to Japan (cf. Hall, 1962). Whichever position a scholar takes on such disputed matters, he is certain to agree that Japan's dominant feature was indigence.[2] The peasants lived on a scale hardly imaginable to a present-day Westerner; and every class, every institution, reflected the poverty of agriculture, the base of the economy. Although about a quarter of the country's rice yield was on land controlled by the shogun, the income from this did not suffice to cover government expenses. The Tokugawa administrators contrived in diverse ways to cover the recurrent deficit, especially by forced "loans" from merchants, debasement of the currency, and borrowing abroad wherever credit could be found.

Associated with the country's poverty was the government's political and military weakness. The bay into which Perry sailed was protected by shore batteries, but his four ships were so overwhelmingly more powerful that opening fire on them would have resulted only in exposing the complete uselessness of the fortifications. Among the gifts that Perry presented to the Japanese plenipotentiaries were copies of Kendall's *War in Mexico* and Ripley's *History of the Mexican War*. "The illustrations to these works were of a rather grim, grisly, and realistic nature, and Abe [Masahiro, head of the shogun's council] is said to have been very uncomfortably impressed whenever he turned to them" (Murdoch, 1926, 3: 619). Once the government yielded to Perry's pressure and signed a treaty opening up two ports to American vessels, representatives of other nations rushed in to demand comparable rights. During one decade the harried Tokugawa officials signed no less than 44 treaties with foreign powers. Their terms were substantially identical: new ports were opened; a tariff and tonnage duties were established; foreigners were given the privilege of residence and extraterritorial rights in specified areas; diplomatic agents were permitted to travel anywhere in Japan. By a general revision of all the treaties in 1866, the maximum tariff on imports of any kind was set at 5 percent; unlike the infant industries of other nations, Japan's could not develop behind the protective wall that most Western economists deemed necessary for their own countries. Extraterritoriality lasted in Japan until 1899, and full control over its own tariffs was not achieved until 1910 (Norman, 1940: 102).

These concessions, enormous when measured against Japanese xenophobia, were obtained almost without force, but with the constant pressure of its threat. The foreigners' easy victory released all the suppressed antigovernment sentiment that had been building up. Several leading shogunate officials were assassinated. The rice riots and peasant revolts recurrent throughout the Tokugawa era increased in number. More and more samurai deserted their lords and joined their fellows in the cities, raising the cry, "Honor the Emperor and expel the barbarians." Japan did not become a colony, but in the view of its leaders over the following decades, this was a fate that always threatened.

THE RISE OF MODERN JAPAN

The year 1968 was the hundredth anniversary of the Meiji Restoration, and the overall economic advance during that century was unique in world history. The analysis of Japan's success, in the West initially hampered by the barrier of an inordinately difficult language, has grown both in volume and in the range of interpretations offered.[3] Of this considerable literature, it is appropriate in this context to present only the barest summary, focused on the background to Japanese emigration.

"Modern economic growth," as this term is used by economists, comprises four main characteristics: (1) international contacts; (2) the application of science and modern technology to industry; (3) a shift of workers, capital, and entrepreneurs out of agriculture into manufacturing and services; and (4) a rapid and sustained rise in real product per capita, in spite of the usual accompanying increase in population.[4] The precise measurement of this process in Japan is difficult, of course, for early data are incomplete and inaccurate, and the relative monetary value of the many new products introduced into the economy cannot be fixed exactly. Yet the main features are well established, and reasonable approximations can be set even for some of the principal quantitative indices.

Most obviously, modernization meant Westernization. The trickle of Dutch learning had broadened into a stream during the fifteen years since Perry's expedition, and under the new government it became a flood. In 1868, Emperor Meiji signed the Five Articles, the Magna Carta of New Japan. One of them proclaimed that "knowledge shall be sought throughout the world, so that the foundations of the Empire may be strengthened." By 1872 at least two hundred foreign technical experts were in Japan as employees of the government, each chosen from the country that had excelled in that man's specialty (Allen, 1946: 28). The intelligent pragmatism that suggested these choices dictated no absolute commitments. The army was reorganized by the French, but within a few months of France's defeat in 1871 Japan shifted to the German military organization. The banking system, based at first on the American model, was soon changed to include elements of British central banking, long-term credit institutions copied from the French, and some innovations particularly suited to the local scene.

Only a few years after young noblemen and samurai had risked their lives to be smuggled aboard a foreign vessel, Japanese were offered special inducements to travel abroad and acquire Western knowledge. The country had laid a good foundation in literacy; by the end of the Tokugawa era, according to Dore's rough estimate (1965a: 321), some 43 percent of boys and 10 percent of girls received "some kind of schooling." As the very figures indicate, the students were not limited to the upper classes; and though the curriculum was hardly suited to the needs of modernization, it at least trained in being trained. The development from this base was both rapid and, in terms of the government's goals, supremely successful. Universal primary education plus the opportunity to advance through such higher institutions helped create a population diverse in its skills but remarkably single-minded in its national character. By 1940, the "almost total uniformity of education experience in the first six school years of the life of every Japanese child" produced "a homogeneity of popular intellectual culture which has probably never been equaled in any society of 70 million people" (Dore, 1964).

From the decision of the Meiji government to foster modernization to the actual beginning of "modern economic growth" took less than two decades (Rosovsky, 1966). The ruthlessly utilitarian policies of this early period were exercised, according to one estimate, by an oligarchy of "fewer than one hundred young men" (E. O. Reischauer, 1965: 123). Since Japan's development could hardly have been started without strong state intervention, this tiny group had its hands in everything. According to the usual interpretation, the government was preeminent as promoter, owner, and manager of the new enterprises until 1880, when an impending financial crisis forced it to sell them to private entrepreneurs.[5] Thereafter, government investment in railroads and other capital goods continued to shape the course of industrialization significantly (Rosovsky, 1959). However, with the partial decentralization of industry, the ruling elite voluntarily gave up some of its political power and established the beginnings of a democratic system.[6]

The importance of large-scale industry, great as it was, can easily be exaggerated. "It was the expansion of Japan's basic economy—agriculture and small-scale industry built on traditional foundations—which accounted for most of the growth of national productivity and income" (Lockwood, 1954: 25). The silk industry, as a prime example, was based on rural households, nearly a third of which derived a supplementary income from cultivating cocoons. The textile industry as a whole was largely rural, with nine-tenths of the operatives female, one-quarter of them under sixteen years of age. The girls, generally recruited through contracts with their peasant fathers, were housed and fed in company dormitories, which blended the factory system of the West with the paternalism and strict discipline of Japanese tradition. Wages were low even by local standards; and often a portion of the girls' meager income was returned regularly to their fathers, another portion set aside for their dowries. After this kind of brief and restricted association with new industrialism, many returned to their villages and married local farmboys. With this combination of Western techniques and extraordinarily cheap laborers (who were afforded no legal protection of any kind until after the turn of the century), Japan could compete successfully against established industrial powers. The periodic rotation of industrial workers, with the consequence that many of the temporary operatives remained rural in their outlook, probably contributed greatly to the country's political stability during this fundamental economic transformation.

Those who guided Japanese industrialization made money by their activity; taxes on dividends and profits were lenient. The extraordinary expenses of the government—commuting the feudal pensions of the 400,000 samurai, the wide range of development programs in the early decades, the later concentration on investment in capital goods and military outlays—all were paid for mainly by the peasants. The new land tax of 1873 provided 94 percent of the government's tax revenue at the time of the decree, and over half until almost 1900. However startling the rise of Japan as a whole, for several generations most of the peasants remained mired in their poverty, and for them, at least, the economic impetus to emigrate was strong.

Despite faults or limitations in Japan's policy of modernization, its overall success was amazing. According to informed estimates, gross national product measured in constant prices increased between 30 and 45 times over the hundred years following the Meiji Restoration. Since the population tripled, product per capita increased between ten and fifteen times.[7] Certainly no one would have predicted anything like this remarkable rise in productivity. Much of the country was in chaos for a decade or more after the inauguration of the new regime, and social order was restored by an obsolete class of warrior knights supremely unfit, it would seem, to lead their people into modern industrialism. Was their success due not to their own leadership so much as to the quality of the people they led?

THE JAPANESE· "NATIONAL CHARACTER"

Virtually by definition, each nation is distinctive in its culture; and the inculcation of its specific beliefs, attitudes, and patterns of behavior, one can reasonably hypothesize, differentiates the modal national of each country from the rest of the world's population. And in several crucial respects, as we have noted, post-1868 Japan was unitary to a high degree. The men who emigrated during those exciting and unsettling decades surely were decisively shaped by the unique events that, before their departure, they either took part in or at least witnessed.

Even a sympathetic observer of the psychological analysis of national character, however, cannot characterize this subdiscipline as well grounded in conceptual clarity and empirical fact, and Americans' analyses of the national character of the Japanese are not the best examples of the genre. They have too often followed the pattern set by Ruth Benedict's *The Chrysanthemum and the Sword,* written during World War II for the military leaders of the United States as a guide to the enemy's psychology by an anthropologist who had never been to Japan, knew no Japanese, and had done no prior work on the country or its people.[8] In such works, genuine insights can easily be colored by negative appellations—for example, when concern over the fate of one's family is denoted as "lack of individuality," a disposition to follow legitimate norms as "rigidity," and so on. Similarly, traits characteristic of the West, or perhaps even universal ones, can easily be given an exotic flavor and pictured as specific to the Japanese. Other limitations characterize many of the analyses of Japanese Americans' character. The reaction to so exceptional an experience as forced evacuation and internment in camps should not, one would suppose, be generalized into a presumed modal personality that had developed apart from this experience. Yet recent inmates just arrived in Chicago provided the basis for several of the best known statements on the matter (Caudill, 1952; Caudill and DeVos, 1956; Uyeki, 1960).

What can one say, in spite of these difficulties, about the national character of the Japanese? New Japan broke with the Tokugawa era under the influence of Western advisers, but also continued the traditional native culture. The counterpart to Western revolutions was a "restoration"; to usher in modern times, the emperor and the national religion of Shinto were given again their ancient, even legendary, prerogatives. Industrialization in Japan neither depleted the rural population nor shattered such rural institutions as the family. Analysts trying to solve the puzzle of Japan's modernization have mostly found a partial answer either in the preindustrial society as a whole or in such elements of it as education (Dore, 1965a), religion (Bellah, 1957), law (Von Mehren, 1958), the larger cities (Robert Smith, 1960), the castle-towns (Hall, 1955), or even the agrarian economy itself (Thomas Smith, 1959). All these studies are part of a developing consensus on the relation between old and new Japan: because modern Japan was constructed on the already existent foundation, it was possible to build an industrial society with minimum disruption and in record time.

The individuals caught up in this transformation were expected both to retain the old and acquire the new. The psychological type that resulted from such counterpressures, at least as seen from the outside, is an array of self-contradictions. In a sense this was true even of the traditional culture, in which ancient Chinese borrowings often lay side by side with half-antagonistic native traits, together forming a composite that struck every foreigner as inordinately complex. "Whichever period of Japanese history one cares to examine, 'traditional' culture and 'modern' culture are invariably found to be flourishing side by side" (Hasegawa, 1965: 59). Commentaries on the Japanese character usually point to the antinomies contained in it. "The Japanese combine a rather Latin taste for extremes with an almost Anglo-Saxon pragmatism. They are progressive, and at the same time conservative; at one moment they seem to be peace-loving, at another bellicose" (Hasegawa, 1965: 87). The stylized formalism of Japanese art must be contrasted with the planlessness of Tokyo; an active and richly endowed intelligentsia is addicted to vulgar Marxism; the acute awareness of status becomes, in playful moods, a complete indifference to it (D. Bell, 1958)—in short, "the chrysanthemum and the sword."

The ability to live simultaneously in two worlds—for instance, to be both a Buddhist and a Shintoist even though the two religions conflict at almost every point—is hardly an indication of the "rigidity" that is supposed, according to various analysts, to characterize the Japanese. By the logic of most measures of an "authoritarian" personality (in particular, the famous F-scale),[9] a people capable of such flexibility is the opposite of "authoritarian." Perhaps we should draw no greater conclusion than that Japanese were trained by their multilayered culture to live effectively with complexities; in this sense, even the villagers had an "urban" cast, a readiness for industrialism.

One of the self-contradictory patterns is of especial importance—that in the modernization of Japan the knightly code of the samurai retained its power to guide. During the Tokugawa era, it would seem, a bit of the spirit of bushido was transferred to commoners. A man who borrowed money, for instance, would often offer no more security than the formula common in the mid-nineteenth century: "In the event of my nonpayment of the said amount, I declare that you may openly laugh at me before the eyes of other people" (Hatoyama and Sakamoto, 1919). The leaders and educators of Meiji Japan, most of whom were ex-samurai, were virtually unanimous in their determination that "something of the samurai ideal—the sense of social commitment, the courage and seriousness of individual responsibility—should be kept alive for future generations" (Jansen and Stone, 1967). This ideal was transmitted mainly, though not exclusively, through the schools.

The ethic of achievement has also been prominent in Japanese education. Dore (1965a: 323) cites a number of precepts from the Tokugawa days—"Determine to succeed, study with all your might, never forgetting the shame of failure"—that had their full counterparts, of course, in the meritocracy of Meiji Japan. "University study was so seriously thought about that a scholar who failed through his own fault would have been considered a criminal" (Hearn, 1917: 465).[10]

The language in which the expanded education was given, since it had been cut off from Western influences for several centuries, was not well suited for the transmission of a modernizing curriculum. The Japanese medical student, for instance, was required to write his dissertation in German, and until well into the twentieth century physicians often expressed technical ideas in German or, at best, in germanized Japanese. "The concept of 'nation' was not even available and had to be freshly coined: *kokka*. Beyond that, whole categories of new conceptions had to be clothed in newly created words: the people, citizens, freedom, rights, political party, individualism, and a host of others" (Yamagiwa, 1965). These gaps in the vocabulary denoted not only Japan's lack of Western technology but, more important in this context, fundamental differences in the ways of life. In Japan, "privacy does not exist; nothing can be hidden; everybody's vices and virtues are known to everybody else" (Hearn, 1917: 112). Thus, "there is no Japanese word for 'privacy,' and the only words which convey the idea inevitably suggest loneliness or selfishness" (Keene, 1959: 7). Even today, there is still not a nonpejorative word for "curiosity" (Dore, 1967).

The distinctive features of Japanese as compared especially with Western languages constitute another clue to the national character of the people who use it. According to Benjamin Whorf, the structure of Japanese "limits free plasticity and rigidifies channels of development"; in the view of Edwin Reischauer, "Perhaps the greatest single misfortune in the history of Japan was that, because of her geographic position, Chinese characters and not one of the Western alphabets became the basis of her writing system."[11] Without subscribing to such extreme statements, one can offer some suggestive examples. For instance, a Japanese psychiatrist (L. T. Doi, 1962) has termed one word "a key concept for understanding Japanese personality structure." It is *amae*, the noun form of *amaeru*, which means "to depend and presume upon another's benevolence." Doi states that no exact equivalent exists in any European language. The connotation is that, among Japanese, the special quality (*amai,* the word for "sweet," derives from the same root) of the mother-child relation is expected also in associations between adults.

The clearest relation between language and social structure is in the sharp distinctions that Japanese provides for honorific, polite, ordinary, and humble levels of usage. "It is probably true that until modern times no 'egalitarian' form of Japanese speech existed" (Yamagiwa, 1965). There are not only counterparts of such a differentiation as between *Sie* and *du* in German, but also separate forms for many other words. When a male is speaking, for instance, the word for "I" may be *ore, boku,* or *watakushi,* in ascending order of deference.

> Honorific forms go beyond mere politeness to make explicit the actual or implied superiority of the person being addressed. Humble forms serve to deprecate the speaker and thus place the person spoken to on a higher footing. . . . The failure to use familiar language toward a person who is obviously an inferior (that is, professor to student, husband to wife) is equally poor form (Yamagiwa, 1965).

A few of these hierarchical usages have become less common in the post-1945 period; but as recently as 1953, 60 percent of a sample of respondents, undifferentiated on this question by age, sex, or education, held that the status distinctions denoted by the multiple forms of "I" and "you" are "good," only 28 percent that they are "bad" (Tsuneishi, 1966: 19 cf. Nakane, 1970: 25–40).

In sum, what can be deduced from these various types of data about the Japanese national character? In several respects, there is a marked contrast with the modal types in industrialized Western nations, and the latter, one should remember, furnished the data for the supposedly universal truths of the social sciences. According to the conventional wisdom of the sociologist, for example, industrialization inevitably brings about a progressive disintegration of the preindustrial social forms; the family-like *Gemeinschaft* gives way to the corporation-like *Gesellschaft.* With the consequent individuation (a more neutral term than the positive "individualism" or the negative "alienation"), large numbers of persons can no longer associate through established structures or institutions; they become elements of an amorphous mass. But the social individualism of Northwest Europeans and their overseas cousins is both anomalous on a world scale and, except in their uniquely prosperous environments, inefficient. The average Japanese of the mid-nineteenth century was too firmly embedded in his culture to be dislodged by even a hyperrapid industrialization. A Japanese acting alone derived motivation and strength from his recognition that, in fact, he was less an individual than a representative of a larger group. No matter how one identifies this group—whether as the family with its many ramifications, the village, the state, or the Japanese people—it was always far more significant than the elements comprising it. Each group, moreover, was structured into a hierarchy of authority, so that every member knew to whom deference was due, from whom it could be expected.

The faults of such a social system, as seen by a Western democrat, have often been pointed out, and in any case they are obvious enough. Structural lines as strong and clear as those in Japanese institutions easily merge into authoritarian control; political democracy is possible, as several periods of modern Japanese history have demonstrated, but not easily achieved or maintained. American commentaries have less often stressed the virtues of the system. The lack of privacy, the absence of even a word for civil rights, are symptoms of an organic strength that, on the one hand, motivated each Japanese to contribute his utmost and thus, on the other hand, enabled the nation to jump from an almost pathetic weakness to parity with the greatest powers in half a century.

Notes

1 The Dutch were suffered to remain because, since they had not sent any missionaries, it was believed that unlike the other Europeans they were not Christians—an impression they did nothing to discourage. P.-F. von Siebold, a German physician, lived in Nagasaki during the 1820s and wrote a book about the country, up to that time the most complete in any Western language. He was allowed to stay only because of a happy translation of *Hochdeutscher* as "Dutch mountaineer."

2 A measure of the government's desperation can be gleaned from

one incident. The shogunate had proposed to make a government monopoly of human excrement, which scavengers collected each evening to sell as fertilizer. One of them protested, recalling the heroic resistance at the Boston Tea Party, of which he had somehow heard: "The government is determined to take over all the profit from nightsoil, disregarding the rights of the brokers. . . . The ladies of America gave up all use of tea and even the pleasure of tea parties. Now, let us follow the example of those Americans and give up the entire production of nightsoil in order to resist the despotism of our government" (quoted in Russell, 1939: 130).

[3] For collections of papers that are both characteristic and better than the average, see Jansen, 1965; Lockwood, 1965; and Dore, 1967. These are volumes in a series, "Studies in the Modernization of Japan," sponsored by the Conference on Modern Japan of the Association for Asian Studies and published by the Princeton University Press.

[4] Simon Kuznets, *Six Lectures on Economic Growth* (New York: Free Press, 1959), Lecture I.

[5] Thomas Smith, 1955: 86–87, 100. Smith notes two other theories that have been offered to explain the sale, a crude and a more subtle Marxist interpretation of the events, but his evidence that the financial need was decisive is convincing.

[6] See Thomas Smith, 1960–61. This interesting article begins with a quotation from Tocqueville—"An aristocracy seldom yields [its privileges] without a protracted struggle, in the course of which implacable animosities are kindled between the different classes of society"—in order to make the point that also in this respect Japan does not fit the usual model.

[7] For a technical and detailed analysis of this century of growth, see Ohkawa and Rosovsky, 1965.

[8] There was a rash of such works also about the national character of Germans. For other, essentially similar statements about the Japanese, see Geoffrey Gorer, "Themes in Japanese Culture," *Transactions of the New York Academy of Science*, 2nd Series, 5 (1943), 106–24; Weston LaBarre, "Some Observations on Character Structure in the Orient: The Japanese," *Psychiatry*, 8 (1945), 319–42.

[9] T. W. Adorno *et al.*, *The Authoritarian Personality* (New York: Harper & Row, 1950).

[10] Dore (1965a: 211) quotes the following passage from a contemporary memoir: "We went all out that month. If one of us got a page ahead, the others would turn pale. We hardly took time off to chew our food properly, and we drank as little water as pos-

sible in order that the others should not get ahead in the time wasted going to the lavatory—so keen were we to get a line or two ahead of the others." See also Thomas Smith, 1967, and for a discussion of the same norm in twentieth-century Japan, Vogel, 1965: chap. 3. Concerning the same kind of behavior among Japanese Americans, see Caudill and DeVos, 1956.

11 Both statements are quoted in Yamagiwa, 1965. The argument posed here is not a special case of the Whorf (or Sapir-Whorf) hypothesis that the structure of any language partly determines the ideas that can be expressed in it and thus the typical behavior of the people that use it—in a word, that language *is* culture. The presuppositions underlying my discussion are much more modest: that there is a relation between the language and the culture of any people and, therefore, that differences particularly in vocabulary are one useful index to national character.

Chapter 8 ◉ Religion

The supposition offered at the beginning of the previous chapter, that the exceptionally rapid rise of modern Japan to economic parity with the West is somehow related to the no less unusual characteristics of Japanese Americans, seems more probable after reviewing the transformation of their home country during the decades when most of the Issei were emigrating. The problem is to determine how the values of Meiji Japan were transmitted to American Nisei.

In any society the institution that typically defines and clarifies its moral norms and passes them on from one generation to the next is the church; and this is a good place to start. What religious guides to correct behavior did the emigrants learn before leaving Japan? What kind of churches did they establish in Hawaii and in the United States? How did these interact with other institutions that parents used for the inculcation of ethical standards?

THE RELIGIONS OF JAPAN

Modern Japan has had a great diversity of religions. It is usual to identify three main faiths—Buddhism, Shinto, and Confucianism—but whether three is the correct number depends on the analyst's purpose. On the one hand, each religion has been divided into many sects, with a sometimes great divergence in doctrine and ritual; on the other hand, all have interacted and partly converged. During the Meiji era, moreover, religious institutions were in ferment; nothing that can be said about them would necessarily be true for the whole period, or of all regions, or about the entire population irrespective of social class. It would be manifestly inappropriate in this book to delve into these complexities. What follows is the barest outline, designed only to introduce the reader to a more detailed account of the Japanese American churches.

The growth of Japanese civilization was closely linked to the spread of Buddhism, without which painting, sculpture, architecture, music, and drama would all have been unrecognizably different, as well as even such minor arts as landscape gardening, the tea cult, flower arrangement, fencing, and printing (Suzuki, 1938). And the range of Buddhist theology is as great as these cultural influences. As the religion spread north and east from its birthplace in India, it acquired accretions in every country, so that Mahāyāna Buddhism (literally, "Greater Vehicle," as contrasted with the "Little Vehicle" of Hīhayāna, or Southern Buddhism) offers its followers an authoritative canon of more than five thousand books in half a dozen languages. "There is little that has ever entered the heart or mind of man which does not find its counterpart in Buddhism somewhere" (A. K. Reischauer, 1925: 9). Yet in a different sense, the moral view its adherents derived from it was thin, for the major concern of the Buddhist seers had generally not been the problem of good and evil but rather the nature of being.[1]

As the de facto state religion of the Tokugawa shogunate, Buddhism had become corrupt and sterile. Priests were honored who lived in licentious luxury and performed few sacerdotal functions; scholarship consisted in arid exegeses on others' commentaries. In line with the nationalism of the Meiji Restoration, its leaders disestablished Buddhism as an alien importation. Many temples and monasteries were demolished, their priests and nuns sent back to secular life, their treasures sold or destroyed, their lands confiscated by the government. The victims of this persecution defended themselves in riots and insurrections, and within a few years Tokyo relaxed its hostility. From the core of the genuine adherents to "the Way of the greatest Good," cleansed of opportunists and restimulated by new contacts with Sanskrit scholars in India and the West, there developed a spiritual awakening in modern Japanese Buddhism (J. M. Kitagawa, 1966: 225–29).

The Meiji government revived Shinto as the one true faith for Japan,[2] so that "Shinto" denotes both the primitive pantheism of the earliest period of Japanese history and, in a somewhat altered form, the established religion of the modern state. Over the centuries much of Shinto magic-superstitious doctrine had been absorbed into Buddhism, either as a folk appendage to upper-class beliefs or, following the strong Shinto revivals in the eighteenth century or during the Meiji era, as the dominant element. Of some gods in the Japanese pantheon, thus, one cannot say whether they are Buddhist or Shinto. This facile association has not been blocked by the contrast between the sometimes dry rationality of Buddhism and Shinto's emphasis on spontaneity, sentiment, and the unity of man with all of nature.

As one important element of the Shinto faith, the emperor was regarded as a living *kami*.[3]

> [The emperor] is to the Japanese mind the Supreme Being in the cosmos of Japan, as God is in the universe of the pantheistic philosopher. From him everything emanates, in him everything subsists. . . . He is supreme in all temporal affairs of the state as well as in all spiritual matters (Herbert, 1967: 389).

Apart from its direct support to Japanese nationalism, the Shinto ethic[4] also bolstered the hierarchical structure by its advocacy of such moral tenets as duty and honor.

> A very important element . . . is *kenshin*, from *ken*, to offer, and *shin*, individual person. It means total, perfectly spontaneous offering of what one has and is. . . . It is not a sense of duty, because it stems from the heart and not from the mind. It is stronger than love, because it is more imperative and admits of no compromise or distortion. . . . It has been defined as "devotion to the common interest" (Herbert, 1967: 74).

"Honor is the only tie that binds the Japanese to the ethical world [of Shinto]." An act is not thought of as "sinful," but rather as depriving one of honor, or "shameful." "In the absence of any written commandments, the . . . consciousness of shame is the last and highest court of appeal" (Herbert, 1967: 76).[5]

Even while the government was unifying religious sentiment into "State Shinto," it was compelled to recognize the legitimacy of what was called "Sect Shinto." Some of the sects were in fact loose confederations of more or less distinct subsects; some

stressed magic and miracles, others the correct ritual; some derived more from Buddhism than from primitive Shinto. In addition to the dozen half-recognized denominations, splinter
sects, devotional grouplets, "pseudoreligions," and "quasi-reli-
gious associations" continually arose under the guidance of local
charismatic leaders, who typically bolstered their simple doc-
trines with promises to heal their adherents, to bring them
prosperity and happiness (J. M. Kitagawa, 1966: 214–21).
Their limited erudition sometimes resulted in a renewed emphasis on this or that doctrinal singularity and thus, over all, in
an intermittent reinforcement of the considerable differences
among Buddhist, Shinto, and Confucian orthodoxies.

As several Japanese writers have pointed out, Shinto *kami*
guard over earthly fortunes and Buddhist deities over the life
beyond, but morality itself is the province of Confucianism, the
third Japanese religion. After it was introduced from China
early in the Christian era, the Confucian philosophy lay dor-
mant for more than a millennium. Ieyasu, the first of the Tokugawa shoguns, had the Confucian classics printed in Japan for
the first time, and during the next two and a half centuries, the
Japanese intellect was molded to their hierarchical model. Its
influence was notable on such diverse elements of Japanese
culture as the development of bushido, Zen Buddhism, and nature poetry. Its main ethical force, however, was to reinforce the
legitimacy of subordination in the state and the family.

> The duty of every individual is to live and act in accord-
> ance with the status ordained for him in the hierarchy of
> social life. . . . The essence of moral and social conduct
> amounts to subordination, obedience, and dutifulness
> (Anesaki, 1938: 45).

A fourth religion, Christianity, though of little general importance in Meiji Japan, must be noted in a book primarily on
Japanese Americans. At the beginning of the seventeenth century, Christianity had been banned and some 40,000 converts
massacred. Shortly after the Meiji Restoration, when officials
discovered a group of Catholics who for two centuries had successfully evaded the Tokugawa police, thirteen of the leaders
were beheaded as an example to the others. Christianity was

viewed, officially and popularly, as the equivalent of sorcery; one usual designation was "the evil religion." Within a few years, however, the anti-Christian policy of the Meiji government was relaxed, and Japan's first Protestant church was established with nine parishioners, including two Buddhist priests sent in to spy on its operations. From this slight beginning the missions and their associated schools and social services grew rapidly, in part reflecting the craze for all things Western that—with government assistance—swept the country in the 1880s. Yet the hostility to this latest alien intrusion never completely abated; unlike Buddhism and Confucianism, Christianity was not fitted into an overall faith of the country. The number of converts was never large, and in some periods it declined. However, since they included members of the upper class (as well as, for instance, most of the women with feminist ideals), Christian influence was sometimes greater than one might suppose (Ōhata and Ikado, 1956; Anesaki, 1938: chap. 5).

According to one analyst, other scholars' "compartmentalization of the several religious traditions in Japan" has impeded them from seeing that Japanese religious history has formed one major tradition.

> Shinto and Buddhism, to mention only the two most conspicuous religious traditions, became so thoroughly mixed in actual practice and popular belief that even the official policy of the Meiji Restoration could not separate them. To this day there remains much evidence to deny that a separation ever took place in popular piety (Earhart, 1967).

Indeed, in religion as in other matters, the Japanese have shown a genius for reconciling opposites into a paradoxical compendium that uniquely suits them. But even those who argue that there has been such a genuine synthesis do not describe it with the same ingredients. According to Tasuku Harada (1914), as one example, "the faith of Japan" consists in *kami,* the Shinto deities; *michi,* which means teaching, doctrine, gospel, or—literally—the Way; *satori,* or the awakening to full consciousness of reality, enlightenment in the Buddhist sense; *sukui,* the doctrine of salvation; *chugi,* the spirit of loyalty, the alpha and omega of bushido; and *mirai,* life after death or, for some believers, future life in the present world. But the list that Ichirō Hori (1968: 10–13) gives of the "significant common tendencies . . . [in] Japanese religion as one entity" is quite different: "emphasis on filial piety (*kō*) and ancestor worship connected with the Japanese family system; emphasis on *on* (debts or favors given by superiors) and *hō-on* (the return of *on*); . . . belief in the continuity between man and deity, or easy deification of human beings; coexistence of different religions in one family or even in one person."

In sum, the religious life of Japan, as seen in a Western perspective, is puzzlingly complex. Shinto and Buddhism have coexisted for centuries, each continually splitting into sects and subsects, each borrowing ritual, gods, and ideas from the other, and each yet remaining organizationally distinct. Moreover, neither of the two, nor even both in combination, provide the rounded ethical guide that a Westerner gets from Judaism or Christianity. This is given in Confucianism, more a moral philosophy than a religion, whose precepts have been incorporated to some degree—but to some degree only—into the ideologies of the other two. Nor is the typical behavior of the individual participant any more fitting by Western standards. In 1961, when the country's population was something under 90 million, 145 million were listed as members of the various religious denominations. More than half of the total, in other words, adhered to more than one religion (Beardsley, 1965).

> A popular religious leader of the early nineteenth century urged his followers, "Revere Shinto, Buddhism, and Confucianism, and cherish sincerity in all." A literal observance of this command obliged a man to believe simultaneously in the Shinto gods, Buddha, and the nonexistence of both; yet this contradiction did not disturb the Japanese (Keene, 1959: 108).

What of this melange did the emigrants to Hawaii or the United States take with them as moral baggage? There is no direct evidence on this point. Statistical data on religious affiliation are generally poor in the United States, and those on Japanese are even less complete and accurate than for the population as a whole. According to a survey of almost a tenth of California's Japanese population in the early 1930s, three-quarters of the Issei were Buddhists, one-fifth were Christians. Among the Nisei, on the contrary, almost half the males and more than half the females were Christians. A small percentage of Issei and an only slightly larger one of Nisei reported no religious affiliation (Strong, 1933: chap. 9). As a typical example of more recent approximations, the War Relocation Authority estimated right after World War II that "the proportion of Japanese Americans who claim[ed] church membership and who attend[ed] regular religious services [was] about the same as that in the general population"—whatever that may have been—and that "about half" of this imprecisely defined total was Buddhist (U.S. Dept. of the Interior, 1947: 226). In spite of the much larger percentage of Japanese in Hawaii, the statistics there have been no better. In several of the censuses before annexation, detailed questions on religion were asked—but only of whites. Possibly the best of recent data, labeled "very general estimates, very gross figures" for around 1963, give a total of 150,000 Buddhists in Hawaii, of whom about 90 percent were Japanese. The estimated affiliations of Christian churches give no breakdown by race.[6]

Such overall statistics, if they existed, would in any case be only a first indication of the religious distribution of Japanese Americans, for apparently many Buddhists have attended Christian churches, and many Christians have been segregated in the Japanese sectors of their denominations, where very often a strong dose of Confucian-Buddhist ethic is mixed in with church dogma. These religious trends have been similar in Hawaii and on the mainland, except for the direct consequences of either the sparser Japanese population on the West Coast or the evacuation. In a general discussion, thus, analyses based in either locale are pertinent to the whole subnation.

BUDDHISM A L'AMERICAINE

The Buddhism established in America was initially no less diverse than its parent institution in Japan. All the major denominations—Tendai, Zen, Shingon, Nichiren, Jōdo, and especially Shin—have been represented, as well as folk sects vaguely associated with either Shinto or Buddhism.[7] The changes that took place in the new setting can be illustrated by detailed descriptions of two temples, both of the Shin (or Hong-wanji) sect,[8] one in the small town of Kona in the late 1930s, the other in a suburb of Honolulu in the late 1960s.

> The Hongwanji temple in Kona has a following of about 200 families. Many of these the priest never sees, as they never attend temple affairs, and it is not unusual for him to conduct a funeral service in a household the members of which he has not met before. . . . The primary function of the temple—to look after the souls of the ancestors of its members—is carried on in Kona just as it is in Japan. The Buddhist "churches," as the temples are called in English by the Japanese of Hawaii, have adopted the Christian Sunday as a day for activity and, unlike Japan, sermons are given every Sunday (Embree, 1941: 105–7).

The Honolulu Hongwanji Temple, the largest and most influential in the United States, exemplifies a further acculturation. It is a branch of the Honpa Hongwanji in Kyoto, but from the very beginning its leaders saw part of their task to be Americanization. According to a short history by the present head's father, Bishop Yemyo Imamura, in 1904 the Mission (predecessor to the Temple) interceded in the plantation strike (cf. pp. 26–27) and helped bring about an amicable settlement. Thereafter, "our activities in the plantations enjoyed the hearty cooperation of the plantation officials," and in 1907 the Mission was granted official status by the territorial government. "My first step," wrote Bishop Imamura (1927), "was to organize the Young Men's Buddhist Association and . . . the night school to teach English." From this unorthodox beginning, the Temple's activities diversified as much as those of the most activist Community Church of suburban American Protestantism.

In Japan, the priest is the legal owner of the temple building and its surrounding property. One priest, of the fourteenth generation that succeeded to the hereditary position, moved from a temple in rural Japan to Hongwanji in Honolulu. There, he found, an abstract entity called "the Mission" owned the property; and its members, following the Congregational principle, elected officers that in fact controlled many of the priest's activities (Akahoshi, 1963). In Japan, Buddhist priests are not preachers; at Hongwanji there are four services every Sunday, a morning and an afternoon one in Japanese, and two in English, one for children and one labeled "teen-adult." In Japan, religious feeling is expressed through painting and sculpture, rarely through music; but a notable feature of the service in the United States is the singing of "Buddhist hymns," accompanied by a Western instrument (Tajima, 1935: 46–47).

The affiliated organizations of the Hongwanji Temple as listed in a promotional brochure, "Honpa Hongwanji Is for You," include activities for all ages: Cub Scouts, Brownies, Boy Scouts, Junior and Cadette Girl Scouts, and Explorers; the Young Buddhist Association of Honolulu and a second "teen group," the Club Dharma; the Sudhana Fellowship, a "teen-adult worship group"; the Upasika Society, a women's group with "a varied program geared to the interests of its members"; a choir and a Sunday School Teachers Association; the Fujinkai, or "older women's group"; and ad hoc study groups organized periodically. The facilities available for these activities include meeting rooms and social halls, complete with kitchen, a library, and a girls' dormitory. The Temple has published two monthly newsletters, one bilingual and one for the YBA, as well as the quarterly *Pacific Buddhist*. Associated with Hongwanji are eight branch temples in Hawaii, two Japanese-language schools, a day-care center, and an English-language school for foreign students.

The Buddhist Sunday schools operate in unabashed imitation of their Christian counterparts. They are equipped with such furnishings—all of which a native Japanese would find exotic —as an organ or piano; hymn books; blackboards, pictures, and charts; children's books, magazines, and games; and a school flag. The curriculum most widely used in Hawaii was compiled by N. Ozaeki, a priest of the Hongwanji Temple, with topics like diligence, concentration, endurance, sobriety, contentment, honesty, charity, friendship, cooperation, filial piety, and so on. Only after the pupils have been led through this garden of virtues are they introduced to the elements of Shin Buddhism, somewhat adapted to the American scene. To the tune familiar to Christian moppets, they sing, "Buddha loves me, this I know." The very word *love* an orthodox Buddhist in Japan would find out of place: man fears and worships God but does not "love" him, and God feels compassion for man but not "love." The spirit of optimism and happiness in Americanized Buddhism, in short, has altered the substance as well as the form of the religion (Tajima, 1935: 59–64). Even more remarkably, Bishop Imamura offered this gloss on the theme of filial piety:

> Parents may feel lonesome in some way or other, and they will need your consolation. Give them solace. Tell them that good parents must think more of the future of their children than their own. To give in this life is to receive in another (Imamura, 1927: 17).[9]

A good example of a transformed ritual is the *Bon* dance as it is now performed in Hawaii. The observance of Bon as a ceremony to entertain the spirits during their visit to the site of their former existence antedates the introduction of Buddhism to Japan. Today the three-day festival has been extended from late June to early September, so that the dances sponsored by various temples will not compete. Traditionally held in a graveyard, the ritual now more often takes place in an empty lot. Fine points of the old-country dances have been lost, and a group of new dances set to modern music, the *ondo*, were incorporated, together with the saxophone, guitar, and other Western instruments. During the summer semiprofessional musicians and dance leaders, the latter usually women of the older generation, travel from one community to another to lead the fun. Even the strictest parents permit their daughters to participate, and non-Buddhists come to watch or even try to learn the unfamiliar steps. The festival "has been almost completely secularized and is now regarded as a purely social affair and to be enjoyed as such" (Onishi, 1938).

The Americanization of Buddhism on the mainland has been no less thorough. Before the war, the Hongwanji Buddhist Temple in Los Angeles sponsored a baseball team, irreverently called "the Wanjies." Even Shinto, despite its closer ties to Japan, accommodated to the point of constructing " 'a beautiful

California-style Spanish-style building that has all the dignity of a Shinto shrine' " (Modell, 1969a: chap. 4). Part of the loss the evacuees suffered during their detention in camps was in communal religious property. Of the 28 temples in Los Angeles, 22 were damaged, some almost beyond repair; in Seattle the Navy took over the temple for its use. And after the evacuation order was rescinded, many temples were temporarily converted into hostels for the returning Japanese. When services were reorganized, either on the West Coast or wherever else Japanese communities were established, the initial response was generally enthusiastic. By the summer of 1946 four temples had been founded in Chicago, including a "Nonsectarian Buddhist Church" that tried to accommodate even more than the prewar norm to the American milieu (U.S. Dept. of the Interior, 1947: 234–35).

Buddhism in the United States must now cope with that familiar dilemma of an acculturating institution: as it adapts more and more to the style of American churches, there is less and less point to its separate identity; but if it fails to do so, it will seemingly lose the bulk of the Sansei generation. The student body at the University of Hawaii includes a large number of nominal Buddhists among its sizable Japanese sector, but the Rainbow Young Buddhist Association on campus, after a recruitment drive over several years, was able to enlist the support of only "30 or 35" members, mostly girls. Students were generally not much interested in religion, my informant told me, and in particular they were unwilling to identify themselves with Buddhism, which marked them as different, old-fashioned, and perhaps lower-class.[10]

CHRISTIANITY AMONG JAPANESE AMERICANS

However much Buddhism adapted to the forms or even the inner faith of American religiosity, in a predominantly Christian country it has been seen as an exotic intrusion. The situation of converted Christians, however, was not markedly different. In either case, Japanese Americans belonged to branch units of institutions controlled by others. It is difficult to judge whether churches constituted a more effective acculturative bridge than temples, for the dominant membership of the two has been, respectively, Nisei and Issei.

Several Christian denominations began missionary efforts in California only months after the arrival of the first Japanese immigrants. By 1910, Los Angeles had five Christian missions competing with a single Buddhist one. The following year the Dendo-Dan, or Japanese Interdenominational Board of Missions, was founded, with joint headquarters in San Francisco and Los Angeles. It distributed some 4,000 copies of its monthly paper to Japanese communities all over the Western states. Many of its activities reflected the marginality of Japanese Americans: on the one hand, it sent a special delegation to Japan to present a Bible to the emperor on the occasion of his coronation; on the other hand, it proclaimed that " 'the Americanization Movement' is one of the chief features of the work of this society" (Dendo-Dan, 1916). Though formally an activity of the main Christian churches, in fact Dendo-Dan was largely self-financed: for example, out of a total budget of $4,075.56 in 1913, contributions from four American Mission Boards made up only $491.65, or somewhat less than the "self-denial offering" of Japanese pastors just in San Francisco (Dendo-Dan, 1914).

When the numbers of Japanese warranted it, the "missions" were generally converted into segregated branches of the various Protestant churches—in particular, Methodist, Presbyterian, and Congregational. In the early 1930s the thirty such Japanese churches in California, affiliated with most of the important Protestant denominations, had a total membership of slightly more than 2,000 and a total attendance at Sunday schools of almost 4,500 (Strong, 1933: 171). Interdenominational cooperation among Japanese Christians continued to develop, with proselytizing and social service as the principal avowed purposes. One side effect, however, was to reinforce the separation of the Japanese branches from the main churches; their services were generally given in both languages, and acceptance of the denomination's ecclesiastical form, doctrine, and ritual did not prevent a considerable persistence in Buddhist moral values. When I interviewed a number of Japanese

American clergymen in the 1960s, Christians as well as Buddhists told me that their parishioners were distinguished from the general American population by their deeper attachment to family, their greater respect for parental and other authority. The facts that some Japanese were affiliated with Christian churches *and* that this affiliation was marginal were both to become important. When evacuation threatened, most of the non-Japanese organizations that expressed opposition were church-related, but the main bodies of the churches themselves never exerted anything like their full power to prevent internment.

After the war, the home missions boards decided, with one exception, to dissolve the segregated Japanese churches and invite their former members to join regular congregations. This effort at integration failed, partly because the Japanese resented being deprived of churches that they had largely paid for, mainly because the racial antagonisms engendered or aggravated by the camp experience could not simply be wished away. By the summer of 1946, the policy had been generally abandoned, and segregated churches were being reestablished (U.S. Dept. of the Interior, 1947: 231–34). Over the following decades, more slowly and experimentally, various degrees of integration were achieved, depending on the proportion of Japanese in the community, the relevance of the language question, and sometimes the personality of the clergymen involved.

The development of Christian missions in Hawaii began in a similar fashion. Initially, all the immigrants were Buddhists, and in some early cases the conversions may have had little to do with religion per se.

> A Japanese Christian rates a little higher with the white community [of Kona] than does a Buddhist, and this fact sometimes enters into a conversion. Some say a Christian finds it easier to borrow money at the bank (Embree, 1941: 127).

Such allegations intensified any religious antagonism that may have existed, but "as a rule Christians and Buddhists [got] along together amicably" (Embree, 1941: 128).

A Christian counterpart of Honolulu's Hongwanji Temple is

the Harris Memorial Methodist Church, established in 1888 and now undoubtedly the country's largest Christian congregation with a predominantly Japanese membership. It was at one time entirely Japanese, but since the 1920s an effort has been made to convert it into a cosmopolitan institution. In line with this policy, no ethnic statistics are maintained; but it is estimated that about 75 percent of the members are Japanese, 20 percent other non-Caucasians, and 5 percent Caucasians. One need hardly say which group is the most influential. According to a brochure celebrating the church's diamond jubilee, "We are now settled in a beautifully designed, functionally planned church plant purchased and built at a total cost of $750,000." The architecture of this "plant" deliberately mixes Oriental and Western motifs. One feature is a repository for the ashes of the dead, which are typically kept in the home of the family until the Confucian calendar indicates an appropriate day for the church ceremony. Another specialty is an enormous kitchen and dining hall, where parties of up to 800 persons can be served nine-course banquets. Among middle-class Japanese Christians of any denomination, it is *the* thing to be married at "Harris," and its facilities are generally booked a year or more ahead.

Even so, the previous leadership had been losing parishioners and support. When a new chief minister, Rev. Rhodes B. Martin, was appointed to the post around 1960, his main charge was to build up the church again. He has been studying Buddhism, and he believes he must promote a combination of its principles with those of Christianity, "broadly defined." With his enthusiastic support, the church gave a mammoth Bon dance; his suggestion that it also sponsor a kite-flying ceremony on the day that this is traditionally observed in Japan was vetoed by his board, which wants also to foster Americanization. In his role as counselor, Mr. Martin felt he could be far less frank than he might be with whites. Some of the weddings at which he officiated had been arranged by marriage brokers, who "probably" checked the two families' genealogies in Japan; but he did not think this happened very often any more among his parishioners. So far as he knew, the one important remnant of the traditional concern about blood lines is the continuing reluctance of Naichi to marry Okinawans (cf. pp. 198–199).[11]

This degree of heterodoxy is unusual, or at least so candid a statement defending it by a Christian clergyman. A step in the same direction was the establishment of a joint Christian-Buddhist federation, the American Nisei Council of Religion, based in Sacramento. According to a publicity letter addressed to "Dear Fellow Japanese Americans":

> Although we were brought up with the Oriental culture in an Occidental world, we tend today to lean toward the American culture. This is good and well, but if we leave out the finer ethics of respect to parents, reverence to God, courtesy to fellowmen, and other related moral principles, we may be denying our children an important heritage.
>
> Of all the moral principles of life, perhaps the one that seems to be weakest in our generation is that of our religious life. Could it be that many of us are Buddhists and Christians in name only? . . . Are we departing from the path of our forefathers, who taught us discipline, reverence, and honor toward our fellowmen and God?[12]

MORAL INDOCTRINATION

Both Buddhist temples and Christian churches, however varied in other respects, taught their parishioners the same Buddhist-Confucian ethics. And the moral instruction in Sunday schools of whatever denomination was reinforced through every institution of the Japanese community.

> In the Japanese schools, the Japanese churches, and any organization where the older generation have a part, the subject of obedience and filial piety is frequently brought to the forefront. . . . Because of the total agreement in the community about these primary ideals, no propaganda gets a more effective reiteration (S. F. Miyamoto, 1939: 96).

It is convenient to analyze these universally inculcated moral norms in the context of the Japanese-language schools, for as objects of official denigration they and their curricula were much studied.

In their principal ostensible purpose, the schools were generally ineffective. Whether on the mainland or in Hawaii, the schools did a poor job of teaching Japanese (e.g., S. F. Miyamoto, 1939: 111; Onishi, 1943: 27–28). Since many Issei spoke little or no English and most Nisei learned only the rudiments of Japanese, communication between the generations of a typical Hawaiian Japanese family was often "limited and awkward," conducted in "a hybrid tongue made up of a smattering of Japanese and island dialect" (Mizuta, 1938).[13] In fact, many of the Nisei generation spoke no language really well (Strong and Bell, 1933: 127–30). Though their Japanese was poor, their English was often well below the native standard (Kono, 1934; Inouye, 1967: 44; Reinecke, 1969).

The language schools were ordinarily more effective in moral instruction. According to an analysis of the first six books in this subject used by all the member schools of Hawaii's Japanese Language Association, the number of pages devoted to each of the designated topics was as follows:

> Filial piety, 42.5; respect for elders, 7; gratitude, 11
> Honesty, 27
> Industry, 23; responsibility, 4.5; reliability, 2.5
> Cooperation, 13.5; friendliness, 8
> Kindness, 13; forgiveness, 7.5
> Courage, 9.5
> Courtesy, 9; orderliness, 3; habits, 3; obedience to rules, 2.5; regularity, 2; neatness, 2; punctuality, 1; carefulness, 1
> Self-confidence, 7.5; self-reliance, 5
> Public-mindedness, 6.5; school spirit, 3.5; neighborliness, 3
> Patience, 6; self-control, 6; perseverance, 5.5
> Conscience, 6
> Lack of superstition, 5
> Creative thinking, 3.5; progressiveness, 3; enthusiasm, 1
> Health, 3

Several of the items demand explication:

Filial piety is . . . the core of all morality. It is not mere obedience to parents. . . . Giving any cause for worry to parents, even sickness, is being undutiful to them. . . . Gratitude is a phase of filial piety. One should always be grateful to one's benefactors as, for example, teachers, who are thought of as one's second parents. . . .

Courtesy includes such ideas as propriety, politeness, etiquette. . . . There is always a correct way in doing everything—closing a door, passing out a cup of tea, receiving a bowl of rice. . . . In whatever station in life one may be, . . . there is always a definite way . . . befitting one's position. . . . Courtesy is not mere outward ceremony. Each action or speech is based on respect for the other's feelings, and whatever one does or says must be sincere, for these acts are the expressions of one's personality (Hayashida, 1933).

The author divided character traits into two broad types. The cardinal virtues of an "aristocratic society" were said to be "obedience, humility, contentment, courtesy, and respect for superiors." The traits characteristic of a democracy (culled, perhaps a bit naively, from John Dewey's *Democracy and Education*, which is hardly a representative statement) were said to be "initiative, creative thinking, cooperation, judgment, responsibility, moral courage, and respect for everyone." If one accepts this dichotomy, then the norms taught in the language schools were certainly more "aristocratic" than "democratic." The Japanese teachers rated filial piety highest among the important virtues, while among a sample of public school teachers it was rated next to last. The very last items on the two lists were, respectively, sportsmanship and humility.

How effective were the religious institutions, including the ancillary language schools, in establishing the moral norms of Japanese Americans? American officialdom, backed by a good portion of public opinion, was certain that the "aristocratic" virtues linked Buddhists to the Japanese state. Not only Shinto but also Buddhist priests, as well as teachers in language schools associated with any of the religions, were subject to earlier and more stringent custody during World War II. Even in Hawaii, Buddhist temples and schools were closed and most of the priests were interned. When the generalization behind such policies was disproved, some Buddhists argued that, on the contrary, the extraordinary heroism of Nisei soldiers derived from their Buddhist upbringing. Having acquired the spirit of bushido and learned to be loyal, Japanese Americans were better patriots, irrespective of which country commanded their allegiance. Whatever empirical evidence exists does not support the thesis.

> Rev. Hiro Higuchi, himself a member of the famed 442nd Combat Team, . . . [took] a census of the religious preferences of some 5,000 men in the regiment. The results . . . proved only that "to the average Nisei religion was not very important." . . . 35 percent "preferred" Protestantism, 13 percent Buddhism, 5 percent Catholicism, and 1 percent Mormonism. 46 percent professed no religion at all (Hunter, 1966: 341–43).

To place Buddhism in a causal relation to behavior patterns is difficult in any Japanese American context, for at either end of the supposed link it is virtually impossible to make the necessary discrimination. On the supposed causal side, nominally Christian churches have assimilated important elements of the Buddhist-Confucian ethic, and nominally Buddhist temples have adapted to the moral content of modern American Protestantism. And on the side of the supposed effects, there is also a general lack of differentiation: virtually all Japanese are diligent, law-abiding, loyal to family and country, and so on through a list of civic virtues that, however exceptional among other Americans, are in this instance routine. "How has it been possible for an ethnic community which is religiously so divided, confused, uncertain, and loosely identified . . . to continue to send out into the wider community such a large proportion of persons of integrity and poise?" (Hormann, 1961–62).

Was there a single "folk religion" in the late Meiji period, one "faith of Japan" to which all, or even most, of the emigrants held and from which the characteristics specific to Nisei and Sansei in part derived? If so, its features cannot be found in this or that sect. In America, as historically in Japan, there has been a relative indifference to denominational identity and thus to doctrinal purity. This does not connote, however, any of the moral flabbiness so often associated with an ecumenical movement. Japanese Americans obviously believe in the crucial importance of ethical standards, but this belief is grounded in a heritage broader than any portion of their variegated religious faiths. Sometimes this strong moral bent seems to determine the religion rather than the other way around; thus, in recent decades a relatively large number converted to the Mormon and Seventh-Day Adventist churches. And sometimes, as among the sample of Nisei soldiers, the lack of any professed religion makes no discernible difference in behavior. Indeed, perhaps the most important element of the Buddhist-Shinto patrimony was its separation of religion, concerned mainly with epistemology or eschatology, from day-to-day ethics. One could reasonably expect, then, that a weakening of religious faith was less likely than among Christians to reduce moral concern.

As a minority in an alien and frequently hostile land, the Japanese undoubtedly stressed those elements of their ethical heritage that promoted *kenshin,* "devotion to the common interest." The communal worrying over "the Japanese image," the concerted effort of not merely families but the whole subnation to control the behavior of all its members—these were expressed in such religious manifestations as sermons, counseling by clergymen, and the efforts of churches or temples to enroll children and young people in instructional activities. But the moral and institutional strength of this people has derived only in part—one could even say only in small part—from religious faith and its ecclesiastical supports. One must extend "religion" to the moral lessons taught in the language schools, to the race pride and group coherence maintained by secular institutions, to argue plausibly for a religious-behavioral link (cf. Uyeki, 1960).

In its old-country form, this group coherence had a strongly hierarchical structure: one owed deference to all in a higher status. But acculturation has meant precisely that many of the links defined by obligation have eroded. Even among the Buddhists, who maintain some of its outer forms (like the Bon dance), ancestor worship is hardly a viable tradition in the

United States. When I questioned various respondents on whether, for instance, household shrines were reinstituted after the war, I evinced mostly embarrassed evasions. The worship of the emperor as a living *kami*, as well as the secularized deference to the authority of the Japanese state, began to disappear once Issei opted for permanent residence abroad; and their final end came when the Japanese-American war forced those marginal to both loyalties to choose between them. Some have argued, as we have noted, that *on* and *hō-on*—the patterns of reciprocal obligation—have been transmuted into group loyalty, either narrowly to the subnation or broadly to the whole of the American nation; but it is a thesis that would be hard to test with empirical data of any kind. In something like its original form, the hierarchical structure has been retained in only one place, the Japanese American family.

Notes

[1] Thus, all moral principles are founded in enlightenment: the good varies with the true. The cardinal vice is ignorance expressing itself in egoism; the cardinal virtue is the suppression of egoism through knowledge. According to the orthodox epistemology of most Japanese sects, only our ignorance induces us to distinguish among seemingly different things, for in reality everything is one. It is not even possible to say whether things are or are not, since no sharp gap separates being from nonbeing. This pertains even to whether there is a deity. Adherents of three branches of Zen Buddhism are atheists; most Buddhist philosophers and members of some sects are monotheists of one sort or another; and many of the common people worship a large number of gods, some of Indian or Chinese origin, others taken over from Shinto, and still others a mixture of all three elements (A. K. Reischauer, 1925: chap. 6).

[2] The early effort fully to unite church and state soon foundered, it is true, and the Constitution of 1889 guaranteed all Japanese freedom of religious belief "within limits not prejudicial to peace and order and not antagonistic to their duties as subjects" (Hori and Toda, 1956). This guarantee did not much reduce Shinto's favored place, however, particularly after liberal governments lost out to ones dominated by militarists.

[3] The word is usually, but inadequately, translated "god." *Kami*

applies to anything high or above oneself, such as a deity, an emperor, or an elevated place.

[4] If there *is* such a thing as specific Shinto ethic. "Is Shinto a religion? . . . Where they find no creed, no code of ethics, hardly any metaphysics, no clear line of demarcation between man and God, it is hard for [Western authors] to imagine that Shinto fulfills the necessary conditions to be deemed a religion" (Herbert, 1967: 34).

[5] In the view of one analyst, "In spite of the fact that various religious cults and moral codes have existed in Japan from ancient times right down to the present, Shinto alone expresses the true spirit of the Japanese people. . . . The heart of the cult is not religion at all in the ordinary sense; it is . . . the fundamental psychological characteristics of the Japanese people. According to Tanaka [Yoshitō, lecturer on Shinto at the Tokyo Imperial University], these are three in number: (1) an intellectual nature capacitating for orderliness and unification; (2) a vivacious and practical (literally, 'this-worldly') emotional nature; and (3) a disposition toward development and expansion" (Holtom, 1922: 78–79).

[6] Seido Ogawa and Mildred Christopherson, "The Contemporary Church Situation in Hawaii," prepared for the Cooperative Planning and Strategy Conference, Honolulu, January 12–13, 1965. The authors remark: "With the Japanese in particular, Buddhism has persisted as a mark of ethnic and cultural identity. Indeed its strength may be seen in the fact that even the express strictures placed on Buddhist operations by the demands of World War II, plus the psychological disadvantages of Buddhist identification, did not materially weaken its function within Japanese life." Another set of data as of the early 1960s comes from a sample of 2,106 adults on Oahu Island, who were asked about their drinking habits for a study by the Honolulu Liquor Commission and, incidentally, also about their religion. With no breakdown by race, 15.8 percent reported themselves as Buddhist, 41.7 percent as Protestant (including Mormon), 27.6 percent as Roman Catholic, and the balance as none, other, or not reported. But these findings have been disputed by several local authorities (Schmitt, 1968: 139–40). Within two pages of one study, the number of Buddhists in Hawaii was given as 100,000 in 1963 and 50,000 in 1965 (Hunter, 1966: 373–75).

[7] In Hawaii there was also an intermixture with the other magic-religious elements—"a grass-roots process of exchanging charms, folk remedies, and practitioners among the different racial groups as they mingle in plantation camps and Honolulu's slums. This

parallels the . . . attrition of ancestral languages . . . [into] 'pidgin' English, . . . and this exchange of what sophisticated urban people would regard as superstitions would then be the pidgin religion of Hawaii" (Hormann, 1961–62; cf. Lind, 1952).

8 *Jōdo-shinshū*, literally, "the true Jōdo sect," teaches that man cannot be saved by his works or prayers, but only by the mercy of Amida, "the supreme Buddha of the Paradise of the Pure-Earth of the West." "It is the Buddhist Protestantism of Japan." The most prosperous Buddhist sect, in the mid-1960s it had more than 12.5 million adherents and almost 20,000 temples, among them the largest and most beautiful in Japan (Papinot, 1964, 1:15, 233).

9 Compare the commentary ascribed to Buddha: "Nothing is greater than filial piety, for it is the culmination of virtue. The culmination of all wickedness is ungratefulness to parents."

10 Interview with Miss Joanne Mujata, a past president of the Rainbow Young Buddhist Association, August 1968. My impression from Tom Tonemura, a past president of the Intervarsity Church Fellowship, was that religious life was fairly active on campus, but directed toward an almost nondoctrinal ecumenical association including Buddhism but concentrated on the larger Protestant denominations.

11 Interview with Rev. Rhodes B. Martin, Harris Memorial Methodist Church, August 1968.

12 Form letter from Rev. Isao Horinouchi, Chairman, American Nisei Council of Religion, May 1, 1965.

13 The experience of a bilingual Episcopal priest, assigned in 1939 to a rural church in Washington state, is suggestive. Asked to address the Japanese youth of the area, he "merrily proceeded to speak for a good half hour in eloquent Japanese," only to find out that no one had understood. Some days later, when he was called on to speak to an assemblage of Issei, he did so in English, assuming that persons who had lived in the United States for 25 to 50 years had mastered the language. "When I sat down, everyone applauded—not for what I said, but out of politeness. Gently, an elder informed me that to be understood by the older Japanese, . . . I would have to use Japanese" (D. Kitagawa, 1967: 2). The only statement I found that the pupils of language schools had learned Japanese well was based on responses from the students of one Honolulu school, who presumably exaggerated their competence (Shichiro Miyamoto, 1937).

Chapter 9 ⊚ Family

If the religions of Japan were not efficient in transmitting social values overseas, as we concluded from an analysis of their principal characteristics, then the institution next most likely to have done so would seem to be the Japanese American family. Indeed, as we have seen, the most prominent residue of the Buddhist-Confucian ethic in the United States has been a reinforcement of the family structure. But if one tries to explain the deviation of Nisei from the American norm by the greater authority that Issei exerted over them, this interpretation also raises almost as many questions as it settles. In this chapter on the family, an effort is made both to analyze the influence of Japanese parents over their children and, no less, to describe the inherent limits of that influence.

THE KIN GROUPS OF JAPAN

The phrase "Japanese tradition," when used to denote a base line from which to measure recent changes in the family, can be quite ambiguous. In the new constitution adopted after Japan's defeat in 1945, dramatic changes were instituted in familial relations; and many of the subsequent analyses of these reforms (or of earlier attempts by Japanese liberals to effect them) contrast the "modern" post-1945 family with the earlier "traditionalist" one. But the revolution brought about by the Meiji Restoration does not fit into such unidimensional simplicity. The uniquely rapid metamorphosis of some elements of the economy and society was made possible in part by deliberately retaining, or even revivifying, other elements of the preindustrial past. Thus, with respect to the family Fukutake (1967: chap. 4) notes, for instance, that "the go-between marriage has *become* the standard form," that one clause in the civil code of 1897 "required parental consent for marriage up to the age of 30 for men and 25 for women, thus *reinforcing* the social custom which gave the power of decision over marriage to parents" (italics added).

An analysis of "the" family of Japan, moreover, can easily founder on the very definition of the term. By traditional norms, reconfirmed in the nineteenth century, the nuclear family of man, wife, and children was embedded in a larger and in many respects more important kin group, through which a conscious continuity was maintained over many generations. Under the Meiji code of family law, the basic unit was the *ie*, or house— meaning not the building, of course (though like the English word *ie* also denotes the physical domicile), and also not the household, but rather the "legal institution which came into being when the family was legally recorded in the family register" (George, 1965). Once this registration was made, persons remained members of the house irrespective of their place of residence (cf. the discussion of the *honseki*, pp. 18–19). The admission of new members to the house by birth or adoption, such changes in civil status as marriage and divorce, and the expulsion of recalcitrant members—all these became legal facts only when they were recorded in the register. Property was generally owned not by an individual, but by a house; and the head of the house also usually controlled any income earned by its members, who had to ask him even for their own pocket money.

The structure of the *ie* fitted in with the constraints set by a small, self-sufficient family farm, the dominant type in Japanese agriculture. Continual division of these often tiny holdings would shortly have led to disaster, and a Tokugawa decree had prescribed unitary inheritance as the norm. In general, the oldest son (or, if he was deemed unsuitable, one other son or son-in-law) could expect to take over control of the whole property; and he and his wife and children usually lived with his father until this took place. The pattern was not the same as in classical China or India, where at least the intent was to accommodate all living persons of several generations within a single joint household. In Japan, younger sons stayed on after their marriage only if there were no other possibilities, as in isolated districts far from urban labor markets. Conditions permitting, Japan's response to increasing numbers was fission, the establishment of branch families and, over a sufficient time, of subbranch families. The manner by which these supplementary *ie* could be created was also legally prescribed, as well as the relation among them. The whole clan (or *dōzoku*) was arranged in a hierarchical pyramid: at the top, the stem family carried out special rituals to worship the house ancestors or *kami,* and in reciprocation the branch families owed it various specified kinds of deference and service (Fukutake, 1967: chap. 5).

The relevance of these institutions to emigration is not entirely clear. Immediately after the Meiji Restoration, when the ban on the division of holdings was eased, there was probably a sharp increase in the creation of branch families. Thereafter, however, the number of farm families remained virtually constant at around 5.5 million, with the population growth absorbed into urban industry. In many cases—how many one cannot know—the settlements overseas were undoubtedly established as branch families,[1] so that the sizable remittances sent home sometimes represented more than sentimental ties. So far as one can tell from various post-1945 surveys, some portions of the institutional structure persisted even after its legal base had been eliminated.[2] In short, we can reasonably assume that most of those who emigrated to Hawaii or mainland United States had been raised to see the *ie* and the *dōzoku* as the dominant parts of the familial system and to accept the values implicit in this definition.

The formation of a conjugal unit within the *ie* was regarded primarily as a means of transmitting the house name and property to the next generation. Marriage was more a bond between the representatives of two *ie* than between two persons. Before 1868, Japanese had no word even for *marry,* but only more or less equivalent locutions that meant "to get a wife" for one's son and "to give away" one's daughter. Love was denigrated as animalic; according to a proverbial saying, "Those who come together in passion stay together in tears." Of course, with the partial Westernization of Japanese culture, young people came to desire marriages based on personal attraction.[3] But this view was still deviant during the major period of emigration, especially among the lower-class rural population from which most of the migrants came. As late as the 1920s, according to a survey of 49 hamlets widely distributed over Japan, just under half the male respondents, and only slightly more than a third of the female, believed that "marriage of acquaintances, or individual choice of mate, should be permitted" (Jones, 1926: 38–39).[4]

When a young person of either sex reached the appropriate age, the parents sought out a person suited to act as a go-between, or *nakōdo*. His role was generally honorific: except for the rare semiprofessional, he was reimbursed with gifts and community respect rather than directly with a fee. The go-between saw to it that the two families were of roughly equal standing—though if the bride came from one slightly less well off, that could be an advantage, since the future daughter-in-law would then be easier to control. An especially important part of his task was to check carefully the two families' genealogies, in order to make certain that both bride and groom came of good stock—meaning, in particular, that neither family derived from the Eta or one of Japan's other subcastes.[5] For a respectable Japanese, even one of the lower classes, marriage to an Eta would be unthinkably disgusting. According to a number of local legends, there was a man who married against the wishes of his parents, lived happily for a short period with his beautiful wife, who then gave birth to an idiot child with a spotted complexion; only then was it discovered that she was an Eta. "This is probably the most widespread myth, as it is employed by parents to discourage children from affairs that might result in a 'love marriage'" (DeVos and Wagatsuma, 1966: 139–40).

Once both families satisfied themselves that the prospective bride and groom were acceptable, a marriage was arranged. The wedding was typically a small, secular affair, with only the couple, their parents, and the go-between present. If there was a religious ceremony, it was performed by a Shinto priest, for even to invite a Buddhist priest to a wedding feast would have been a bad omen.[6] Even after the marriage was consummated, the household could withhold registration until the daughter-in-law proved herself to be dutiful, industrious, and capable of bearing healthy children. Until the marriage was registered, she could be packed ignominiously back to her parents' home, together perhaps with her "illegitimate" child (George, 1965).

For a farm family, fecundity was quintessential. Ideally there were three children—first a girl, to be given away in marriage; then a son, the heir to the family property and status; and then a second son, an understudy in case of disaster. According to another proverb, the birth of three daughters could ruin any family's fortune; and until well into the twentieth century surplus infants, especially female ones, were exposed to die. Those that survived were typically raised with singular indulgence; the young wife, deprived of love from her husband and harassed by her in-laws, generally lavished on her children the affection she could feel for no one else (Fukutake, 1967: 47–51; cf. Jones, 1926: 53–54).

Spoiled when young, children were increasingly repressed as they approached maturity, for absolute obedience was incumbent on all past the age of puberty. Filial piety was virtually a religion, with "piety" to be understood in the sense of the ancient Roman *pietas*—that is, the religious sense of household duty.

> There are no greater favorites with the people of Japan than the "Four-and-Twenty Paragons of Filial Piety." . . . For instance, one of the Paragons, . . . though of tender years and having a delicate skin, insisted on sleeping uncovered at night, in order that the mosquitoes should fasten on him alone and allow his parents to slumber undisturbed. . . . But the drollest of all is the story of Rōraishi. This Paragon, though seventy years old, used to dress in baby's clothes and sprawl about upon the floor. His object was piously to delude his parents, who were really over ninety years of age, into the idea that they could not be so very old after all, seeing that they had such a puerile son (Chamberlain, 1905: 165).

That the family (in the broadest sense of the word) was in many respects Japan's dominant institution should be apparent from even so short a sketch of its main features. Its position was reinforced, moreover, by the fact that the law governing it became a general model for the regulation of other kinds of social relationships. The Western family is tied very closely to its biological links; adoption is used mainly to provide homes for orphans or illegitimate children and, from the other side, to enable barren couples to acquire social offspring and heirs. The functions of adoption in Japan, as in most non-Western societies, have been much wider. A man described as the best authority on the subject at the turn of the century, Shigeno Aneki, enumerated no less than ten different categories of adopted persons (Chamberlain, 1905: 17–19). The words *oya-ko*, meaning ordinarily "parent and child," gradually took on a much wider significance. A peasant living constantly on the edge of disaster might get a measure of security through a formal ceremony designating a somewhat wealthier neighbor as his fictional father; another might raise his social status by seeking out an *oya* of a powerful house (Fukutake, 1967: 67). "The notion that a business firm (or enterprise) is analogous to the family persists and colors the entire field of labor relations, especially for small and middle-sized business" (Von Mehren, 1958). "A professor often acts like a father to his disciples, arranging their marriages (woe betide a disciple who marries without his permission!) and choosing his most promising student for his own daughter" (Keene, 1959: 37). Similarly, a distinguished painter, potter, or actor almost always had a son of equal distinction in the same art, suggesting to those who interpret genealogies literally that artistic ability must be more often inherited than among Western races.[7] During the Meiji era, "the sole way in which a foreigner could be naturalized was by getting a Japanese with a daughter to adopt him, and then marrying the daughter" (Chamberlain, 1905: 18).

In sum, what held the conjugal family of Meiji Japan together was not the sometimes ephemeral bonds of romantic love, but the transpersonal and virtually timeless interests of the house, reinforced by admonitions to filial piety so extreme that to modern Western ears they sound almost like caricatures. So many other social relationships imitated the pattern of the family that, for a person brought up in this culture, this was *the* institution, the model for all others. Yet its seemingly invincible strength was time-bound, closely associated with other elements of the Meiji culture, and thus in some degree an anachronism in Japanese cities today or in the overseas settlements of Japanese emigrants.

THE FORMATION OF JAPANESE
AMERICAN FAMILIES

The adaptation of any migrant population to its new environment can be analyzed by contrasting the life styles of the several generations, and this commonplace, as we have noted, is
especially true of Japanese Americans. The disparity between
the cultures of Japan and the United States is greater in most
respects than among the various nations of the Western world,
and thus also the potential differences between immigrants and
their native-born offspring. Far more than with any European
people, moreover, the rates of immigration and of assimilation
were set by political decisions, marked with much greater preci-
sion than vaguer economic and social forces.

During the first decades of Japanese immigration, the sex
ratio of the immigrants, particularly to the mainland, was very
high (Table 9-1).[8] Most of the male migrants were single; and

Table 9-1. Males per 100 Females among
Japanese Americans, 1890–1960

CENSUS YEAR	MAINLAND UNITED STATES	HAWAII
1890	687.3	*
1900	2,369.6	349.2
1910	694.1	220.1
1920	189.8	134.3
1930	143.3	116.1
1940	130.9	110.3
1950	117.7	102.1
1960	92.0	96.9

* Not available.

SOURCES: U.S. Bureau of the Census, *Historical Statistics of the United
States,* 1960, Series A62, 68. *U.S. Census of Population: 1960,* Vol. I,
Part 3, "Alaska," Table 15; Part 13, "Hawaii," Table 15; *Subject
Reports,* "Nonwhite Population by Race," Final Report PC(2)–1C,
Table 3.

of those who were married, many left their wives (and children,
if any) at home, intending to return to them after a relatively

short stay abroad. As with almost any population with so skewed a sex ratio, those few females available were often shared among the males. According to a survey of Honolulu's red-light district in the early years of this century, 82 out of the 107 prostitutes were Japanese (Gulick, 1915: 8–9). On most of the plantations, however, there was no prostitution, and the Japanese had less venereal disease than any other subnation. "Some of the physicians and managers made amazingly strong statements on this point." Even so, managers favored married men over single in both employment and the assignment of jobs, not only because wives helped in the work at lower rates of pay, but chiefly because they found married men to be "more contented, more steady, more diligent, and more free from venereal disease" (Gulick, 1915). The same criterion, one can assume, probably prevailed among mainland employers. To one degree or another, biological or social motives for getting married (or for having one's wife in Japan emigrate) were reinforced by such attitudes.

Since marriage was not primarily a union between two individuals, it was not necessary for the man to return to Japan to seek out a spouse. In the somewhat ethnocentric account of the U.S. Commissioner of Labor, such "ideals and conventionalities of the West" did not exist among Japanese laborers in Hawaii.

> Marriage is a business contract, and many women arrive
> in Honolulu to meet husbands whom they have never seen.
> They have been practically purchased by friends or agents
> of the latter in the home country.[9]

These marriages followed the usual procedure arranged by a go-between, with a friend or relative standing in for the groom at the wedding ceremony. Following the Gentlemen's Agreement of 1907, after which Japan issued passports only to wives of established residents of the United States, among other categories (see pp. 42–44), marriages by proxy became a heated political issue. Following a net remigration to Japan of about 2,500 during each of the two years after the agreement, a renewed migration during the next decade included a large proportion of so-called "picture brides." They joined husbands generally much older than they; among the mainland population in 1942, the median age of Issei males was 55, that of Issei females eight years less (D. S. Thomas, 1952: 18–19).

A high sex ratio is common in the earliest immigration of any nationality, and a frequent response to the consequent deprivation is intermarriage. Not every female, of course, would become the wife of an alien, particularly one of another race; nor would every immigrant, however anxious he might be to acculturate in other respects, want to accommodate to a spouse completely ignorant of his homeland traditions. In Hawaii, of all places on earth, such inhibitions to intermarriage have been least in evidence, and the resultant mixture of races has become a favorite topic of social analysis[10] since the classic study by Romanzo Adams.

> The outstanding fact about the marriage of Japanese in Hawaii [, however,] is that they have married within their own group in higher proportion than any other of the peoples of Hawaii. . . . Marriage is undertaken in the interest of the family, and . . . when the selection is made in this way, marriage with persons of another race or people never takes place (Adams, 1937: 160–61).

The go-between, whether operating in Japan or among Japanese in the United States, investigates thoroughly not only the two candidates' personal characteristics and immediate family background, but their forebears through as many generations as the data permit. Japanese consulates maintain records of Japanese citizens (formerly of all persons of Japanese origin; cf. pp. 18–19) according to their prefectural origin, and these leads can be followed to the more complete lists maintained in each prefecture itself. As Adams noted, "If a Japanese son has an ancestor or an uncle, cousin or other relative, who has suffered from any one of certain diseases or who has been convicted of an infamous crime, he suffers in his status and the chance for a good marriage is lessened." Anyone with a hint of Eta background is automatically excluded, and subgroups within the marriageable population are ranked by relative suitability. In particular, Naichi (or Japanese originating in the main archipelago) look down on Okinawans (a sizable minority among Hawaiian Japanese, whom official records do not distinguish), and marriage between the two subgroups is uncommon (Yamamoto, 1957). In sum, "it is not enough to marry just a Japanese; he should belong to the same prefecture and be of equal rank, and of course so much the better if his family are from the same community in Japan" (Yoshizawa, 1937).

Once the "picture brides" joined their husbands, most Japanese Americans began to have children. The birth rate rose sharply; in California it reached a maximum of 68 in 1920, or four times that of the whites. In the view of West Coast racists, the "invasion" of Japanese, seemingly blocked by the Gentlemen's Agreement, was being realized surreptitiously through this uncommon fertility. In part, the argument rested on the use (whether inadvertent or not) of a measure inappropriate to compare populations with grossly different age structures—namely, the crude birth rate, or the number of births during a year per 1,000 persons in the whole midyear population. Ordinarily the denominator of this fraction contains large proportions of infants, children, and aged; but so long as most of the Japanese were recent immigrants, most were also potential parents. By measures independent of the age structure, the fertility of mainland Japanese was less anomalous, though for a period still comparatively high. In 1920, the gross reproduction rate[11] of mainland Japanese was 3.4, or three times that of West Coast whites. Over the next two decades, however, Japanese fertility fell off rapidly, converging with the white rate by about 1940 (D. S. Thomas, 1950; 1952: 12–13).

In the decades since 1945, the fertility of Japanese·Americans, especially that of urban Nisei, has fallen well below the norm set by native whites (Table 9-2). The reasons, one can hypothesize, are not only such general social-economic factors as residence in cities and high-level occupations, but also the ethnic identity itself.

> Identification with a minority group which does not have a normative system encouraging large families, and which does not prohibit or discourage the use of efficient methods of contraception, depresses fertility below majority levels. . . . The struggle to advance . . . appears to be harder for minority-group members. As [they] enter more generally into competition with the majority community, they

Table 9-2. Fertility Rates of Native Whites and Japanese, by Age and Residence, United States, 1960

| | CHILDREN EVER BORN, PER | | | |
| AGE CATEGORY AND SUBNATION | 1,000 Women | | 1,000 Ever Married Women | |
	Total	Urban	Total	Urban
20–24				
Native white	1,000	866	1,376	1,269
Japanese	436	370	940	860
25–29				
Native white	1,980	1,806	2,189	2,047
Japanese	1,279	1,178	1,469	1,381
30–34				
Native white	2,418	2,244	2,584	2,434
Japanese	1,798	1,672	1,968	1,865
35–39				
Native white	2,488	2,273	2,643	2,445
Japanese	2,165	2,073	2,379	2,314

SOURCE: 1960 Census data, as organized in Calvin Goldscheider and Peter R. Uhlenberg, "Minority Group Status and Fertility," *American Journal of Sociology,* 74 (1969), 361–72. Reprinted by permission of The University of Chicago Press. © 1969 by The University of Chicago. All rights reserved.

may . . . counteract some of their disadvantages by deferring or limiting child-bearing. . . . [Indeed,] achievement values must be present for minority group members to translate the "goals" of social mobility and concomitant acculturation for themselves and their children into "means" which include family-size limitation (Goldscheider and Uhlenberg, 1969).

In sum, the family of Japanese Americans has been in many respects a remarkably powerful institution, both reflecting the strength of the broader community and contributing to it. One reason was the emphasis on filial piety in the Buddhist-Confucian tradition, which Japanese immigrants shared with Chinese. Among the Chinese, however, normal family life based on endogamous marriages was all but impossible for the immigrant generation. When the Oriental Exclusion Act was passed in 1882, there were fifteen Chinese males to one female, and from that date to 1943 not even the few men who had acquired American citizenship were permitted to bring alien wives into the country. The interlude during which "picture brides" were permitted entry, in contrast, reduced the Japanese American sex ratio much closer to parity; most Issei males could marry, even if relatively late in life. Once formed, the marriages were remarkably stable. The rate of divorce among Japanese has generally been the lowest (or, with the Chinese, one of the two lowest) among all the country's subnations (Monahan, 1966).[12]

Manifestly, there is some truth to the hypothesis that the family constituted one important link between the somewhat similar social norms of Meiji Japan and the Nisei generation in the United States. But it is also true that the family's rigidity itself proved to be a source of weakness in the more permissive environment of American culture.

ISSEI AND NISEI

The authoritarian control of the family is stressed so often that one can forget that the rearing of children starts in a quite different mood. As in Japan, among Japanese Americans infancy and early childhood are perhaps the happiest years of the typical life—or so one gathers from such personal documents as an account of a Seattle girlhood (Sone, 1953: 44–47). A familistic culture, virtually by definition, ascribes the highest importance to the next generation, and Japanese American mothers have generally permitted nothing to interfere with the care of their children. As a consequence, for example, Oriental children suffer far fewer accidents than either Caucasian or Negro children of the same ages,[13] especially when neither the parents nor the child had yet adapted to American norms. The acculturated child of acculturated parents, closer to his Caucasian counterparts, was exposed to hazards more often, while the acculturated child of nonacculturated parents had not been taught to cope with whatever dangers he encountered (Kurokawa, 1970).

Some time around puberty, this relative indulgence gives

way to a straiter discipline than the usual American child ever knows. The effect of strict upbringing on the subsequent behavior of the children is to some degree a moot question. But the usual thesis, particularly concerning immigrant parents and their native-born children, is that close parental control is likely to boomerang: a foreign-born father lacks both the status in American society and the requisite knowledge of it to train his offspring efficiently (cf. p. 139). That is, according to a near consensus among criminologists and family sociologists, the rearing of children is more likely to fail when the training has to cross a cultural divide. The thesis appeals to one's common sense, and it has at least some empirical evidence to support it. If we accept this premise, the Japanese family in the United States was as though designed to develop intergenerational revolt, for not only was the discipline more stringent but in several respects the distance between the two generations was greater than in any other subnation:

AGE. The gap between Issei and Nisei was large. In 1942, when (as we have noted) the median ages of Issei males and females on the mainland were, respectively, 55 and 47, the Nisei had a median age of only 17 years. Though not quite so extreme, the same disparity existed in Hawaii, where virtually the whole of the second generation acquired legal maturity in the few years following World War II (see pp. 110–113). Because the immigration had been set largely by political controls, a whole generation was skipped: in their age, and thus in their outlook and authority, Issei fathers were more like grandfathers.

DISCRIMINATION. Impediments to the assimilation of Issei cut them off not only from American society but also to some degree from their native-born sons and daughters. Ineligible for citizenship, Issei were generally excluded also from trades and professions that require a license; in the mainland states where most Japanese lived, they were forbidden to own land. Young as they were, therefore, Nisei often had to act as intermediaries between their families and the broader community—for instance, as the legal owners of the land their fathers worked or, in the camps, as the interpreters to the older inmates of the rulings that governed all their lives. If the restrictions that Issei parents set were unreasonable by general American standards, then they must have seemed triply so to adolescents, or even children, called upon to play adult roles.

The point should not be exaggerated, for some circumstances also brought the two generations closer together. Once they had abandoned the prospect of remigrating to Japan, most of the immigrants did what they could to acculturate to their new homeland. In response to a query about their self-perception in the 1960s, half of Issei respondents rated themselves as mostly American, only 15 percent still as mostly Japanese. "Asked 'In your opinion what is *Seiko*?' (a Japanese word roughly translated into English as 'success,' but classically carrying a much less material connotation), one-third answered in terms of strictly economic success, having assimilated an American meaning to the Japanese concept" (Modell, 1968). On the other hand, many Nisei were far less Americanized than they sometimes imagined. Often the public schools they attended were segregated, or virtually so; and few had close personal relations with whites. According to so sympathetic an observer as Galen Fisher, for many years secretary of the YMCA in Japan, "The fear of intermarriages . . . will continue to act like a wet blanket on all efforts to bring about close and equal friendships and cooperation between the races" (Strong, 1934: 30).

CULTURE. Because Japan is stranger to an American than any Western country of emigration, the cultural distance between the first and second generations was ordinarily greater than in any community of European immigrants. In particular, in many families neither parents nor children were able really to master the others' language, so that communication was necessarily limited to the simplest of statements (p. 183, n. 13). The Japanese-language schools—whose most important function was to link the first and second generations—in fact did no such thing. As we have noted, their pupils typically learned neither Japanese nor English really well. In their moral instruction, the schools reinforced the traditionalist authority of the parents rather than building a bridge between them and their children.

Nihon Gakko [the Japanese American school that Monica Sone attended] was so different from grammar school I found myself switching my personality back and forth daily like a chameleon. At [the grammar school] I was a jumping, screaming, roustabout Yankee, but at the stroke of three . . . I suddenly became a modest, faltering, earnest little Japanese girl with a small, timid voice. . . . [In the Japanese school] the model child is one with deep *rigor mortis*—no noise, no trouble, no back talk (Sone, 1953: 22–25).

The churches, though all were more or less segregated from the white population, also separated the two generations of Japanese. As early as the 1930s, the reader will recall, more than half the Nisei had become Christians, while three-quarters of their parents' generation still remained Buddhists.

KIBEI. Differences between Issei and Nisei were accentuated by the American-born sons who had been sent to Japan to be educated and, on their return, could often fit in nowhere. With the six or more years of schooling that most of them had acquired abroad, they had fewer years of American residence than most of their first-generation parents (D. S. Thomas, 1950). Some soaked up the aggressive Japanese nationalism of the 1930s, and these were prominent in the Tule Lake riots. In other cases, the effect of dispatching provincial adolescents alone into Japan's tumultuous student world was to make them pro-Communist; and during World War II many Kibei taught in U.S. Army language schools or even worked for the OSS and other American intelligence services. In short, the ambivalence characteristic of Japanese Americans' status was likely to be sharpest among those who combined the American citizenship of the Nisei with the greater knowledge of Japanese culture characteristic of Issei.

Kazuo [a Kibei] looked sad and vulnerable. I knew Nisei girls turned up their noses at dating a Kibei. A Nisei girl felt insulted if a man sailed grandly through the door in front of her. She was mortified when he slouched in a chair and leaned back grandly to acknowledge introductions. Kazuo did these things, but he meant no harm. In

Japan he had been waited on by females (Sone, 1953: 128; cf. Arkoff, 1964).

Intergenerational conflict affected every element of domestic life,[14] for both sides could regard even the slightest detail as symbolic. One girl recalled how her mother had tied or slapped her hands to cure her of left-handedness. "It was a shame and a disgrace for a girl to be left-handed. In Japan it is a mark against a maiden and certainly a hindrance to marriage" (Yoshizawa, 1937). According to one of the Nisei who contributed life histories to Dorothy Swaine Thomas and her collaborators, "It was a victory for us whenever my sister was allowed to prepare an American meal" (D. S. Thomas, 1952: 211). He summed up the second-generation point of view as follows: "I could never understand why the Issei were so sensitive and suspicious about the Nisei. Nothing we ever did was right." From the other side, many a parent must have echoed the Hawaiian Japanese mother who said, "I feel like a chicken that has hatched a duck's egg" (Embree, 1941: 145).

One of the recurrent issues was parental control of adolescent behavior. "Dad was strict to the point of tyranny. He wanted to shut me away by myself and not have any contacts with any children my age" (D. S. Thomas, 1952: 481). Another respondent: "My father was always puritanical in his attitudes and he never talked about sex to his children" (p. 323). The mother of one would "raise holy heck" when a 17-year-old boy stayed out till eleven o'clock. After working on the family farm without pay for four years, he went to Los Angeles on his own. "This revolt process then went down to my next sister and so on down the line" (p. 153).

Love matches, even between two Nisei, were frowned on, and many parents tried to prevent them by prohibiting dating. Two "love-stricken" high school students, able to see each other only twice in two years, communicated with letters delivered by "a furtive-eyed boy." The romance came to an abrupt end when they met again in the same class of the Japanese-language school, for the girl had grown to be a good head taller than the boy (Sone, 1953: 129–30). For old-fashioned parents, the only proper marriage was one arranged by a go-between at the initiative of the two families, but on this crucial point they were forced to yield halfway.

> When [my fiancee] and I decided to get married, I told her to write to her parents for permission. Her folks were very surprised and refused to give consent. . . . I wrote to her folks in the best Japanese I could and told them that we were engaged and that I planned to be honorable toward their daughter. . . . Her folks wrote and said that they would have to have full particulars of my family before they would give their consent. . . . A mutual family friend acted as the middleman. It took about a month and a half, . . . and he corresponded with both sides of the family until they were satisfied. . . . It didn't matter if we had a [go-between] or not because we were going to get married regardless of the findings of the family investigations (D. S. Thomas, 1952: 259–60).

So far as I can judge from scattered reports (for example, Embree, 1941: 76) or the interviews that I myself conducted, this has become the standard pattern. Young people fall in love and decide to marry on their own; then a go-between investigates the two families' genealogies and, if his findings are satisfactory, "arranges" the wedding. Seemingly, this is a compromise by which the young people get their way while the parents retain only the empty remnants of an old ritual, but in some instances the form may still be significant. For the pattern reinforces both endogamy within the Japanese community and the exclusion of Eta, since in neither case would traditionalist parents go along with the fiction that they have exercised their "right" to choose their offspring's spouse. Knowing how far their parents will go, young Japanese act accordingly—for only a wholly anomalous one would invite a complete break with his family. Thus, as I was told by an undergraduate at the University of Hawaii, Japanese girls went out occasionally with boys of other races but they would marry only another Japanese, because otherwise "there would be too many differences of opinion on things like how to raise the children." Her own parents, though preferring that she marry a Buddhist, would not object if she acquired a Christian Japanese husband: even the conventional older generation see racial homogeneity as much more important than religion.

Second to courtship and marriage, the main issue that separated Issei and Nisei was politics. The vernacular press was bilingual for years before the internment, with parents reading the Japanese section and children the English. According to a detailed analysis of three Los Angeles newspapers in 1941, "the content of the two [sections] was often quite different, and just before the outbreak of the war, divergencies in editorial policy and in the handling of political reports were especially noteworthy" (D. S. Thomas, 1952: 59). The division in political orientation was reinforced by the JACL, whose periodical—published only in English—stressed the advantages of full and self-conscious Americanization. While in some respects the camp experience obviously bound the whole of the mainland Japanese community together, the extremity of their common state also exacerbated any divisions within it. "Every faction found its convenient scapegoat." Christians and Buddhists suspected each other; those denounced as "collaborators" in turn denounced the "Issei agitators" (D. S. Thomas, 1952: 90). Since most of these disputes pitted one generation against the other, for many the camp experience inhibited even more any significant contact between parent and child.

SANSEI, YONSEI, AND MORE ISSEI

The Issei who entered the United States before Asian immigration was cut off in the 1920s are today a dwindling remnant of old men and women, and even the average Nisei is well into middle age. The experience of the first two generations, the main drama played by any immigrant group, is largely history. The future lies with a progeny for whom most of the events recounted in this volume have been experienced only vicariously.

The very success of the second generation in overcoming discrimination and establishing comfortable places in the middle-class world has meant that their children, the Sansei, have grown up in generally pleasant circumstances. Among all the Nisei I spoke to, whether in Hawaii or especially on the mainland, every one voiced some concern about Japanese teenagers and, if he became frank enough, especially his own children. For the Sansei, an approximation to the general American norm represents a deterioration from their parents' uncommonly high standards and implausible achievements. The delinquency rate among Japanese American youth today, though still lower than that of any other subnation, is both higher than it used to be and possibly rising (pp. 139–142). While the academic record of Sansei students is generally respectable, as a group they are less driven than their parents' generation, more often willing to accept a place in society somewhat less prestigious than the utmost they might have been able to realize. The JACL, *par excellence* the organization of the second generation, worries about the incessant difficulty in recruiting young members; for the typical Sansei, a society designed to foster Americanism among Japanese and to defend their civil rights has outlived its purpose.[15]

There is thus a marked opposition also between the second and third generations. However little of Japanese culture Nisei absorbed from their parents, and however unwillingly, they generally demand obedience (an up-to-date version of the "filial piety" that they had rejected). On the other hand, many Nisei consciously indulge their children just because they remember the harsh loneliness of their own childhood (Howard, 1957; Lyman, n.d.). As Sansei reach the age of marriage and bring into the world the fourth generation, the Yonsei, they give every indication of disappearing into the anonymity of American normality. But this would be, in my opinion, a false prognosis. Like the third generation of many nationalities,[16] Sansei are seeking their roots in the culture of their grandparents' homeland. Courses to foster this interest at the University of Hawaii, I was told, attract many students; and Japanese movies are well attended by young people, most of whom can barely understand a word of the dialogue.[17] Among a minority, a vogue has developed for such refined pastimes as flower arrangement or the tea ceremony. When I attended an exposition of such traditional Japanese arts, youths of the Sansei age bracket were much in evidence as both participants and observers.[18]

It is possible that this sentimental interest in things Japanese among thoroughly American Sansei will be fed by contacts with new immigrants from the old country. After the drastic post-war revisions in American legislation, movement from the countries of Asia was once again permitted. An annual average of some 4,300 immigrated from Japan during 1951–1968,[19] settling mainly in areas with existent concentrations of Japanese Americans. In the literal sense these are also Issei, indistinguishable in the place-of-birth records of the census (except implicitly by age) from those who had immigrated before 1924. But post-1945 Japan is hardly the same country from which those first Issei departed, and at least some of the new immigrants seem to be quite different types.

The one group of new Issei that has been studied is the considerable number of Japanese war brides. American servicemen of all races brought back wives from both Europe and Japan. A *priori*, one might expect racially homogamous marriages to be more successful, even in the tolerant milieu of Hawaii, but the contrary seems to have been the case. Both European girls who wed Nisei and Japanese girls who wed non-Nisei Americans reported general satisfaction with their marriages, but this was not true of Japanese girls wed to Nisei (Table 9-3).

Young females in Japan, like those in any of the other war-ravaged countries, undoubtedly felt they were marrying up when they wed a representative of the affluent victor. Many prepared for life in their new country by learning English and attending classes that the American Red Cross sponsored in such mysteries as American cooking, table manners, child care, and the like.

Table 9-3. *Percentage of 324 War Brides Who Reported a "Good" Marital Adjustment in Hawaii, by the Race of the Two Spouses*

| | HUSBAND | |
WIFE	Japanese	Not Japanese
Japanese	39	75
Caucasian	70	51

SOURCE: Yukiko Kimura, "War Brides in Hawaii and Their In-laws," *American Journal of Sociology*, 63 (1957), 70–76. Reprinted by permission of The University of Chicago Press. Copyright 1957 by The University of Chicago.

If their husbands were Nisei, they perceived them as Americans; for as Japanese, most of them were seen by the brides' families as of rather inferior status and lineage. Between the husband and wife, this ambiguity could probably have been resolved, but it was sharper in the relations between the sophisticated, generally well educated native of modern Japan and her Hawaiian mother-in-law, who usually expected some of the deference traditionally due her. Even to converse was difficult, for the war brides, all of whom spoke standard Japanese, felt contempt for the rural dialect (well interspersed with English and Hawaiian pidgin) that their in-laws typically used. The Japanese language, as we have noted, still indicates in every phrase and nuance the social status of the person being addressed, and the brides found the speech their in-laws used often "vulgar and extremely uncouth," "insulting to the point of being unendurable." Some portion of this antipathy, obviously, was reflected in the attitudes of the wife toward her husband, and vice versa (Kimura, 1957; cf. Kimura, 1963).

In sum, the thesis most generally offered to explain the extraordinary success of Nisei—that the strong family structure of Japanese Americans afforded the young the best possible chance to overcome even vicious discrimination—is also not wholly adequate. The discrepancy is enormous between Japanese Americans of the first and second generations—in age, in culture, in occupational level, in social roles. Far smaller intergenerational differences in other minorities have repeatedly been cited as the cause of precisely the social pathologies so markedly lacking among Nisei. Whatever made this second generation different, whatever gave the Nisei the strength to thrive on adversity, it was more than the continuity from the culture of Meiji Japan that their family and religion effected.

Notes

[1] On the other hand, Vogel (1967) found in his analysis of recent rural-urban migration within Japan that "the family which established itself in the city was typically a nuclear family of husband and wife with considerable independence from the rural *ie*. This

is in striking contrast, for example, to many areas in China and to the Batak of Indonesia, where the migrants to the city maintained ownership or some hope of eventual ownership of property in the rural areas." Since most overseas migrants from Japan initially intended to return, this contrast suggests that they may well have retained stronger links to their house than those who moved to cities.

2 In the 1950s, about 43 percent of a sample of villagers (as contrasted with only 16 percent of an urban sample) preferred the prewar civil code that had given the *ie* a legal status, and 72 percent (as contrasted with 19 percent) still believed that when the oldest son marries he should continue to live with his parents (Fukutake, 1967: 53). From 1920 to 1960, the proportion of households in small towns and villages that included only a single nuclear family remained almost constant at approximately 55 percent, while in the country as a whole it rose from 60 to 65 percent (*ibid.:* 38). In his study of postwar rural Japan, Dore (1959: 393ff.) found a remarkable persistence of the submissive acceptance of the authority structure associated with a household's dominance.

3 The changes in familial attitudes in Japan and consequently in the conflict between generations have been parallel to the same process among Japanese Americans, but the topic is too peripheral to the main theme to analyze it here. Several of the general works on Japan already cited in other contexts (e.g., Beardsley, Hall, and Ward, 1959; Hall and Beardsley, 1965; Fukutake, 1967) discuss it; and more specific analyses of changes in family structure and behavior are to be found in many books (e.g., Sugimoto, 1966; Koyama, 1961; Blood, 1967) and, of course, still more journal articles (e.g., Vogel, 1961; Wagatsuma and DeVos, 1962; Koyano, 1964; Kurokawa, 1968).

4 As one of the earliest attempts to use surveys in the analysis of any non-Western society, Jones's almost unknown work is of considerable interest. Included in his "questionary" were, for instance, such indices of primitiveness as the belief in various superstitions: about a third of his respondents held that a fox can bewitch a person; 59 percent of the male respondents and 64 percent of the female affirmed that "charms or prayers issued by the temples [are] useful in keeping away sickness or in curing disease" (pp. 64–67). Other queries tested the importance of group controls of individual behavior; thus, to the question "If you were assaulted, lied to, or basely insulted, what would you do?" three-quarters of the males and two-thirds of the females checked the reply "Control yourself and not mind," with the bal-

ance of the responses distributed over "Strike back," "Seek revenge later," and "Call the police" (pp. 55–56).

[5] As with most oppressed minorities, there is no neutral designation for the Eta. During the Tokugawa era, this was the official term, used in government documents and census classifications. Then as now, it was pejorative and offensive; the Chinese characters used to write the word mean literally "full of filth." From the beginning of the Meiji era, various euphemisms were adopted and successively abandoned. The most common terms in present-day Japan are *buraku* (which means simply "hamlet" or "community") for an Eta ghetto and thus *burakumin* for a resident of such a community. In the United States, however, those who know of the existence of the Eta recognize no other name for them—and carefully avoid using this designation in polite society (cf. pp. 228–229).

[6] How faulty the cultural continuity can be among Japanese Americans is suggested in the description offered by a Nisei author: "Buddhist weddings have been shortened and thereby resemble Christian ceremonies" (Kitano, 1969: 87).

[7] Anyone who has tried to learn something of classical Japanese prints soon becomes aware of the confusion of names, which were in many cases changed several times as an apprentice moved from one master to another. Take Katsukawa Shunshō as an example. "Shunshō had a number of talented pupils; among them were Shunkō, Shunei, Shunchō, Shunzan, Shunsen, Shunjō, and Shunrō (this last was an early name of Hokusai)"; in each case the first syllable was the same as in the master's name—Muneshige Narazaki, *The Japanese Print: Its Evolution and Essence* (Palo Alto, Calif.: Kodansha International, 1966), p. 130.

[8] At the time of writing, data from the 1970 census were not yet available, but the lack is not significant for the point being made —that for two generations or so the unbalanced sex ratio made endogamous marriages impossible for a large portion of the Japanese immigrants, especially, but not exclusively, on the mainland.

[9] U.S. Bureau of Labor Statistics, *Report of the Commissioner of Labor on Hawaii, 1902* (Washington, D.C.: Government Printing Office, 1903), p. 37. Marriages by proxy occasionally took place also among the resident population if convenience so dictated (cf. Blood, 1967: 4).

[10] For bibliographic guidance, see in particular Schmitt, 1965; Parkman and Sawyer, 1967. Concerning the genetics of interracial crossing, see Morton, 1967.

11 That is, the number of daughters imputed to the average woman passing through her fecund period, on the assumption that the current age-specific fertility would continue.

12 Also in Japan, contrary to the tenets of American sociology, the family "became more stable in the period of economic development and urbanization" (Taeuber, 1958: 30–31).

13 Bureau of Maternal and Child Health, California Department of Public Health, "Epidemiology of Childhood Accidents" (Berkeley, California, 1960–63).

14 It is not meant to suggest that no Japanese American family escaped such conflicts. One respondent reported, for instance, "I've had a very happy childhood and I never did have any big conflicts" (D. S. Thomas, 1952: 456). But such recollections were unusual among the sample that contributed the life histories assembled in *The Salvage*, and in this case, it should be noted, the respondent was not a Nisei but an Issei who had immigrated as a child.

15 The editor of the JACL weekly discussed a debate he had had with some young Japanese on the question of whether the "JACL has 'outgrown' its usefulness because the challenges which served as a basis for its organization thirty years ago do not exist today." One suggestion was to go beyond the issues specific to the organization and "join the fight with other Americans to make America and the rest of the world a better place in which to live" (*Pacific Citizen*, September 10, 1965).

16 See Marcus Lee Hansen, *The Problem of the Third-Generation Immigrant* (Rock Island, Ill.: Augustana Historical Society, 1938); reprinted in *Commentary*, November 1952.

17 In 1968 there were six Honolulu theaters that showed only Japanese movies, usually with English subtitles. In that year the star feature was *Yoake No Futari* (Rainbow over the Pacific), filmed in Hawaii to commemorate the centenary of the first Japanese immigration.

18 Every Sunday Honolulu's Japanese Chamber of Commerce and the Consulate General of Japan jointly sponsor a Culture Show, which includes Japanese music, dancing, clothing, and household ceremonies.

19 U.S. Bureau of the Census, *Statistical Abstract of the United States, 1969* (Washington, D.C.: U.S. Government Printing Office, 1969), Table 125.

Chapter 10 ◉ Subnation

The conclusions of the last two chapters were negative, but not entirely so. To some degree, of course, the values of Meiji Japan were inculcated in each American Nisei within his family, just as to a probably lesser degree they were included in children's religious upbringing. What is noteworthy is that the propositions are only partly valid, for they pertain, after all, to the two principal socializing institutions. If family and church were not the only entities that instilled distinctive ethical norms and behavior patterns in the second generation, what other factor can explain the Japanese American anomaly?

The reader who has come this far will recall that the boundaries Japanese draw in their institutional controls very often include the whole of the ethnic community. The main bond of the Japanese American family, for instance, has been neither mutual affection, as with the modern Western type, nor authoritarian control, as in the Buddhist-Confucian model; its strength derives principally from the fact that the family is solidly embedded in a supportive Japanese community. Even old-fashioned parents are relatively indifferent to an interfaith marriage of their son or daughter, while even thoroughly Americanized Sansei typically avoid one that crosses racial lines. Trade unions, whether of Hawaiian plantation workers or, later, of Los Angeles fruit vendors, initially excluded all but Japanese as members. Often Nisei students provided prospective employers with recommendations from Japanese American professors in academic disciplines totally alien to their own studies. In one situation after another, in short, the individual Japanese has derived moral and financial support from not merely this or that specialized institution, but from the whole of what I have chosen to term his "subnation"; and in reciprocation he has manifested a group loyalty usually designated by such half-pejorative labels as "race pride" or "nationalism."

This chapter offers the thesis that the principal solution to the anomaly we have been examining lies in that relation between individual and ethnic group.

THE CONCEPT OF SUBNATION

The statuses of an individual are usually divided, following Ralph Linton's apt suggestion, into two types—ascribed and achieved. In analyses of a society, the counterpart of an individual's achieved status is social class. To measure the movement of a person up the social ladder, or of a nation toward full economic development and cultural modernity, analysts use changes in occupation, education, income, and rural-urbanmetropolitan residence—all as indices of social class. In contrast, some classifications are defined by criteria that are (or are perceived to be) more or less immutable: race, origin, national stock, language, citizenship, religion, and region (in the sense of a cultural rather than a political subdivision). These define what Harold Isaacs has called a person's "basic group identity."

> By "basic group identity" I mean the set of identifications which every individual shares with others from the moment of his birth: his ethnic being, his family and group name, his color and physical characteristics, the whole culture-past providing him with, among other things, his language, religion, arts, modes and styles of life, and inherited value system. . . . The primary function of this basic group identity is to provide a person with some measure of supporting self-acceptance and self-esteem.[1]

On a world scale, the institution associated with each basic group identity is, of course, the nation. The etymology of *nation* (the word derives from Latin for "to be born") suggests a people linked by common descent from a putative ancestor; and other generally accepted characteristics are a common territory, history, language, religion, and way of life.[2] Obviously not all nations conform to every element of this definition. No single set of ancestors produced the varied immigrants who made up the population of the United States; some nations comprise several language or religious groups; the Gypsy nation has no common territory; nearly all the new African nations lack all the criteria except a common territory, and very often that was arbitrarily demarcated by an alien power. The key characteristic, which can make up for a lack of any of the others, is group consciousness, a sense of identity with kind. For as members of a nation, "human beings interact not so much in terms of what they actually are but in terms of the conceptions that they form of themselves and of one another."[3]

Within most nations are smaller units that also depend on the individuals' ascribed status or basic group identity, but there is no unambiguous word for this second broad type of population classifications. I have used "subnation" as the most appropriate term. Except for their smaller size, subnations have the main features that we associate with nationality: an actual or putative biological descent from common forebears, a common territory, an easier communication inside than outside the group, a sentimental identification with insiders and thus a relative hostility toward outsiders. As with nations, not all subnations need show every distinguishing characteristic.

Subnations are also like nations in that their precise boundaries are often difficult to fix, especially when they lack a formal organization (the counterpart of a state). This imprecision is not a fault of the concept,[4] for it reflects reality exactly. For example, some Jews see themselves (and are seen by others) as a religious group; others insist that Jews are an ethnic stock, members of a nation partly in exile, carriers of a particular culture, or some combination of these. As another instance, persons in Mexico who wear huaraches and speak an Indian language are designated in the census as "Indians," and those who wear shoes and speak Spanish are not. That some "races" are defined by cultural characteristics, some "ethnic groups" by racial characteristics, and so on through all the vagaries of the many systems of classification—these are problems unavoidable to one using the statistics (cf. Petersen, 1969). But at a conceptual level, the genus of *subnation* can be defined without concern about how one species in it is differentiated from another.

The large literature on subnations (by whatever designations) includes many works supposedly showing that, in some sense, the object of the analysis does not exist. This curious notion derives mainly, one supposes, from Marx. In his conception of any society, since the "real" (virtually in the Platonic sense) structure is set by the individuals' relations to the productive system, any culturally defined social group is either pathological (religion is "the opium of the people") or false ("the workers have no fatherland"). Enthusiastic ecumenicists, similarly, have sometimes come close to asserting that no differences exist among religions, vehement internationalists that none distinguish one nation from another. This persistent denial of man's basic group identity takes several forms, the most important of which are noted briefly:

IMPRECISE BOUNDARIES. The most pervasive expression of the thesis, of course, has been to deny biological differences. Since "there are no pure races," some conclude that "there is only one race—the human race" or that, in a shorter paraphrase, "there are no races."[5] Even at a biological level the argument is fallacious, since from the slightest knowledge of systematics we know that not merely subspecies (that is, races) but species, and indeed all classificatory divisions up to and including phyla, have both characteristic features *and* vague boundaries, and that this follows from the process of evolution itself. To apply the criterion of precise limits across the board would eliminate all biological classification and every category used in social analysis as well. For the distinction is also inexact between rural and urban, between working-class and middle-class, between employed and unemployed, even between male and female if we are interested in social roles rather than physiology.

NO INNATE DIFFERENCES. Races that do exist, according to a second line of argument, are of no social importance, for they are distinguished only by superficial characteristics. Curiously, those social scientists who believe themselves farthest from biological determinism are the most likely to express it in this context. Since no significant genetic variations set one race off from another, they aver, there are no significant differences of any kind.[6] Even before an audience of professional social scientists, one must hesitate today to assert that Negroes as a group are inferior—inferior in education, in health, in family structure, in motivation, in various other attributes decidedly relevant to their place in society. That these several kinds of inferiority originated in social conditions rather than genetic inheritance is true, but this does not mean that it can be abolished quickly or easily. In his "principle of cumulation," the underlying theory of *An American Dilemma* (see p. 3), Myrdal pictures the Negro as a passive object of either white prejudice or liberal reform. The theory has been proved inadequate. For with the substantial improvements gained during the past two decades,[7] Negroes shifted their reference group: once pleased to have risen above their fathers' status, now many blacks are aggressively dissatisfied that they have not yet achieved full equality with whites. One consequence of massive civil-rights programs has been to exacerbate racial conflict, to encourage the rise of black violence and white backlash. That this came as a surprise to everyone in the field of race relations was due, at least in part, to sociologists' fixation on biological equality (in analyses of postcolonial economies, "the revolution of rising expectations" had become a cliché).

DIFFERENCES ONLY TEMPORARY. How often have we been told that communication and therefore mutual understanding are everywhere improving? The trends since 1945 have provided a needed shock to such a theory of ethnic relations. Whether it is religion that distinguishes one subnation from another (as in Northern Ireland and the Netherlands), or language (as in Belgium and Norway), or race (as in Kenya and the United States), or various combinations of these (as in Canada and India), the increase has been notable in the number, self-awareness, and pugnacity of subnations. To say that this was not in accord with dominant theory would be an understatement.

The most important American theorist of the last generation, and one whose influence is still considerable, was Robert E.

Park of the University of Chicago. He developed the thesis that all interethnic relations go through an invariable and irreversible four-stage succession of contact, competition, accommodation, and assimilation. Progress along this line is inevitable—except when something interferes with it. Once its premises are accepted, the schema is unassailable; for the numberless subnations that have remained distinct for decades, or even for centuries, can be explained away by the specific circumstances, and the dogma that full amalgamation will be attained "eventually" remains intact.[8] For example, according to Winifred Raushenbush (an associate of Park's who applied his theory to the Japanese in California), the orderly progression from competition to accommodation was impeded in Florin by the fact that the Japanese who had congregated there too visibly dominated the town, which in any case was too close to Sacramento, the state capital and therefore the center of California's anti-Oriental agitation. Since these impediments were lacking in Livingston, another town in California, she found the race-relations cycle there to be proceeding on schedule.[9]

At the time that Park was writing his essays, immigration was an important political issue. Those who favored restrictive legislation argued that immigrants were unassimilable; and liberal professors, who opposed such legislation, countered with the theory that assimilation was not only possible but inevitable. At that time, immigrants also felt too insecure to aspire to any fate but full integration, but with the partial realization of this goal, their attitude typically changed.

The writings of several American Jews, who as a group were both the least secure and the best educated of the new immigration from Southern and Eastern Europe, marked successive stages in a theory of acculturation. In his play titled *The Melting-Pot*, Israel Zangwill paid homage to "the great Alchemist [who] melts and fuses them with his purging flame—Celt and Latin, Slav and Teuton, Greek and Syrian," and, as represented in the play's hero and heroine, Jew and Gentile. Horace Kallen used the phrase "cultural pluralism" to legitimize, on the contrary, the retention of those old-country traits consistent with a political loyalty to the new country; and Samuel Lubell argued that in fact, and correctly for all minorities, such a pluralism also includes vestigial loyalties to foreign states. The series reached a kind of climax in Will Herberg's division of American subnations into the remarkable triad, Protestant-Catholic-Jew—whose numbers at the time that he wrote the book approximated, respectively, 79 million, 31 million, and under 4 million.[10] Within one generation, if we accept these widely read and quoted books as representative, an immigrant group went from a joyful anticipation of its disappearance in native American society to a demand for full corporate equality with the far larger subnations of the earlier settlers.

Were there then no theorists who, by present standards, can be judged better than these? Paradoxically, America's first significant analysis of subnations, published originally in 1906, was in some respects the most perceptive. This was William Graham Sumner's *Folkways*. Folkways—a word that he coined —are "the habits of the individual and the customs of the society," developed originally perhaps to satisfy some need but eventually followed out of simple tradition, which becomes "its own warrant, not held subject to verification by experience." Folkways are assumed to be "right" and "true"; if they have to be rationalized with general ethical or epistemological principles, Sumner termed them *mores*, a Latin word he introduced into English. Mores "do not stimulate to thought, but the contrary. The thinking is already done and is embodied in the mores." Each nation and subnation—to one degree or another, by definition—is associated with its own set of folkways and mores; and each, therefore, has a "view of things in which one's own group is the center of everything, and all others are scaled and rated with reference to it." To this universal characteristic, Sumner gave the name "ethnocentrism." And in its ethnocentric view every group divides the world into two parts—itself, the "in-group," and everyone else, the "out-group" (again terms, since become routine in sociological analysis, that as a pioneer Sumner had to invent). Group differences, because they are based on distinctions regarded as relatively immutable, are likely to persevere. "It is not possible to change [the mores] by any artifice or device, to a great extent, or suddenly, or in any essential element. . . . Changes which are opposed to the mores require long and patient effort, if they are possible at all."[11]

JAPANESE AMERICANS AS A SUBNATION

An attempt has been made in this book to go beyond mere description or moral indignation. The main point has been to pose a fundamental analytical question—why one colored minority subjected to unusually harsh discrimination has not reacted in accord with current popular notions and sociological theory, which in this case are the same. Here the intent is both to offer an answer to that question and, in the process, to amend some of the deficient portions of earlier theorizing. The discussion is arranged, following Blalock's stimulating initiative,[12] under a series of general propositions.

1. *Subnations exist.*

According to the classificatory system of the census, the Japanese constitute a separate race in the population of the United States. That is to say, they are distinguished by a number of inherited characteristics (a gene pool) which derive from both their origin and their boundary-maintaining endogamy. In a painstaking study, Shapiro showed that nonmigrants in the main areas of Japanese emigration, Hawaiian Issei, and Hawaiian Nisei of homogamous unions differed significantly in a long list of physical traits. Like the earlier study by Franz Boas, Shapiro's work has often been cited as evidence that heredity and environment interact—a point that has since become a commonplace. The plasticity of a genetically unmixed line, however, is limited: "I emphatically do not believe that the Japanese will ever become [physically] identical with Hawaiians as a result of enjoying an identical environment, and I do not expect to find that the Japanese in Hawaii will eventually lose all similarity to the stock from which they came" (Shapiro, 1939: 202).

Whether Japanese should be classified as a separate race depends on whether a particular analysis is better served by a smaller (for example, only Naichi) or a larger (for example, Oriental Americans) gene constellation. But apart from how the genetically defined group is bounded, the concept of *race* is ordinarily less appropriate than *subnation*, since Japanese are distinguished by cultural as well as physical characteristics. Their unity in some instances may have depended on a nationalist identification with Japan, in others on their common language or religion, in others on the effect of physical differences, in others on a sense of identity with the group. Since it is usually impossible to determine which factor was most important in each situation, classificatory systems based on narrowly defined, overlapping criteria are unsatisfactory. We solve the problem by using a broader term that leaves this question open.

2. *Subnations ordinarily persist, and often those that disappear are replaced by others.*

Apart from his general importance as an influential theorist of race relations, Park is significant in this context because he both wrote about Japanese Americans and influenced others (in particular, the sociology department of the University of Hawaii) who analyzed them in greater detail. The four essays reprinted in *Race and Culture* that deal with Japanese (Park, 1950: chaps. 9, 14, 17, 19) are prime instances of the author's typical ambiguity. "Race prejudice is a function of visibility," and, of course, "physical traits do not change" (pp. 247, 252). Even so, "the race problem turns out . . . to be a problem of communication," and "there is no way of preserving existing social barriers except by preserving the existing animosities that buttress them" (pp. 253–54). Thus, "isolation is at once a cause and an effect of race prejudice" (p. 228), and everywhere isolation is breaking down. "The melting pot is the world" (p. 149). In short:

> Race relations . . . can best be interpreted if what they seem to be at any time and place is regarded merely as a phase in a cycle of change which, once initiated, inevitably continues until it terminates in some predestined racial configuration . . . consistent with an established social order of which it is a part. Race relations in Hawaii today seem to be approaching the terminus of such a cycle (p. 195).

Most of those who have written about race mixture in Hawaii have accepted this "optimistic" prognosis. For one important example:

> Looking forward two or three hundred years, one may envisage the population of Hawaii as made up almost wholly of . . . descendants of the old Hawaiians . . . [and] peoples of Europe and . . . Asia. They will be approaching a condition of a stable race mixture and they will call themselves Hawaiians. They will be culturally homogeneous (Adams, 1937: 113).

Or, as a more extreme statement, characteristic of the author's buoyant view of all aspects of Hawaiian society:

> It [is] only a question of time—certainly less than another generation—before Hawaii's population will have become so extensively interbred as to make the retention of the present system of racial categories a useless pretense (Lind, 1961–62).[13]

The only important exception to this consensus is in a work about Hawaii written by a foreigner and published abroad:

> There is a consciousness of racial differentiation in general as . . . in the United States at large—and of the ethnic composition of Hawaiian society in particular. In other words, there is no blurring of the ethnic distinctions in spite of common citizenship and of frequent intermarriage. . . . The present residential pattern is that of a number of subsections, each with a specific [ethnic or ethnic-class] character. . . . There are occupations filled by a succession of ethnic categories in much the same way as the slums serve as a transitional stage for people of many ethnic categories. . . .
> Recreational and civic associations are frequently based on ethnic descent. . . . Once established [for whatever reason], such associations grow stronger on account of accumulative sentiments [favoring] particularistic cultural patterns. . . . It is among these voluntary social and religious associations in particular that it is possible to see the emergence of a [centrifugal] movement. Instead of the

earlier centripetal one of integration, assimilation, Americanization—in short, the melting-pot concept—we see a
persistence and reemergence of voluntary associations on
an ethnocultural basis (Wittermans, 1964: 68–69, 94–97,
109–11).

In my opinion, this last analysis of Hawaii's multi-ethnic society is by far the more accurate. Two trends are apparent. Subnations have successfully demanded that the definition of their
public roles be color-blind, and in many instances they have
consciously retained the means of carrying out their private
roles in relative seclusion.

Marriages across race lines are so frequent in Hawaii compared to any other place in the world that one is tempted to
exaggerate their importance. It is true that the offspring from
some of these marriages lose their ethnic identity (or, better,
acquire the new one of "Cosmopolitan"), but culturally—rather
than racially—most acquire the ethnic identity of only one of
their parents. The two dominant groups in the islands, whites
and Japanese, remain entirely distinct, with their edges barely
blurred. Especially the Japanese, who in less than a generation
have gone from wartime obloquy to political and economic
power, are thoroughly conscious of their group identity. Sometimes the prognosis in Hawaii of a melting-pot amalgamation
(as on the mainland in the 1920s) is intended less as a forecast
than as a defensive gesture by Orientals or white liberals, not
yet certain that racial hostility is entirely dissipated.

3. *As subnations acculturate in some respects, they thereby attain the status and the self-confidence to maintain or reassert
their independence in other respects.*

This is why Park was mistaken in his assertion that the race-
relations cycle, "once initiated, inevitably continues until it
terminates in some predestined racial configuration." Three examples have been given of a contrary trend—the manifestations
among Sansei of third-generation nativism, in line with Hansen's thesis (pp. 208–209); the response of black militants to
improved opportunities for social-economic assimilation; and

the successive definitions of acculturation that four prominent Jewish analysts offered.

4. *Identification with an in-group implies a comparative rejection of all out-groups.*

A *Dictionary of International Slurs* lists what the author terms "ethnophaulisms," which denigrate in the language of every people all other peoples with whom it has been in contact. A volunteer collaborator was able to collect some 1,800 such slurs in Japanese, but unfortunately before his manuscript could be published, it was destroyed in a fire.[14] The universality of the phenomenon suggests that praise of one's own kind and disparagement of all others will not easily give way to antidefamation leagues. The campaign to abolish prejudice and discrimination, which constitutes a considerable part of the field of ethnic relations,[15] will never be completed.

In their concern with what they think of as "relevant" issues, few analysts of ethnic relations pose the question whether efforts to abolish prejudice and discrimination may not be, even in moral terms, partly ill considered. The vision of the earth's population *gleichgeschaltet* into one-world uniformity has an obverse side—the universal loss of each individual's basic group identity, the epidemic spread of alienation. One important reason that Japanese Americans overcame their extraordinary hardships is that they truly believe (as do Jews) that they are innately superior, that others are inferior. And an important reason that Negroes have made far less progress against no greater odds is that too many of them (like most other colored minorities in the United States) accept as valid the depreciation expressed in others' prejudices. From the point of view of a democrat, the balance that Wittermans saw in Hawaii is a healthy one, with the bureaucratic anonymity of public life balanced by continuing group identity in cultural relations.

5. *All ethnocentrism is founded on myth to some degree, but peoples who can base their self-esteem on little else than myth make poor neighbors.*

The rich become richer, and of no kind of capital is this aphorism truer than of group pride. The self-confidence attained from identifying with Meiji Japan's amazing record gave Issei a psychological edge, which became larger when they and their sons were also able to overcome every obstacle. The article of Shinto faith that the emperor is a direct descendant of the sun god (compare Jews' self-appraisal as the chosen people), or the common legends of family exploits and honors—these myths counted little against the solid reality of Japanese achievement. The very fact that Japanese Americans retained vestigial ties, at least of sentiment, to an alien land and culture enabled them —however paradoxically—to acculturate more readily to their new homeland.

In contrast, the minority most thoroughly imbedded in American culture, with the fewest meaningful ties to an overseas fatherland, are American Negroes. As black intellectuals who have visited Africa discovered, their links to *négritude* are usually too artificial to survive a close association with this—to them, as to other Americans—strange and fascinating continent.[16] Since a Negro can name no other homeland, he has no refuge when the United States rejects him. Placed at the bottom of this country's scale, he finds it difficult to salvage his ego by self-evaluation in another currency. And the efforts to construct a heroic past, either somewhere in Africa or in the prosaic or squalid history of American Negroes, have probably only aggravated this subnation's psychological insecurity.

With the large postwar influx of Negroes to West Coast cities, they came into contact with Japanese for the first time. The meeting was not the most cordial, for reasons pointed out by the English-language editor of one of San Francisco's two Japanese newspapers.

We have had the pleasure of meeting some outstanding Negro leaders, . . . [but] more occasions to come in contact with lesser Negroes who make a great number of our people afraid to come out to Nihonmachi [the Japanese quarter] at night. Some of our respected Negro leaders . . . will tell you the reason that there is a large number of crimes being committed by the Negroes is because the colored people are not equally treated. They will tell you that the reason there are more Negro dropouts from high schools is because the colored children are not given an opportunity to follow the kind of work they want after graduation. They blame society for their womenfolk's giving birth to illegitimate children and living on welfare checks, . . . for the petty thefts and rapes being perpetrated by their men in Nihonmachi. In short, they blame all of their antisocial habits and cultural maladjustment on the "unjust" community in which they live.

We have yet to hear any Negro voice "blaming" themselves for their social maladjustment. . . . There is a crying need on the part of the Negro community as a whole to make a concerted effort to better themselves.[17]

6. *A people that enjoys cultural unity is not shattered by internal divisions, but sometimes the contrary.*

Nineteenth-century Japan was unitary to a remarkable degree, with ethnic, linguistic, and religious uniformity and geographical isolation. "Westernization of Japanese intellectual and cultural life had the paradoxical effect of heightening the Japanese' sense of their separateness . . . [and] the alienness of Western intellectual culture" (Dore, 1964). But within this singularity, Japanese society was also split along many dimensions. The rigid class structure was reflected in language and other elements of the culture. Regional, prefectural, and village patriotisms were strong. Not only did these divisive attitudes persist overseas, but emigrant communities developed some types of their own. Mainland Japanese look down on the uncouth peasant types in Hawaii, who return the compliment with the derisive term *kotonk*, meaning a person of mental and moral hypersophistication (cf. Steiner, 1949). In the camps there were sharp differences between Californian inmates and those from the Pacific Northwest. Generational disputes were aggravated by differences over religion, politics, and way of life. Two cleavages are of especial interest and worth examining in detail.

Long before they had any contact with either Caucasians or Africans, the Japanese valued "white" skin as beautiful and deprecated "black" skin as ugly. As far back as the Nara era (710–793), descriptions of feminine beauty emphasized "a fragrant white skin," and over the following centuries, though the ideal changed in other respects, this valuation remained constant. Ladies of the Tokugawa period used parasols, face hoods, generously applied powder, and a poultice made of nightingale droppings to keep their face, neck, and shoulders as pale as possible. In written or pictorial descriptions of the period, Europeans were distinguished by their height, hair color and hairiness, and large eyes and nose, but the faces of Japanese females were painted a lighter hue than those of the Dutch. In the twentieth century, even when Japan fought the "whites" as the "champion of the colored nations," a trend toward idealizing Western physical features remained a hidden subcurrent, to emerge in the postwar years in artificially waved hair, operations to remove the epicanthic fold, and, still, efforts to whiten the skin. In present-day Japan, most respondents refused to describe themselves as "yellow," though they know that the Japanese are part of the "yellow race" (*Oshoku jinshu*, the technical term for Mongoloid). It is only among those who have spent some time abroad, or especially those who live in the United States, that ethnic Japanese refer to themselves as "yellow," sometimes with a defensiveness perhaps presaging a future Yonsei slogan, "Yellow is beautiful" (Wagatsuma, 1967). At the present time, according to a study of perceived social distance among a Hawaiian sample, "the Japanese feel at greater distance from the 'dark' groups than do the Caucasians" (Samuels, 1969).[18]

A second important distinction made in Japanese society and carried over to American communities was the several types of outcastes, known collectively in the United States as Eta (see p. 212, n. 5). According to legends apparently widely accepted today, they are not really Japanese but of alien or even animal origin. In fact, they probably developed as specialists in such defiling occupations as tanning. When Buddhism was made the state religion under the Tokugawa shogunate, those who ate meat and worked with animal products were pushed still farther outside acceptable society. In 1871, the Eta were officially "emancipated"—meaning that their tax-exempt land was made subject to taxation by redefining its owners as "commoners" without any compensation for the loss of earlier special privileges. The always latent hostility of the populace erupted occasionally into "Eta-hunts" or "campaigns to exterminate the Eta." During the Meiji era, the response to this persecution was wholly assimilationist; the victims demanded only that discrimination in schools, government offices, and the army and navy be abolished, and that programs be subsidized to assist them in finding respectable places in the existent social structure (DeVos and Wagatsuma, 1966: chaps. 1–2).

To collect information on the Eta in the United States is almost impossible,[19] and the only extended analysis available was published under a pseudonym (DeVos and Wagatsuma, 1966: chap. 10). The author hypothesized that as a group the Eta would try to escape from their low status by a fuller acculturation to general American society (cf. Adams, 1937: 170–71), but this proved to be mistaken. Almost all avoided occupations traditionally associated with Eta and concentrated on vegetable or fruit farming. They were more conscientious Buddhists than non-Eta of the same community, and a disproportionately large number were segregated at Tule Lake and renounced their American citizenship. They tried to escape their shameful status, in other words, not by moving into a society that saw them only as Japanese, but by covering up their origin and proving themselves to be better Japanese than their neighbors. Rated by objective indices, the Eta were somewhat better off, but no respectable Japanese would consider a marriage with one of them. In the Florin area at least two and probably several more marriages between Eta and non-Eta were annulled when the previously hidden status of one partner was revealed.

Though not defined by the same criteria, these various patterns of differentiation among Japanese are reminiscent of the sometimes quite acrimonious difference among American Jews —between Sephardic and Ashkenazic, German and East European, Orthodox and Reformed, Zionist and American Council for Judaism, liberal and radical, and so on. In both cases, the disputes often heighten the overall sense of ethnic identification, since the "true" meaning of being a Japanese (or a Jew) has been one recurrent issue.

7. Marginality is psychologically deleterious to a person who judges himself by a culture he cannot enter, but beneficial to one adequately based in a subnation that serves as his reference group.

When Park (1950: chaps. 26–29) coined the term "marginal man" and Stonequist developed his concept in a book-length exposition, these writings, like the race-relations cycle itself, were part of a liberal alibi for immigrants' deficiencies. Through no fault of his own, the thesis went, a newcomer (or the product of a mixed marriage) falls between two cultures, one half-lost and the other not yet fully gained. According to a number of later critics, far from being a handicap, marginality can result in greater insight and creativity.[20] Most of these later papers were written by Jews, and their critique is parallel to the second generation's rejection, noted earlier, of the melting-pot thesis. Today few sociologists would accept the theory of marginality in its original form, but among the lay public its essence is still widely accepted. As one important example, the notion that institutionalized minority status necessarily harms the psyches of the individuals concerned was one basis of the Supreme Court's desegregation decision in 1954. Even much of professional discussion consists of arguments on one side or the other, rather than efforts to resolve the contradiction by stipulating under what conditions marginality is harmful or the contrary. (The much larger literature on bilingualism is similar: some hold simply that learning a second language impedes, others that it reinforces, the acquisition of the first.)

In his study of a sample of New Haven Jews, Antonovsky found that the "core variable" in each person's marginal status is: "Does he look for participation, self-expression, and security toward the Jewish community or toward some part of the world beyond its confines?"[21] The Japanese community has consistently acted as the prime judge of each person's behavior, and the vast majority of Japanese accept their own subnation in this role. In the Hawthorne district, outside Los Angeles, in the 1930s:

Comparatively little contact had been made between Japanese and whites, [for] it is not essential. The Japanese do

not seek the whites in this district, for "they are not worthy
of attention," according to a Japanese leader. The self-
sufficiency of the Japanese is apparent on every hand . . .
their own stores, professional people, publications, and
cultural and recreational activities (Strong, 1934: 23–24).

In the abundant analysis of the 1954 desegregation decision, the
concept of *congregation* (that is, the voluntary association of
members of a subnation) has been almost lost. All persons who
live together are said to be "segregated" in a "ghetto." In an
empirical study the two attitudes might be difficult to distinguish, but to confuse the concepts is inexcusable (cf. Yinger,
1962–63).

Contacts with the larger world were inevitable even for a
Japanese who lived in such an almost self-sufficient *Nihonmachi*, but under such circumstances affronts could be avoided
(rather than invited by aggressive confrontations). For example, a man who enjoyed playing golf on the Los Angeles
municipal course claimed that he had never experienced any
unpleasantness there because of his race. The reason was that
he and his friends always played early in the morning, avoiding
Sundays and holidays.

He did not suffer from discrimination because he "dodged"
the possibilities of its being shown. The "dodging" may be
a more important factor in the life of the Japanese than
the actual mortification that occasionally occurs from
overt discrimination (Yinger, 1962–63).

With the upward mobility possible since 1945, such tight little
communities have been partly dissolved, particularly on the
mainland. In their public roles, most Japanese now live in the
larger American world. But as Wittermans pointed out, they
also retain a private world to which they can retire in their
domestic life, there to be measured by an "Oriental in-group"
(Samuels, 1970) that makes of marginality a status with few
frustrations and dual satisfactions.

In sum, the Japanese Americans have lived in a genuine
community, stronger and more cohesive at the time the Nisei
generation was growing up, but still today a dominant fact of

their social environment. In effect, this community's dimensions are those of the subnation. Each person, each family, each locality has owed the community allegiance: nothing is done without fully considering its effect on "the Japanese image." In return, the community has bolstered every such part with material and moral support. Each family, each institution, has been more effective by working within a context of accord. Differences there have been aplenty, but in the main they have had the paradoxical effect of reinforcing the overall cohesion.

When the proponents of Japanese exclusion denounced the immigrants as "clannish," it was not only a correct description but a marvelously apt word, for the social cohesion had a clanlike base. And when those who opposed exclusion denied the clannishness, asserting that all races are essentially the same and that any initial differences would inevitably disappear in a predestined, four-stage succession, they were defending correct policy with false fact and weak theory. Indeed, in many respects the Japanese Americans are now more American than Japanese—in political loyalty, language, and way of life. Let us hope, however, that the subnation is not to be completely melted into the national pot, that it will continue to train its members in the courage, perseverance, and dignified self-esteem that have marked this people's history in the United States.

Notes

1 Harold R. Isaacs, "Group Identity and Political Change: Nationalism Revisited," *Survey*, No. 69 (1968), 76–98.

2 This follows the usage of "ethnicists," who define *nation* as "a politically conscious and large-scale ethnic group," rather than that of "statists," who define it as "an effective, i.e. loyalty-inspiring, territorial political unit," with nationality linked to "legal citizenship, not cultural origin"—Anthony D. Smith, "Theories and Types of Nationalism," *European Journal of Sociology*, 10 (1969), 119–30. I find it less confusing to designate the latter entity a "state" or, if the cultural element is to be emphasized, a "nation-state."

3 Tamotsu Shibutani and Kian M. Kwan, *Ethnic Stratification: A Comparative Approach* (New York: Macmillan, 1965), p. 38.

4 "The demand for . . . precise definition of terms can easily have a pernicious effect, as I believe it often has had in behavioral science. It is the dogmatisms outside science that proliferate closed systems of meaning; the scientist is in no hurry for closure. Tolerance of ambiguity is as important for creativity in science as it is anywhere else"—Abraham Kaplan, *The Conduct of Inquiry: Methodology for Behavioral Sciences* (San Francisco: Chandler, 1964), pp. 70–71.

5 The most important statement, perhaps, is Ashley Montagu, *Man's Most Dangerous Myth: The Fallacy of Race*, 4th ed. (New York: World, 1964). But the view is not idiosyncratic to this one physical anthropologist. A symposium in *Current Anthropology* (three full issues in 1962–1964) indicated how little consensus, how little even of a tolerant appreciation of other views, exists among the world's professionals on this subject. Some term is needed to designate a human group associated with a distinguishable genetic inheritance, and those who object to *race* because of its unpleasant connotations have struggled to find another denotation of subspecies of *Homo sapiens*. Montagu (1964: Appendix B) has suggested, for instance, that scholars substitute "ethnic group" for "race." But even if one accepts the dubious contention that such word magic helps in achieving understanding, the choice is especially inept. By its usual definition, an "ethnic group" is set off mainly by its cultural characteristics, and it is the hallmark of racist writings to confound physical and cultural attributes.

6 How seriously this confusion can fault analysis is especially clear in a recent work on race relations in Britain. Colored children, we are told, "being products of our educational system, will be as well equipped as their white contemporaries." On the other hand, such pupils, since they "have had their natural ability and energy thwarted" in various ways, require a whole series of expensive remedial programs—E. J. B. Rose *et al.*, *Colour and Citizenship: A Report on British Race Relations* (New York: Oxford University Press, 1969), pp. 285, 477, 698–710.

7 See, for example, U.S. Bureau of the Census, "The Social and Economic Status of Negroes in the United States, 1969," *Current Population Reports*, Series P-23, No. 29 (Washington, D.C.: U.S. Government Printing Office, 1970). The overall improvements in education, employment, income, housing, living conditions, and health are all significant. These averages for the whole subnation, moreover, include both middle-aged products of the pre-reform period and virtually illiterate teenage dropouts, and the data therefore understate the opportunities realized by younger Negroes

who have developed some usable capabilities. None of the figures, it is true, indicate that Negroes as a group have reached parity with the rest of the population, only that they are moving toward that goal with unprecedented speed.

8 Most of the material pertinent to this discussion is included in the first of three posthumous volumes of collected essays (Park, 1950). For incisive criticisms of Park's theory, see Brewton Berry, *Race and Ethnic Relations*, 3rd ed. (Boston: Houghton Mifflin, 1965); Stanford M. Lyman, "The Race Relations Cycle of Robert E. Park," *Pacific Sociological Review*, 11 (1968), 16–22; Amitai Etzioni, "The Ghetto: A Re-evaluation," *Social Forces*, 37 (1959), 255–62.

9 Cited in Lyman, *op. cit.*

10 Israel Zangwill, *The Melting-Pot*, rev. ed. (New York: Macmillan, 1920); Horace M. Kallen, *Culture and Democracy in the United States* (New York: Boni & Liveright, 1924); Samuel Lubell, *The Future of American Politics*, 2nd ed. (Garden City, N.Y.: Doubleday, 1956); Will Herberg, *Protestant, Catholic, Jew: An Essay in American Religious Sociology* (Garden City, N.Y.: Doubleday, 1955).

11 William Graham Sumner, *Folkways: A Study of the Sociological Importance of Usages, Manners, Customs, Mores, and Morals* (Boston: Ginn, 1940), chaps. 1–2. After his death, Sumner's enormous reputation waned (except at Yale, where he had been Professor of Political and Social Science for thirty-seven years). For a characteristic attack, see Donald Fleming, "Social Darwinism," in Arthur M. Schlesinger, Jr., and Morton White (eds.), *Paths of American Thought* (Boston: Houghton Mifflin, 1970), chap. 7. "Social Darwinism" is a loose pejorative, and whether it applies justly to Sumner depends on what the term signifies. Following Herbert Spencer, Sumner held that there has been an evolution of human societies; but today, after a hiatus of anti-evolutionary thought, most social scientists would agree. This cultural evolution is conceptually parallel to Darwin's schema, but Sumner was not naive enough to import terms and ideas directly from biology (as did, for example, the human ecologists of the Chicago school). He was unequivocally antiracist: "modern scholars," he wrote in *Folkways*, "have made the mistake of attributing to [physical] race much which belongs to the [cultural] ethos." Probably the principal reason for Sumner's declining influence (as compared, for instance, with that other superb dogmatist, Thorstein Veblen) was his politics. Though a functionalist, he used

what is currently termed a conflict model to analyze politics and society, and like all classical liberals he feared the power of government more than he welcomed its benefits.

12 Hubert M. Blalock, Jr., *Toward a Theory of Minority-Group Relations* (New York: Wiley, 1967).

13 Other expressions of the same prediction, among others that could be cited, include DuPuy, 1932: 115–17; Cheng, 1953; Lind, 1967: 115.

14 A. A. Roback, *A Dictionary of International Slurs (Ethnophaulisms)* (Cambridge, Mass.: SCI-Art Publishers, 1944), pp. 288–89.

15 See R. A. Schermerhorn, *Comparative Ethnic Relations: A Framework for Theory and Research* (New York: Random House, 1970), pp. 6–8.

16 Harold R. Isaacs, "Back to Africa," *The New Yorker,* May 13, 1961.

17 Howard M. Imazeki, "To Our Negro Neighbor, This Is Our Voice," *Hokubei Mainichi,* June 29, 1963. See also "A Negro-Nisei Dialogue," *ibid.,* January 1, 1966; Kumeo A. Yoshinari, "Civil Rights and the JACL," *Pacific Citizen,* September 3, 1965.

18 See Vinacke, 1949; Arkoff and Weaver, 1966; Shim and Dole, 1967.

19 There is a widespread belief among mainland Japanese that the largest group of Eta are congregated in the California town of Florin. A Nisei professional in nearby Sacramento who had been born and brought up in Florin was kind enough to give me a long interview. He was a highly cultured man, apparently completely assimilated to middle-class life, and I found his informed comments about California's Japanese community of great interest. But when I asked him about the rumor concerning Florin, he broke off the interview abruptly and seemingly had to control himself not to throw me bodily out of his office. Two descriptions of Florin by whites (Brown, n.d.; Gulick, 1914: chap. 5) do not mention the Eta, whether out of friendly discretion or ignorance I do not know.

20 Everett V. Stonequist, *The Marginal Man: A Study in Personality and Culture Conflict* (New York: Scribner's, 1937). For some representative criticisms, see Milton M. Goldberg, "A Qualification of the Marginal Man Theory," *American Sociological Review,* 6 (1941), 52–58; Arnold W. Green, "A Re-examination of the Marginal Man Concept," *Social Forces,* 26 (1947), 167–71; David I. Golovensky, "The Marginal Man Concept: An Analysis and Critique," *Social Forces,* 30 (1952), 333–39; Aaron Antonovsky, "To-

ward a Refinement of the 'Marginal Man' Concept," *Social Forces,* 35 (1956), 57–62; David Riesman, *Individualism Reconsidered* (New York: Free Press, 1954), pp. 153–78; Erwin Flaschberger, "The Marginal Man and His Marginal Attitude: A Theoretical Approach," *REMP Bulletin,* 10 (1962), 89–96.

21 Antonovsky, *op. cit.*

◉ Bibliography

This is not a list of all the works cited in this book, but only of those that pertain more or less directly to Japanese Americans. Nor is it a complete bibliography on that topic. The voluminous but repetitive debate on Oriental exclusion, for example, is represented by only a few typical items on either side. Works especially recommended either as interesting personal memoirs or as scholarly analyses are marked with an asterisk. (By Japanese convention, the family names come first, followed by the personal name, but Westernized Japanese or those writing for a Western audience usually reverse the order. The style follows that in the original work.)

Adams, Romanzo C. [1924?]. *The Japanese in Hawaii: A Statistical Study Bearing on the Future Number and Voting Strength and on the Economic and Social Character of the Hawaiian Japanese.* New York: National Committee on American Japanese Relations.

————. 1929. "Japanese Migration Statistics," *Sociology and Social Research,* 13, 436–45.

————. 1933. *The Peoples of Hawaii.* Honolulu: Institute of Pacific Relations.

*————. 1937. *Interracial Marriage in Hawaii: A Study of the Mutually Conditioned Processes of Acculturation and Amalgamation.* New York: Macmillan.

Akahoshi, Hidefumi. 1963. "Hongwanji in Rural Japan and Cosmopolitan Hawaii," *Social Process,* 26, 80–82.

Allen, G. C. 1946. *A Short Economic History of Modern Japan, 1867–1937.* London: Allen & Unwin.

Anesaki, Masaharu. 1938. *Religious Life of the Japanese People: Its Present Status and Historical Background.* Tokyo: Kokusai Bunka Shinkokai.

Arkoff, Abe, and Donald A. Leton. 1966. "Ethnic and Personality Patterns in College Entrance," *Journal of Experimental Education,* 35, 79–83.

————, Gerald Meredith, and Shinkuro Iwahara. 1964. "Male-Dominant and Equalitarian Attitudes in Japanese, Japanese-American, and Caucasian-American Students," *Journal of Social Psychology*, 64, 225–29.

―――, and Herbert B. Weaver. 1966. "Body Image and Body Dissatisfaction in Japanese-Americans," *Journal of Social Psychology*, 68, 323–30.

Arrington, Leonard J. 1962. *The Price of Prejudice: The Japanese-American Relocation Center in Utah during World War II*. Logan, Utah: Utah State University.

Bailey, Thomas A. 1932. "California, Japan, and the Alien Land Legislation of 1913," *Pacific Historical Review*, 1, 36–59.

*―――. 1934. *Theodore Roosevelt and the Japanese-American Crises: An Account of the International Complications Arising from the Race Problem on the Pacific Coast*. Stanford: Stanford University Press.

Baldwin, Roger. 1948. "The Nisei in Japan," *Common Ground*, 8, 24–29.

Banse, Walter F., ed. 1956. *Adjudications of the Attorney General of the United States*. Vol. I: *Precedent Decisions under the Japanese-American Evacuation Claims Act, 1950–1956*. Washington, D.C.: U.S. Government Printing Office.

Barnhart, Edward N. 1960. "The Individual Exclusion of Japanese Americans in World War II," *Pacific Historical Review*, 29, 111–30.

*―――. 1962. "Japanese Internees from Peru," *Pacific Historical Review*, 31, 169–78.

Beach, Walter G. 1932. *Oriental Crime in California*. Stanford: Stanford University Press.

Beardsley, Richard K. 1965. "Religion and Philosophy," in Hall and Beardsley, 1965: chap. 7.

―――, John W. Hall, and Robert E. Ward. 1959. *Village Japan*. Chicago: University of Chicago Press.

Bell, Daniel. 1958. "Japanese Notebook," *Antioch Review*, 18, 64–73.

Bell, Reginald. 1935. *Public School Education of Second-Generation Japanese in California*. Stanford: Stanford University Press.

Bellah, Robert N. 1957. *Tokugawa Religion*. New York: Free Press.

Bennett, Charles G., George H. Tokuyama, and Paul T. Bruyere. 1963. "Health of Japanese Americans in Hawaii," *Public Health Reports*, 78, 753–62.

Blood, Robert O., Jr. 1967. *Love Match and Arranged Marriage: A Tokyo-Detroit Comparison.* New York: Free Press.

Bloom [Broom], Leonard, and Ruth Riemer. 1949. *Removal and Return: The Socio-economic Effects of the War on Japanese Americans.* Berkeley: University of California Press.

*Bosworth, Allan R. 1967. *America's Concentration Camps.* New York: Norton.

Boyd, Monica. 1968. "The Japanese Americans: A Study in Socio-economic Integration." Paper presented at the annual meeting of the Southern Sociological Society.

*Breslow, Lester, and Bonnie Klein. 1971. "Health and Race in California," *American Journal of Public Health,* 61, 763–75.

Broom, Leonard, and John I. Kitsuse. 1956. *The Managed Casualty: The Japanese-American Family in World War II.* Berkeley: University of California Press.

Brown, Alice M. 1913. *Education, Not Legislation: California and the Japanese.* Privately printed.

———. n.d. *Japanese in Florin.* Privately printed.

*Buell, Raymond Leslie. 1922–23. "The Development of Anti-Japanese Agitation in the United States," *Political Science Quarterly,* 37, 605–38; 38, 57–81.

———. 1923. "Some Legal Aspects of the Japanese Question," *American Journal of International Law,* 17, 29–49.

Caudill, William. 1952. "Japanese-American Personality and Acculturation," *Genetic Psychology Monographs,* 45, 3–102.

———, and George DeVos. 1956. "Achievement, Culture and Personality: The Case of the Japanese Americans," *American Anthropologist,* 58, 1102–26.

*Chamberlain, Basil Hall. 1905. *Things Japanese, Being Notes on Various Subjects Connected with Japan for the Use of Travellers and Others.* London: Murray.

Chambers, John S. 1921. "The Japanese Invasion," *Annals of the American Academy of Political and Social Science,* 93, 23–29.

Cheng, Ch'eng-k'un. 1951. "Assimilation in Hawaii and the Bid for Statehood," *Social Forces,* 30, 16–29.

———. 1953. "A Study of Chinese Assimilation in Hawaii," *Social Forces,* 32, 163–67.

*Conroy, Hilary. 1953. *The Japanese Frontier in Hawaii, 1868–1898.* Berkeley: University of California Press.

*Daniels, Roger. 1962. *The Politics of Prejudice: The Anti-Japanese Movement in California and the Struggle for Japanese Exclusion.* Berkeley: University of California Press.

Dendo-Dan. 1914. *Evangelization of the Japanese on the Pacific Coast.* San Francisco: Japanese Interdenominational Board of Missions.

————. 1916. *Fifth Annual Report, Shintenchi Supplement.* San Francisco: Japanese Interdenominational Board of Missions.

DeVos, George A. 1966. *A Comparison of the Personality Differences in Two Generations of Japanese Americans by Means of the Rorschach Test.* Honolulu: University of Hawaii.

————, Hiroshi Wagatsuma, *et al.* 1966. *Japan's Invisible Race: Caste in Culture and Personality.* Berkeley: University of California Press.

Digman, John M. 1957. "Ethnic Factors in Oahu's 1954 General Election," *Social Process in Hawaii,* 21, 20–24.

Doi, L. Takeo. 1962. "*Amae:* A Key Concept for Understanding Japanese Personality Structures," in Robert Smith and Beardsley, 1962: 132–39.

Doi Yatarō. 1957. "Yamaguchi-ken Ōshima-gun ni okeru Hawaii imin shi," *Yamaguchi Daigaku Nōgakubu gakujutsu hōkoku* ["A History of Emigration to Hawaii from Oshima District, Yamaguchi Prefecture," *Bulletin of the Faculty of Agriculture, Yamaguchi University*], 8, 775–848.

Dole, Arthur A. 1961. *A Study of Values as Determinants of Educational-Vocational Choices in Hawaii.* Honolulu: Hawaii Department of Education.

————, and Eileen E. Iwakami. 1960a. "Statistical Profile of a Freshman Class: A Survey of University of Hawaii 1959 Freshmen." Honolulu: Bureau of Testing and Guidance, University of Hawaii.

———— and ————. 1960b. "Survey of University of Hawaii 1960 Seniors: Why They Came to College." Honolulu: Bureau of Testing and Guidance, University of Hawaii.

————, and Ruth Sherman. 1962. "Determinants of the Choice of a Science Program by Ninth-Grade Males." Honolulu: Psychological Research Center, University of Hawaii.

Dore, R. F. 1959. *Land Reform in Japan.* New York: Oxford University Press.

*————. 1964. "Japan as a Model of Economic Development," *European Journal of Sociology,* 5, 138–54.

————. 1965a. *Education in Tokugawa Japan.* Berkeley: University of California Press.

————. 1965b. "The Legacy of Tokugawa Education," in Jansen, 1965: 99–131.

————, ed. 1967. *Aspects of Social Change in Modern Japan.* Princeton: Princeton University Press.

Dranga, Jane. 1936. "Racial Factors in the Employment of Women," *Social Process in Hawaii*, 2, 11–14.

DuPuy, William Atherton. 1932. *Hawaii and Its Race Problem.* Washington, D.C.: U.S. Government Printing Office.

Earhart, H. Byron. 1967. "Toward a Unified Interpretation of Japanese Religion," in Joseph M. Kitagawa, ed., *The History of Religions: Essays on the Problem of Understanding.* Chicago: University of Chicago Press, chap. 9.

Embree, John F. 1939. *Suye Mura: A Japanese Village.* Chicago: University of Chicago Press.

*————. 1941. "Acculturation among the Japanese of Kona, Hawaii," *American Anthropologist*, Vol. 43, No. 4, Part 2.

*Enright, John B., and Walter R. Jaeckle. 1961–62. "Ethnic Differences in Psychopathology," *Social Process*, 25, 71–77.

Epps, Edgar G. 1967. "Socio-economic Status, Race, Level of Aspiration, and Juvenile Delinquency: A Limited Empirical Test of Merton's Conception of Deviation," *Phylon*, 28, 16–27.

Flowers, Montaville. 1917. *The Japanese Conquest of American Public Opinion.* New York: Doran.

Fuchs, Lawrence H. 1961. *Hawaii Pono: A Social History.* New York: Harcourt Brace Jovanovich.

Fujita, Michinari. 1929. "The Japanese Associations in America," *Sociology and Social Research*, 13, 211–28.

Fukutake, Tadashi. 1962. *Man and Society in Japan.* Tokyo: University of Tokyo Press.

*————. 1967. *Japanese Rural Society.* Tokyo: Oxford University Press.

*George, B. James, Jr. 1965. "Law in Modern Japan," in Hall and Beardsley, 1965: chap. 11.

Girdner, Audrie, and Anne Loftis. 1969. *The Great Betrayal: The Evacuation of the Japanese-Americans during World War II.* New York: Macmillan.

Glick, Clarence E., *et al.* 1958. "Changing Attitudes toward the Care of Aged Japanese Parents in Hawaii," *Social Process in Hawaii,* 22, 9–20.

Goldscheider, Calvin, and Peter R. Uhlenberg. 1969. "Minority Group Status and Fertility," *American Journal of Sociology,* 74, 361–72.

Gordon, Tavia. 1957. "Mortality Experience among the Japanese in the United States, Hawaii, and Japan," *Public Health Reports,* 72, 543–53.

————. 1967. "Further Mortality Experience among Japanese Americans," *Public Health Reports,* 82, 973–84.

Goto, Y. Baron. 1968. *Children of Gan-nen-mono: The First-Year Men.* Honolulu: Bishop Museum Press.

Grodzins, Morton. 1949. *Americans Betrayed: Politics and the Japanese Evacuation.* Chicago: University of Chicago Press.

Gulick, Sidney L. 1914. *The American Japanese Problem: A Study of the Racial Relations of the East and the West.* New York: Scribner's.

————. 1915. *Hawaii's American-Japanese Problem: A Description of the Conditions, a Statement of the Problems, and Suggestions for Their Solution.* Honolulu: Star-Bulletin.

————. 1916. *The Pacific Coast and the New Oriental Policy.* New York: Federal Council of Churches of Christ in America.

Hall, John W. 1955. "The Castle Town and Japan's Modern Urbanization," *Far Eastern Quarterly,* 15, 37–50.

————. 1962. "Feudalism in Japan—A Reassessment," *Comparative Studies in Society and History,* 5, 15–51.

*————, and Richard K. Beardsley, eds. 1965. *Twelve Doors to Japan.* New York: McGraw-Hill.

Harada, Koichi Glenn. 1934. "A Survey of the Japanese-Language Schools in Hawaii." Unpublished master's essay, University of Hawaii.

Harada, Tasuku. 1914. *The Faith of Japan.* New York: Macmillan.

Hasegawa, Nyozekan. 1965. *The Japanese Character: A Cultural Profile.* Palo Alto, Calif.: Kodansha International.

Hatch, F. M. 1914. "The Constitutional Convention of 1894," *Hawaii Historical Society Report,* 23, 50–61.

Hatoyama, Kazuo, and Saburo Sakamoto. 1919. "Japanese Personal Legislation," in Okuma, 1919, 1:251–80.

Hayashida, Akiyoshi. 1933. "Japanese Moral Instruction as a Factor in the Americanization of Citizens of Japanese Ancestry." Unpublished master's essay, University of Hawaii.

Hayner, Norman S. 1934. "Delinquency Areas in the Puget Sound Region," *American Journal of Sociology*, 39, 314–28.

———. 1938. "Social Factors in Oriental Crime," *American Journal of Sociology*, 43, 908–19.

Hearn, Lafcadio. 1917. *Japan: An Attempt at Interpretation.* London: Macmillan.

Herbert, Jean. 1967. *Shinto: At the Fountain-head of Japan.* New York: Stein and Day.

Holtom, D. C. 1922. "The Political Philosophy of Modern Shinto: A Study of the State Religion of Japan," *Transactions of the Asiatic Society of Japan*, Vol. 49, Part 2, pp. 1–325.

Hori, Ichirō. 1968. *Folk Religion in Japan: Continuity and Change.* Chicago: University of Chicago Press.

———, and Toda Yoshio. 1956. "Shinto," in Kishimoto, 1956: 37–98.

Hormann, Bernhard L. 1948. " 'Racial' Statistics in Hawaii," *Social Process in Hawaii*, 12, 27–35.

———. 1957. "Integration in Hawaii's Schools," *Social Process in Hawaii*, 21, 5–14.

———. 1961–62. "Toward a Sociology of Religion in Hawaii," *Social Process*, 25, 58–66.

Hosokawa, Bill. 1969. *Nisei: The Quiet Americans.* New York: Morrow.

Howard, Stuart Alan. 1957. "The Hawaiian Sansei: A Problem in the Study of Psychological Acculturation." Unpublished master's essay, Stanford University.

Hunter, Louise Harris. 1966. "Buddhism in Hawaii: Its Impact on a Yankee Community." Unpublished master's essay, University of Hawaii.

Ichihashi, Yamato. 1915. *Japanese Immigration: Its Status in California.* San Francisco: Marshall Press.

———. 1931. "International Migration of the Japanese," in Walter F. Willcox, ed., *International Migrations*, New York: National Bureau of Economic Research, 2, 617–36.

*———. 1932. *Japanese in the United States: A Critical Study of the Problems of the Japanese Immigrants and Their Children.* Stanford: Stanford University Press.

Iga, Mamoru. 1957. "The Japanese Social Structure and the Source of Mental Strains of Japanese Immigrants in the United States," *Social Forces,* 35, 271–78.

Ikeda, Kiyoshi, Harry V. Ball, and Douglas S. Yamamura. 1962–63. "Ethnocultural Factors in Schizophrenia: The Japanese in Hawaii," *American Journal of Sociology,* 68, 242–48, 593–96.

Imamura, Yemyo. 1927. *A Short History of the Hongwanji Buddhist Mission in Hawaii.* Honolulu: Publishing Bureau of Hongwanji Buddhist Mission.

Inouye, Daniel K., with Lawrence Elliott. 1967. *Journey to Washington.* Englewood Cliffs, N.J.: Prentice-Hall.

Ishikawa Tomonori. 1967a. "Yamaguchi-ken Ōshima-gun Kuga-son shoki Hawaii keiyaku imin no shakai-chirigakuteki kōsatsu," *Chiri Kagaku* ["A Social-Geographical Study of Japanese Indentured Emigrants to Hawaii from Kuga Village, Oshima District, Yamaguchi Prefecture," *Geographical Science*], 7, 25–38.

————. 1967b. "Hiroshima-wangen Jigozen-son keiyaku imin no shakai-chirigakuteki kōsatsu," *Jinbun Chiri* ["A Social-Geographical Study of Contract-labor Emigrants to Hawaii from Jigozen Village on the Shore of Hiroshima Bay," *Human Geography*], 19, 75–91.

————. 1967c. "Hiroshima-ken nanbu Kuchida-son keiyaku imin no shakai-chirigakuteki kōsatsu," *Shigaku Kenkyū* ["A Social-Geographical Study of Japanese Indentured Emigrants to Hawaii from Kuchida Village in Southern Hiroshima Prefecture," *Historical Journal*], 99, 33–52.

*Iwata, Masakuzu. 1962. "The Japanese Immigrants in California Agriculture," *Agricultural History,* 36, 25–37.

Iyenaga, T., and Kenoske Sato. 1921. *Japan and the California Problem.* New York: Putnam's.

Jackman, Norman R. 1957. "Collective Protest in Relocation Centers," *American Journal of Sociology,* 63, 264–72.

Jansen, Marius B., ed. 1965. *Changing Japanese Attitudes toward Modernization.* Princeton: Princeton University Press.

————, and Lawrence Stone. 1967. "Education and Modernization in Japan and England," *Comparative Studies in Society and History,* 9, 208–32.

Japan, Consulate General, San Francisco. 1925. *Documental History of Law Cases Affecting Japanese in the United States, 1916–1924.* San Francisco. 2 vols.

Japanese National Commission for Unesco. 1958. *Manual of Demographic Statistics in Japan.* Tokyo.

Jones, Thomas E. 1926. "Mountain Folk of Japan." Unpublished doctoral dissertation, Columbia University.

Kanagawa, Wayne Yoshito. 1955. "A Study of Old-age Recipients of Japanese Ancestry." Unpublished master's essay, University of Hawaii.

Kawakami, Kiyoshi K. 1912. *American-Japanese Relations: An Inside View of Japan's Policies and Purposes.* New York: Fleming H. Revell.

————. 1921. *The Real Japanese Question.* New York: Macmillan.

*Keene, Donald. 1959. *Living Japan.* Garden City, N.Y.: Doubleday.

Kelsey, Carl, ed. 1921. "Present-day Immigration, with Special Reference to the Japanese," *Annals of the American Academy of Political and Social Science,* 93, 1–120.

*Kihara Ryūkichi. 1935. *Hawaii Nihonjin shi* [A History of the Japanese in Hawaii]. Tokyo: Bunseisha.

Kimura, Yukiko. 1939. "Honolulu Barber Girls—A Study of Culture Conflict," *Social Process in Hawaii,* 5, 22–29.

————. 1957. "War Brides in Hawaii and Their In-laws," *American Journal of Sociology,* 63, 70–76.

————. 1963. "Religious Affiliation of War Brides in Hawaii and Their Marital Adjustment," *Social Process,* 26, 88–95.

Kishimoto Hideo, ed. 1956. *Japanese Religion in the Meiji Era.* Translated and adapted by John F. Howes. Tokyo: Ōbunsha.

*Kitagawa, Daisuke. 1967. *Issei and Nisei: The Internment Years.* New York: Seabury Press.

Kitagawa, Joseph M. 1966. *Religion in Japanese History.* New York: Columbia University Press.

Kitano, Harry H. L. 1960. "Housing of Japanese-Americans in the San Francisco Bay Area," in Nathan Glazer and Davis McEntire, eds., *Studies in Housing and Minority Groups,* Berkeley: University of California Press, pp. 178–97.

————. 1962. "Changing Achievement Patterns of the Japanese in the United States," *Journal of Social Psychology,* 58, 257–64.

————. 1969. *Japanese Americans: The Evolution of a Subculture.* Englewood Cliffs, N.J.: Prentice-Hall.

Kono, Ayoko. 1934. "Language as a Factor in the Achievement of American-born Students of Japanese Ancestry." Unpublished master's essay, University of Hawaii.

Konvitz, Milton R. 1946. *The Alien and the Asiatic in American Law.* Ithaca, N.Y.: Cornell University Press.

Koyama, Takashi. 1961. *The Changing Social Position of Women in Japan.* Paris: Unesco.

Koyano, Shogo. 1964. "Changing Family Behavior in Four Japanese Communities," *Journal of Marriage and the Family,* 26, 149–59.

Kurita, Yayoi. n.d. "Labor Movements among the Japanese Plantation Workers in Hawaii." Unpublished manuscript on file in the library of the University of Hawaii.

Kurokawa, Minako. 1968. "Lineal Orientation in Child Rearing among Japanese," *Journal of Marriage and the Family,* 30, 129–36.

———. 1970. "Childhood Accidents," in Minako Kurokawa, ed., *Minority Responses: Comparative Views of Reactions to Subordination.* New York: Random House, pp. 120–30.

Kuykendall, Ralph S. 1967. *The Hawaiian Kingdom,* Vol. 3: *1874–1893, The Kalakaua Kingdom.* Honolulu: University of Hawaii Press.

Ladenson, Alex. 1940. "The Background of the Hawaiian-Japanese Labor Convention," *Pacific Historical Review,* 9, 389–400.

Leighton, Alexander H. 1945. *The Governing of Men: General Principles and Recommendations Based on Experience at a Japanese Relocation Camp.* Princeton: Princeton University Press.

Lind, Andrew W. 1930a. "Some Ecological Patterns of Community Disorganization in Honolulu," *American Journal of Sociology,* 36, 206–20.

*———. 1930b. "The Ghetto and the Slum," *Social Forces,* 9, 206–15.

———. 1946. *Hawaii's Japanese: An Experiment in Democracy.* Princeton: Princeton University Press.

———. 1951. "The Changing Position of Domestic Service in Hawaii," *Social Process in Hawaii,* 15, 71–87.

———. 1952. "Religious Diversity in Hawaii," *Social Process in Hawaii,* 16, 11–19.

———. 1957. "Racial Bloc Voting in Hawaii," *Social Process in Hawaii,* 21, 16–19.

———. 1961–62. "Hawaii in the Race Relations Continuum of the Pacific," *Social Process,* 25, 7–14.

―――. 1967. *Hawaii's People,* 3rd ed. Honolulu: University of Hawaii Press.

Lockwood, William W. 1954. *The Economic Development of Japan: Growth and Structural Change, 1868–1938.* Princeton: Princeton University Press.

*―――, ed. 1965. *The State and Economic Enterprise in Japan: Essays in the Political Economy of Growth.* Princeton: Princeton University Press.

Luomala, Katharine. 1946. "California Takes Back Its Japanese Evacuees: The Readjustment of California to the Return of the Japanese Evacuees," *Applied Anthropology,* 5, 25–39.

Lyman, Stanford M. 1968. "Contrasts in the Community Organization of Chinese and Japanese in North America," *Canadian Review of Sociology and Anthropology,* 5, 51–67.

―――. n.d. "Generation and Character: The Case of the Japanese Americans." Unpublished manuscript.

Malcolm, Roy. 1921. "American Citizenship and the Japanese," *Annals of the American Academy of Political and Social Science,* 93, 77–81.

Masaoka, Joe Grant. 1969. "Japanese Americans: Perplexities of the Past." Paper read at the World Conference on Records, Salt Lake City, Utah.

Masuda, Ruth N. 1937. "The Japanese 'Tanomoshi,'" *Social Process in Hawaii,* 3, 16–19.

*Matsuda, Mitsugu. 1968. *The Japanese in Hawaii, 1868–1967: A Bibliography of the First Hundred Years.* Honolulu: University of Hawaii.

*McGovney, Dudley O. 1922–23. "Race Discrimination in Naturalization," *Iowa Law Bulletin,* 8, 129–61, 211–44.

―――. 1947. "The Anti-Japanese Laws of California and Ten Other States," *California Law Review,* 35, 7–60.

McKenzie, R. D. 1928. *Oriental Exclusion: The Effect of American Immigration Laws, Regulations, and Judicial Decisions upon the Chinese and Japanese on the American Pacific Coast.* Chicago: University of Chicago Press.

McWilliams, Carey. 1942a. "California and the Japanese," *New Republic,* 106, 295–97.

*―――. 1942b. "Moving the West-Coast Japanese," *Harper's Magazine,* 185, 359–69.

————. 1945. *Prejudice: Japanese-Americans: Symbol of Racial Intolerance*. Boston: Little, Brown.

Mears, Eliot G. 1928. *Resident Orientals on the American Pacific Coast: Their Legal and Economic Status*. Chicago: University of Chicago Press.

Meller, Norman. 1961–62. "Recent Changes in the Composition of Hawaiian Legislatures," *Social Process*, 25, 45–52.

*————, and Daniel W. Tuttle, Jr. 1969. "Hawaii: The Aloha State," in Frank H. Jonas, ed., *Politics in the American West*, Salt Lake City: University of Utah Press, pp. 152–79.

*Metcalf, V. H. 1906. "Japanese in the City of San Francisco, Cal." U.S. Senate, 59th Congress, 2d Session, Document 147. Washington, D.C.: Government Printing Office.

Millis, H. A. 1915. *The Japanese Problem in the United States: An Investigation for the Commission on Relations with Japan Appointed by the Federal Council of the Churches of Christ in America*. New York: Macmillan.

Misaki, H. K. 1933. "Delinquency and Crime," in Strong and Bell, 1933: 155–73.

Miyamoto, Shichiro. 1937. "A Study of the Japanese Language Ability of the Second and Third Generation Japanese Children in a Honolulu Language School." Unpublished master's essay, University of Hawaii.

Miyamoto, Shotaro Frank. 1939. *Social Solidarity among the Japanese in Seattle*. Seattle: University of Washington.

Mizuta, Iwao. 1938. "Changing Attitudes towards the Japanese Language in Hawaii," *Social Process in Hawaii*, 4, 28–36.

Modell, John. 1968. "The Japanese American Family: A Perspective for Future Investigations," *Pacific Historical Review*, 37, 67–81.

*————. 1969a. "The Japanese of Los Angeles: A Study in Growth and Accommodation, 1900–1946." Unpublished doctoral dissertation, Columbia University.

————. 1969b. "Class or Ethnic Solidarity: The Japanese American Company Union," *Pacific Historical Review*, 38, 193–206.

Monahan, Thomas P. 1966. "Interracial Marriage and Divorce in the State of Hawaii," *Eugenics Quarterly*, 13, 40–47.

Morita, Yukio. 1967. "The Japanese Americans in the United States between 1945 and 1965." Unpublished master's essay, Ohio State University.

*Morton, Newton E., Chin S. Chung, and Ming-pi Mi. 1967. *Genetics of Interracial Crosses in Hawaii*. New York: S. Karger.

Murdoch, James. 1926. *A History of Japan*. London: K. Paul, Trench, Trubner. 3 vols.

Murphy, Thomas D. 1954. *Ambassadors in Arms: The Story of Hawaii's 100th Battalion*. Honolulu: University of Hawaii Press.

*Nakane, Chie. 1970. *Japanese Society*. Berkeley: University of California Press.

National Opinion Research Center. 1946. *Attitudes toward "The Japanese in Our Midst."* Report No. 33. Denver: University of Denver.

Nickel, George D. 1942. "Evacuation, American Style," *Survey Midmonthly*, 78, 99–103.

Norman, E. Herbert. 1940. *Japan's Emergence as a Modern State: Political and Economic Problems of the Meiji Period*. New York: Institute of Pacific Relations.

O'Brien, Robert W. 1949. *The College Nisei*. Palo Alto, Calif.: Pacific Books.

Ōhata Kiyoshi and Ikado Fujio. 1956. "Christianity," in Kishimoto, 1956: 171–309.

Ohkawa, Kazushi, and Henry Rosovsky. 1965. "A Century of Japanese Economic Growth," in Lockwood, 1965: chap. 11.

*Okubo, Miné. 1946. *Citizen 13660*. New York: Columbia University Press.

Okuma, Shigenobu, ed. 1919. *Fifty Years of New Japan*. New York: Dutton. 2 vols.

Okumura, Takie, and Umetaro Okumura. 1927. *Hawaii's American-Japanese Problem: A Campaign to Remove Causes of Friction between the American People and Japanese*. Honolulu: Nippu Jiji.

Onishi, Katsumi. 1938. " 'Bon' and 'Bon-odori' in Hawaii," *Social Process in Hawaii*, 4, 49–57.

————. 1943. "A Study of the Attitudes of the Japanese in Hawaii toward the Japanese-Language Schools." Unpublished master's essay, University of Hawaii.

Orchard, John E., and Dorothy J. Orchard. 1930. *Japan's Economic Position: The Progress of Industrialization*. New York: Whittlesey House.

Papinot, E. 1964. *Historical and Geographical Dictionary of Japan.* New York: Frederick Ungar. 2 vols.

Park, Robert Ezra. 1950. *Race and Culture.* New York: Free Press.

Parkman, Margaret A., and Jack Sawyer. 1967. "Dimensions of Ethnic Intermarriage in Hawaii," *American Sociological Review,* 32, 593–607.

Paul, Rodman W. 1936. *The Abrogation of the Gentlemen's Agreement.* Cambridge, Mass.: Phi Beta Kappa Society.

Petersen, William. 1969. "The Classification of Subnations in Hawaii: An Essay in the Sociology of Knowledge," *American Sociological Review,* 34, 863–77.

Population Problems Research Council. 1953. *Influences of Emigrants on Their Home Village: Report of a Survey of "Amerika-Mura."* Tokyo: Mainichi Newspapers.

Reinecke, John E. 1969. *Language and Dialect in Hawaii: A Sociolinguistic History to 1935.* Honolulu: University of Hawaii Press.

*Reischauer, August Karl. 1925. *Studies in Japanese Buddhism.* New York: Macmillan.

Reischauer, Edwin O. 1965. *Japan: Past and Present.* 3rd ed. New York: Knopf.

[Ringle, Kenneth D.], "An Intelligence Officer." 1942. "The Japanese in America: The Problem and the Solution," *Harper's Magazine,* 185, 489–96.

Rosovsky, Henry. 1959. "Japanese Capital Formation: The Role of the Public Sector," *Journal of Economic History,* 19, 350–75.

*———. 1966. "Japan's Transition to Modern Economic Growth, 1868–1885," in Henry Rosovsky, ed., *Industrialization in Two Systems: Essays in Honor of Alexander Gerschenkron,* New York: Wiley.

Russell, Oland D. 1939. *The House of Mitsui.* Boston: Little, Brown.

Samuels, Frederick. 1969. "Colour Sensitivity among Honolulu's Haoles and Japanese," *Race,* 11, 203–12.

———. 1970. "The Oriental In-Group in Hawaii," *Phylon,* 31, 148–56.

Sanjume, Jisoo. 1939. *An Analysis of the New Americans Conference from 1927 to 1938.* Honolulu: New Americans Conference.

Sansom, G. B. 1931. *Japan: A Short Cultural History.* London: Oxford University Press.

*Schmid, Calvin F., and Charles E. Nobbe. 1965. "Socio-economic Differentials among Nonwhite Races," *American Sociological Review*, 30, 909–22.

Schmitt, Robert C. 1956. "Psychosis and Race in Hawaii," *Hawaii Medical Journal*, 16, 144–46.

————. 1965. "Demographic Correlates of Interracial Marriage," *Demography*, 2, 463–73.

————. 1967a. "Shifting Occupational and Class Structure: 1930–1966," in Andrew W. Lind, ed., *Modern Hawaii*, Honolulu: University of Hawaii.

*————. 1967b. "Differential Mortality in Honolulu before 1900," *Hawaii Medical Journal*, 26, 537–41.

*————. 1968. *Demographic Statistics of Hawaii: 1778–1965.* Honolulu: University of Hawaii Press.

Shapiro, H. L. 1939. *Migration and Environment: A Study of the Physical Characteristics of the Japanese Immigrants to Hawaii and the Effects of Environment on Their Descendants.* New York: Oxford University Press.

Shim, Neil, and Arthur A. Dole. 1967. "Components of Social Distance among College Students and Their Parents in Hawaii," *Journal of Social Psychology*, 73, 111–24.

Smith, Robert J. 1960. "Preindustrial Urbanism in Japan: A Consideration of Multiple Traditions in a Feudal Society," *Economic Development and Cultural Change*, 9, 241–57.

————, and Richard K. Beardsley, eds. 1962. *Japanese Culture: Its Development and Characteristics.* Chicago: Aldine.

Smith, Thomas C. 1955. *Political Change and Industrial Development in Japan: Government Enterprise, 1868–1880.* Stanford: Stanford University Press.

*————. 1959. *The Agrarian Origins of Modern Japan.* Stanford: Stanford University Press.

————. 1960–61. "Japan's Aristocratic Revolution," *Yale Review*, 50, 370–83.

————. 1967. " 'Merit' as Ideology in the Tokugawa Period," in Dore, 1967: 71–90.

*Sone, Monica. 1953. *Nisei Daughter.* Boston: Little, Brown.

Spicer, Edward H. 1946. "The Use of Social Scientists by the War Relocation Authority," *Applied Anthropology*, 5, 17–36.

Steiner, Jesse F. 1917. *The Japanese Invasion: A Study in the Psychology of Interracial Contacts.* Chicago: McClurg.

———. 1949. "Japanese Americans on the Mainland: Postwar Status and Problems," *Social Process in Hawaii*, 13, 1–18.

Strong, Edward K., Jr. 1933. *Japanese in California*. Stanford: Stanford University Press.

*———. 1934. *The Second-Generation Japanese Problem*. Stanford: Stanford University Press.

———, and Reginald Bell. 1933. *Vocational Aptitudes of Second-Generation Japanese in the United States*. Stanford: Stanford University Press.

Sugimoto, Etsu Inagaki. 1966. *A Daughter of the Samurai*. Rutland, Vt.: Tuttle.

Suzuki, Daisetz Teitaro. 1938. *Zen Buddhism and Its Influence on Japanese Culture*. Kyoto: Eastern Buddhist Society.

*Taeuber, Irene. 1958. *The Population of Japan*. Princeton: Princeton University Press.

Tajima, Paul J. 1935. "Japanese Buddhism in Hawaii: Its Background, Origin, and Adaptation to Local Conditions." Unpublished master's essay, University of Hawaii.

*tenBroek, Jacobus, Edward N. Barnhart, and Floyd W. Matson. 1968. *Prejudice, War and the Constitution*. Berkeley: University of California Press.

Thomas, Dorothy Swaine. 1950. "Some Social Aspects of Japanese-American Demography," *Proceedings of the American Philosophical Society*, 94, 459–80.

*———. 1962. *The Salvage*. Berkeley: University of California Press.

*———, and Richard S. Nishimoto. 1946. *The Spoilage*. Berkeley: University of California Press.

Thomas, Norman. 1942. "Dark Day for Liberty," *Christian Century*. 59, 929–31.

———. 1943. *Democracy and Japanese Americans*. New York: Postwar World Council.

Trevor, John B. 1925. "Japanese Exclusion: A Study of the Policy and the Law." House Document 600, 68th Congress, 2d Session. Washington, D.C.: U.S. Government Printing Office.

Tsuchiya, Takao. 1937. *An Economic History of Japan*. Tokyo: Asiatic Society of Japan.

Tsuneishi, Warren M. 1966. *Japanese Political Style: An Introduction to the Government and Politics of Modern Japan.* New York: Harper & Row.

U.S. Army, Western Defense Command and Fourth Army. 1943. *Final Report: Japanese Evacuation from the West Coast, 1942.* Washington, D.C.: U.S. Government Printing Office.

U.S. Department of the Interior, War Relocation Authority. 1945a. *Myths and Facts about the Japanese Americans: Answering Common Misconceptions Regarding Americans of Japanese Ancestry.* Washington, D.C.: U.S. Government Printing Office.

————, ————. 1945b. *"What We're Fighting For": Statements by United States Servicemen about Americans of Japanese Descent.* Washington, D.C.: U.S. Government Printing Office.

————, War Agency Liquidation Unit. [1947]. *People in Motion: The Postwar Adjustment of the Evacuated Japanese Americans.* Washington, D.C.: U.S. Government Printing Office.

U.S. House of Representatives, Select Committee Investigating National Defense Migration [The Tolan Committee]. 1942. *Hearings.* 77th Congress, 2d Session. Washington, D.C.: U.S. Government Printing Office.

U.S. Senate, Immigration Commission. 1911. *Report.* Vols. 1–2: "Abstracts of Reports," Senate Document 747, 61st Congress, 3d Session. Vol. 23: "Japanese and East Indians," Senate Document 633, 61st Congress, 2d Session. Washington, D.C.: U.S. Government Printing Office.

Utley, Freda. 1937. *Japan's Feet of Clay.* New York: Norton.

Uyeki, Eugene S. 1960. "Correlates of Ethnic Identification," *American Journal of Sociology,* 65, 468–74.

Varon, Barbara F. 1967. "The Japanese Americans: Comparative Occupational Status, 1960 and 1950," *Demography,* 4, 809–19.

Vinacke, W. Edgar. 1949. "Stereotyping among National-Racial Groups in Hawaii: A Study in Ethnocentrism," *Journal of Social Psychology,* 30, 265–91.

Vogel, Ezra F. 1961. "The Go-Between in a Developing Society: The Case of the Japanese Marriage Arranger," *Human Organization,* 20, 112–20.

————. 1965. *Japan's New Middle Class: The Salary Man and His Family in a Tokyo Suburb.* Berkeley: University of California Press.

————. 1967. "Kinship Structure, Migration to the City, and Modernization," in Dore, 1967: chap. 3.

Von Mehren, Arthur T. 1958. "Some Reflections on Japanese Law," *Harvard Law Review,* 71, 1486–96.

Voss, Harwin Leroy. 1961. "Insulation and Vulnerability to Delinquency: A Comparison of the Hawaiians and Japanese." Unpublished doctoral dissertation, University of Wisconsin.

*Wagatsuma, Hiroshi. 1967. "The Social Perception of Skin Color in Japan," *Daedalus,* 96, 407–43.

————, and George DeVos. 1962. "Attitudes toward Arranged Marriage in Rural Japan," *Human Organization,* 21, 187–200.

Wakukawa, Ernest K. 1938. *A History of the Japanese People in Hawaii.* Honolulu: Toyo Shoin.

Werner, Emmy E., Jessie M. Bierman, and Fern E. French. 1971. *The Children of Kauai: A Longitudinal Study from the Prenatal Period to Age Ten.* Honolulu: University of Hawaii Press.

*Wittermans, Elizabeth. 1964. *Inter-ethnic Relations in a Plural Society.* Groningen: Wolters.

*Yamagiwa, Joseph K. 1965. "Language as an Expression of Japanese Culture," in Hall and Beardsley, 1965: 186–221.

Yamamoto, George K. 1957. "Some Patterns of Mate Selection among Naichi and Okinawans on Oahu," *Social Process in Hawaii,* 21, 42–49.

————. 1959. "Political Participation among Orientals in Hawaii," *Sociology and Social Research,* 43, 359–64.

————. 1968. "The Ethnic Lawyer and Social Structure: The Japanese Attorney in Honolulu." Unpublished manuscript.

Yinger, J. Milton. 1962–63. "Integration and Pluralism Viewed from Hawaii," *Antioch Review,* 22, 397–410.

Yoshizawa, Emi. 1937. "A Japanese Family in Rural Hawaii," *Social Process in Hawaii,* 3, 56–63.

◎ Index

By Japanese convention, the family name comes first, followed by the personal name, but Westernized Japanese or those writing for a Western audience usually reverse the order. The style here follows that in the original work. Note that *b* stands for a bibliographic reference, *f* for a figure, *n* for a footnote, and *t* for a table.

Japanese American(s) (*con't.*)
54–61, 136, 140–143, 186

crime and delinquency, 134–43, 202, 208

culture, 14, 115, 203–204, 209–210, 213*n*

discrimination against, 3, 5–6, 23, 25, 32–34, 39–54, 64*n*, 103–104, 116–117, 129*n*, 202–203

education, 14, 39–42, 59–61, 83, 113–116, 122–123, 175, 183, 203, 208

family, 6–7, 132–133, 181, 187, 196–200, 203, 205–207, 209–210, 212*n*, 229

fertility, 199–200

generational conflict, 7, 8*n*, 86, 110, 139, 141–143, 183, 189*n*, 202–207, 213*n*, 221, 227. *See also* Issei, Kibei, Nisei, Sansei, Yonsei.

geographical distribution of, 30, 36*n*, 86, 227

health, 143–147, 151*n*, 197, 201

housing, 103–104

immigration, 12–20, 127*n*, 196–197, 209

income, 23, 24*t*, 120, 125

labor organizations of, 26–27, 54–55

language schools, 59–62, 65*n*, 67, 102, 176, 182–184, 189*n*, 203–204

"loyalty," 84–88, 91–92, 98*n*

military record of, 86–87, 110, 185, 204

mortality, 147–148

nationality, 48–50, 57–58. *See also honseki*, marginality.

occupations of, 23–30, 51, 103, 115–126

"picture brides," 43–44, 197–198, 201

relations to Japan, 18–19, 59–62

religions. *See* Buddhism, Christianity, Confucianism, Shinto.

remittances to Japan, 13, 24–25

restitution to, 94*n*, 104–107, 126–127*n*

return from camps, 101–104

"sabotage," 66–67, 74, 80–81, 101

sex ratio, 196*t*, 201, 212*n*

social mobility of, 4–5, 23–30, 118–126, 129*n*, 138

social welfare for, 131–134, 149*n*

subnation, 7, 27, 160–161, 199–200, 214, 221–232

war brides, 209–210. *See also* Bon dance, *buraku*, "dodging," Eta, filial piety, Japan, "school crisis."

Japanese American Citizens League, 58, 84, 86, 89, 99*n*, 107–108, 118, 141–142, 207, 208, 213*n*, 235*n*

Japanese-American Committee for Democracy, 74, 75–76, 96*n*. Japanese Associations, 40, 57–58, 67, 126, 149*n*

Japanese Family Guidance Council, 141–142

Japanese National Commission for UNESCO, 35*n*, 244*b*

Jenks, Jeremiah W., 18, 36*n*

Jews, 3, 59, 216, 219–220, 225, 226, 229, 230

Jonas, Frank H., 248*b*

Jonassen, Christen T., 149*n*